The Delaneys of
EDINBURGH

Patricia Delaney Dishon

Grosvenor House
Publishing Limited

This book is published by
Grosvenor House Publishing Ltd
28-30 High Street, Guildford, Surrey, GU1 3EL.
www.grosvenorhousepublishing.co.uk

A CIP record for this book
is available from the British Library

ISBN 978-1-78148-576-7

Author

Patricia Dishon (nee Delaney) is the great-granddaughter of Arthur and Cecilia Delaney. She has a BA (Hons) from the Open University, lectured in Scottish Studies in the Centre of Continuing Education at the University of Edinburgh and is a member of the Scottish Tourist Guides Association.

If you have any relevant information about this story the author can be contacted at

patricia@dishon.eu

Dedication

In memory of my much loved father Arthur Delaney
(1922 – 1974)

and

My dear mother, Elizabeth Coyle,
(1922 – 2000),
who first began the journey into this story with me.

Acknowledgements

Thanks must go first to my long-suffering husband, Brian, who has been with me every step of the way, for his loving patience and support and for editing the manuscript. He has a box of spare commas if anyone needs them! This book would not have been possible were it not for the painstaking research into the Delaney family carried out by my brother Michael Delaney. I thank him for giving me access to his own book – *The Lost Children* (unpublished) - on which I have drawn freely. I would like to thank Seamus McCluskey, author and historian, of Emyvale, Co. Monaghan, for all the help and information on the Delaneys of Emyvale and for the warmth of the welcome given to all the members of the Delaney family who have visited Emyvale in recent times. I appreciate the permission given by Alan Lugton and his publishers, Birlinn Limited of Edinburgh, to reproduce Alan's description of Hibernian Football Club's triumphant return to Edinburgh, with the Scottish Cup in 1887. This is contained in his amazing book, *The Making of Hibernian*. Emma's 'letters' have been adapted from her own book *Our Children in Old Scotland and Nova Scotia* by Emma Maitland Stirling and are mainly in her own words. The Scotsman Newspaper's Archive proved an invaluable source of information into the times the Delaney family lived through. Though this is essentially a family story I have endeavoured to make it as historically accurate as possible.

The Court documents referred to throughout are authentic legal papers from the Court of Session in Edinburgh, Scotland, and the Supreme Court of Nova Scotia in Canada.

Patricia Delaney Dishon

HELEN'S STORY

PART ONE

CHAPTER 1

Edinburgh 1850

Helen Delaney stood beside the freshly-turned earth of her husband Arthur's grave in the Greyfriars churchyard. The burial ground beside the old Kirk was an oasis of green peace in the dirty, smoky town of Edinburgh known far and wide as "Auld Reekie". The new growth of grass spread fresh and green between the old grey tombstones of the 'great and the good' who lay here. The trees were in full bud and birdsong sounded sweetly from the branches. In the near distance the old castle, guardian of the town, sat huddled high on its volcanic rock.

Helen saw or heard nothing. She was far away in another place. The place of memories. Her dearest Arthur was lying still and cold in this grave far from his beloved Ireland. She remembered the first time she had ever seen him. He had been straight off the Irish boat at the Broomielaw in Glasgow. She had gone down to meet him with her cousin, Hugh Collins, who knew Arthur from his young days in County Monaghan. While they had waited for the boat to dock he had told Helen that the Delaneys were a well set up family in Donagh parish in that county. They owned a quarry and ran a stone-mason's business.

'Sure, most of the dear departed of Monaghan lie under stones crafted by the Delaneys,' Hugh had joked.

They also farmed several acres around the village of Emyvale but, Hugh had explained, their prosperity had been undermined when they were asked to build a grand new branch for the Hibernian Bank in Monaghan town. Much quality stone and family labour went into its construction but on completion the Bank had reneged on the agreed costs. The case was still proceeding through the Irish Courts but meanwhile money was tight. The quarry business and farms employed most of James and Mary Delaney's large family but this financial disaster meant they could no longer all be supported by the family concerns. Some of the sons had had to seek employment elsewhere.

Arthur had never been suited to heavy labouring work anyway either at the quarry or on the farms.

'Do you know he can read and write,' Hugh had said. 'He was the ould schoolmaster's best pupil, sure he was.'

Arthur had been apprenticed to a local tailor and learned that trade. 'However, as you know,' said Hugh, 'times are hard over there and people are not after buying new clothes at all.' His employer had had to let Arthur go.

Arthur's sister, Sarah, had left Donagh years ago with her husband, John Skiffington, and settled in Edinburgh.

'Sure they have managed to get Arthur work with a Monaghan man, Philip Boylan. This Boylan man has done very well for himself. He's a master tailor but he has a finger in a lot more pies now apparently,' Hugh had explained.

Arthur had written to Hugh to ask if he could break his journey and stay a few nights with Hugh in Glasgow and his friend had readily agreed.

'He's a grand fellow, I'm sure you'll like him,' her cousin had enthused.

'Hugh, Hugh!'

They had looked up and had seen, coming down the gangway waving with his hat and calling Hugh's name, a tall slender man with a mass of red gold curls now exposed and shining in the sunlight. Hugh had run forward and, shaking his friend's hand then slapping him on the back, he had relieved him of his bag and had brought him towards Helen. She remembered looking up into the greenest eyes she had ever seen. A broad grin creased Arthur's face as they were introduced. He had taken both Helen's hands in his and had stood looking down at her.

'Have I died and gone to Heaven?' a soft Irish voice had said. 'Who is this angel?'

Helen felt again the blush that had spread over her body and up to her face at his look and touch. She remembered being glad when Hugh had broken the spell.

He had nudged Arthur away and had said, 'Ignore him Helen, he always did have a touch of the blarney about him! Though my cousin is quite a pretty colleen, I suppose, now that you mention it, Arthur,' Hugh had teased.

The three had then set off in high spirits for the home that Helen shared with her aunt's family and where Arthur was to lodge.

Arthur had only stayed three days with them but it had been enough for both of them to know that they were meant for one another.

Helen stood remembering the sense of anticipation she had felt every month waiting for the cart that would bring Arthur on a visit. At last the day arrived when Arthur had been able to tell her that he had found a home for them, in one of his boss' properties, and had saved enough for them to be married.

She remembered her first view of Edinburgh, so different from Glasgow where she had been born. The castle on its rock, like something out of a fairy-tale, had fascinated her. Remembering, Helen glanced up at that castle, now so familiar.

Their wedding had taken place on a fine Spring day in April, 1839, just eleven years ago. Kindly Father George Rigg had married them in the priest's house just across the road from this graveyard, in Brown's Square. It had been a simple ceremony and afterwards they had gone to Sarah's house in the High Street for their wedding breakfast. Helen glanced at her sister-in-law, Sarah, standing, weeping beside her. Sarah was Arthur's twin and the two had always been close. Poor Sarah was heartbroken at the loss of her brother.

Sarah and John had been woven into the fabric of her and Arthur's marriage. They had stood as god-parents for their children, James, born the year after their marriage, Thomas, in 1845, and John, three years later.

These had been times of great joy in their life. But they had had times of sorrow also. She remembered the times, the many times, that she and Sarah had laid their dead children to rest in this grave. Some of the children had lived long enough to be baptised but others had gone before they could even know them. Helen felt she had never really recovered from that awful year when their twin daughter Mary had died just weeks after her birth and had been followed within months by her sister Rosanna.

But whenever she was at her lowest ebb Sarah was there for her. Sarah and John had come to believe that they themselves would never have children after many years of childless marriage. Great was their joy then when a lovely son whom they had named Arthur, after Sarah's beloved brother, was born to them. Another son, John, had completed their family but two years later he had followed his cousins to this grave. Then it had been Helen's turn to support her distraught sister-in-law.

The two women had come through those sorrows but how, Helen wondered, would either of them ever get over the loss of lovely, gentle Arthur. Arthur, who had never been robust and had grown more delicate as the years went by, had been unable to resist when fever had swept through the Old Town.

Helen suddenly realised she would never feel his arms around her again, never hear him calling from the stair, 'Where's my angel girl?' She fell to her knees and sobbed as if her heart would break.

Sarah, tears still streaming down her own face, gently raised Helen from the ground. 'Come away Helen,' she said, 'come home, the laddies will be worried, sure they will.'

The two women walked through the great iron gates of the churchyard and out into Candlemaker Row. The street took its name from the old days when those who had made their living making candles had lived here crowded together. The stench from the animal fats used had discouraged any neighbours not in the trade. Now the properties housed the poorest of the poor of the present time. Part of the Row was formed by the massive stone wall supporting the old Greyfriars churchyard above but the rest was lined by crumbling ancient buildings.

Helen and Sarah headed downhill their black mourning clothes and tear-stained faces attracting some curious stares.

To the left the street led into the Grassmarket, scene in the past of religious martyrdom and riots as well as the markets for which it was named. Here in the 17th Century, during the bitter Covenanting wars which had divided Scotland, many had been hanged for their faith, or as the callous parlance of the time declared, "They were sent to glorify God in the Grassmarket." Here, too, some years later the mob had hanged a Captain Porteous from a barber's pole after his orders to the Town Guard to shoot on another mob had resulted in several deaths.

Today, the four sides of the market-place were lined with pawnbrokers, second-hand clothes shops, offal butchers and spirit dealers. Such was the effect of the famine years in Ireland that more than three-quarters of these businesses were owned by Irish immigrants.

An old stone well stood in the middle of the road and Sarah went towards it and splashed cold water on her face.

'Come on, Helen,' she said, 'we can't be letting the bairns see us looking like this.'

After Helen, too, had washed the tear-stains from her face the two women made their way out of the square and walked along the Cowgate. They were almost immediately plunged into gloom, as a span of George IV Bridge above arched over the roadway, cutting out the sun. When they emerged it was as if they had entered Hell itself. Or so it would have seemed to an outsider. But the women scarcely noticed, so familiar was the scene to them. The Cowgate had previously been where some of the grandest houses of the nobility stood in the

Old Town. One building still bore the name of Regent Morton who had once ruled Scotland. These were the homes abandoned to the poor when the drift to the newly emerging New Town of Edinburgh, across the Nor Loch, took the wealthy to a more salubrious environment. Now Morton House, and the others, were subdivided into one-roomed hovels housing the poor Highlanders driven from the north by The Clearances, and of course the Irish. Gaelic voices mingled with Erse and Lowland Scots on the streets. These decaying buildings were grossly over-crowded and lacked a water supply. Water had to be fetched from street wells. Helen and Sarah kept to one side of the road to avoid an open drain running down one side of the street which carried the town's effluent. The whole area was a breeding ground for disease and despair. Like the Grassmarket, the Cowgate was lined with dilapidated shops selling all manner of second hand goods and it seemed that every second one was licensed to sell hard liquor. Many men, and women too, sought escape from the harsh realities of despairing lives in the oblivion of raw whisky.

Helen and Sarah had to pick their way carefully through the noisy, foul-smelling street. They stood aside to let pass two-wheeled, horse-drawn carts, piled high with second-hand household goods, making their way to the premises of the dealers. The women turned left at the end of the Cowgate and climbed the slope up St Mary's Wynd. This narrow street had long ago been the site of St Mary's convent standing in a pleasance of green space and orchards. The Scottish Reformation in the 16th Century had changed all that. Old Catholic Edinburgh and many of its buildings had been swept away. Now, three hundred years on, Edinburgh remained staunchly Protestant. Much hostility was shown to the Irish Catholic population that had flooded in after the Great Famine in Ireland. Today, St Mary's Wynd was at the heart of that Irish ghetto.

Like the other Old Town streets it was lined with shops and stalls at pavement level selling all manner of goods. Second hand clothes hung on hooks outside some shops and trestle tables below extended the shop space. These were piled high with used shoes, battered cooking pots and coarse crockery. The flats above the shops had pulley ropes on poles extending from the windows and the washing hanging from these was blowing in the stiff wind that was rarely absent from the town. Some of the original houses had, quite literally, fallen down, so at intervals along the street new tall stone tenement buildings filled the gaps. It was one of these that Helen and Sarah now entered, climbed the stairs and pushed open the door of a first floor flat.

Three young lads ran forward and threw their arms around their mother's knees, nearly knocking Helen off her feet.

A tall young woman, her red hair and green eyes identifying her as another of Arthur's sisters, rose quickly from her seat by the fire. She attempted to disengage the children from their mother.

'Sure, let your Mammy get her bonnet off, won't ye?' said Jane Delaney. 'What in the name of the Virgin and all the saints is the matter wi ye?'

The eldest son, James, muttered, 'We thought ye were no coming back.'

A silence fell on the room and the three women looked at each other in dismay their eyes filling with tears. Well they understood the children's fear after the sudden loss of their father.

Sarah broke the silence. 'Now then, which of you fine bhoyos would like to help me make yer Mammy a nice cup of tea?' she said.

Helen wearily took off her bonnet and her cloak. 'Thanks for staying with them, Jane, will ye stay for a cup yerself?' she asked.

'No tanks, Helen, a better be getting back. Mistress McLaughlin will be needin me to help wi the meal for maister coming in,' Jane replied.

Jane had only been in Edinburgh for two years and her brogue was still strong.

The situation back home in Donagh had become desperate. The potato blight had returned again and again to Ireland and famine and disease stalked the land. The old folk had sent young Jane to stay with her brother and sister in Edinburgh.

'We will see ye tomorrow morning at mass then,' said Helen.

As Jane called her farewells the boys were helping, or rather hindering, Sarah as she lifted the kettle from its swag over the fire in the range and filled the big china teapot. With the tea brewed Sarah reached into her bag and withdrew three coins.

'Since ye hiv been such good bairnies ye can go up the road to Ma Casey's shop and get yersells some bonbons,' she said.

The children, now reassured by the return of their mother, ran off whooping with delight!

'Keep a guid hold of wee John's hand now James and mind how ye go,' their mother called after them.

The two women settled themselves by the fire, the tea cups in their hands.

'Have ye thought about what yer going to do, Helen?' Sarah asked.

'A dinnae ken, Sarah, I cannae seem to think at a,' Helen replied.

'Well ye know me and John will help a we can,' said Sarah.

Helen reached across and took her sister-in-law's hand. 'A ken that Sarah, where would I hae been withoot ye these past days. An John tae,' she said. 'The truth is a keep thinkin that Arthur will walk back in that door, a cannae believe he's gone,' she cried.

The boys bursting back into the room had put an end to their conversation but later, with Sarah gone, and the children in bed, Helen's mind returned to Sarah's question. What was she going to do? She had some money put by from their meagre savings but some of that would have to go in funeral expenses. Their main income came from Arthur's tailoring skills and with money saved from that they had opened the shop below the flat and were small scale brokers. Helen could not continue with the shop with no other income with which to deal.

For the first time since Arthur's death worry managed to pierce the thick cloud of grief that had enveloped Helen. The laddies! What would happen to their sons, Helen thought, and panic threatened to overwhelm her.

She took Arthur's favourite pipe from the rack by the fire, lay down on their bed in the recess, and, still clutching it, wept herself to sleep.

CHAPTER 2

A month had passed since Helen and Sarah's visit to the graveyard. Helen had re-opened the shop to sell off the remaining stock but with no income to invest in new stock the shop would have to go.

John had offered her a job working with him and Sarah in their grocer shop at 92 High Street.

Helen was touched by their kindness but knew that they didn't really need another pair of hands to help run the store. Nor could they afford to pay Helen enough to keep her and her three sons.

One worry had though been lifted from Helen. Arthur's boss, Philip Boylan, who was also their landlord, called in one day. He insisted that she should not pay rent for the shop or their flat until she had found her feet. Helen was grateful and relieved but some, like Arthur's other sister, might have said that Mr Boylan could well afford the gesture.

'Sure,' Jane had said, 'doesn't he own half the Old Town and his daughter owns the other half!'

This was an exaggeration but the old man did indeed own a considerable number of properties in the town. He had arrived in Edinburgh at the turn of the century well before the famine years. Like Arthur, he had trained as a tailor in his native Ireland and with a little capital saved had crossed the Irish Channel. On landing in

Glasgow he found that city not to his taste and had travelled on to the Capital. He set up in business at East Common Close in the Canongate and in 1821 he married Dorothy Warrick, daughter of an Irish hat-maker in the town. Together they raised a large family while building a highly successful tailoring and alterations business. As it prospered the Boylans had diversified opening a boot and shoe emporium.

Around this time many of the gentry and professional residents of the Old Town had vacated their homes and decanted to the grand New Town rising up on farmland across the Nor Loch. Philip began buying up their houses and sub-dividing them. In this way he turned spacious apartments that had housed one family into single-ends and room and kitchen dwellings that housed many. When later the flood of emigrants from famine-hit Ireland poured into Edinburgh the Boylans were well placed to accommodate them and reap yet more profit from the rents. As some ancient buildings in the town collapsed, or fell into uninhabitable decline, Philip feud the gap sites and erected fine new stone tenements like the one in which Helen now lived.

Arthur and Helen's first home had been in one of his boss' old properties in Boyd's Entry but as their family grew they had moved to a larger flat on St Mary's Wynd.

The Boylans also lived on the street, but in a spacious, three-storey house with their own stable and hayloft behind.

Despite Jane's scathing remarks Helen was grateful to the old man.

Arthur had always said that his boss was a hard task-master but very fair with his workers. "You play fair wi him and he'll see you alright," he would say.

Certainly, anytime Helen had met Mr Boylan in the past, he had seemed kindly and courteous. He would tip his hat to Helen and take a few pennies from his waistcoat pocket for the children, patting them on the head and declaring them "fine fellows".

Their next meeting took place a few weeks later.

Helen had been forced to close the shop and she took the key back to Mr Boylan in his office. He was reluctant to take it and tried to encourage her to hold the property meantime. But Helen was firm. She was concerned that accumulated rent on an unused shop would eventually further drain her small funds. The landlord was forced to accept her decision.

'How are those fine sons of yours doing?' he inquired, as he showed her out. 'They seem sturdy, healthy young lads. Ye must be very proud of them.'

Helen admitted that she was, but, her voice faltering, she told him how much the children were missing their father.

Philip looked at her kindly.

'Well they might,' he said. 'He was a fine man, your Arthur, a fine man. I never had a moment when I regretted taking him on and that's the truth.'

This was too much for Helen and she burst into tears.

The old man looked awkward but pulled a spotless handkerchief from his pocket and handed it to her.

'There, there,' he consoled, and patted her on the shoulder.

At last the storm of weeping subsided and Helen was able to compose herself enough to thank the man, take her leave, and step out into the street.

The next day was Sunday and Helen and the children were leaving morning mass at St Patrick's church on

Lothian Street. The church, as usual, had been packed to bursting point but Helen had spotted Sarah and young Arthur during the service. Outside she was looking around for her sister-in-law when she saw her deep in conversation with Philip Boylan. Helen was puzzled. Not at them conversing, after all Sarah and Mr Boylan had known each other a long time. Indeed it was Sarah who had got her brother, Arthur, the job with the man in the first place. But they looked so serious, their heads close together as if they didn't want to be overheard.

Suddenly, spotting their cousin, wee Arthur, beside his mother, Helen's sons darted forward to greet him before Helen could stop them.

Looking up the couple saw Helen approaching and she thought she saw Sarah give the old man an affirming nod.

Helen apologised for her son's interruption and drew from her bag the handkerchief Mr Boylan had given her the previous day, now freshly laundered.

Helen's initial reaction was replaced with sudden anxiety when the old man said, 'Will ye walk a bit wi me, Mistress?'

At this Sarah darted forward, lifted a protesting toddler, John, in her arms and said, 'Come on laddies – is it hungry ye are? Who's for a plate of good Irish ham and some fine, fresh eggs?'

'Me, me,' the children chorused and followed Sarah happily down the street.

Helen and Philip walked off towards the green space known as The Meadows. This was a favourite place for St Patrick's parishioners to stroll after church. It was a fine May day and the trees that lined the walkways were putting forth fresh green shoots. The area had once been meadowland surrounding the Borough Loch, which had been one of the main sources of water for the old town. Later it was drained and landscaped to create a fine green space in the heart of the town. The main walkway was lined with cherry trees and the branches were heavy with pink blossom. Couples strolled arm and arm enjoying the warm sunshine of one of the finest days of the Spring so far. Children chased each other round and round and a couple of boys kicked a ball back and forth to each other.

Philip and Helen walked for a bit in silence until she could stand it no longer.

'Is it about the rent?' she burst out.

'No, no Mistress,' Philip reassured her, 'do not distress yourself on that score. Your home will not be taken from you no matter the decision you take.'

Helen's immediate fear subsided somewhat at these words but was replaced with puzzlement. What decision, she wondered?

Philip stopped and removed his hat. Though he was a man past his middle years he still had a fine head of hair. In his youth it had been almost black but now it was a silvery grey. He wore his dark, finely tailored suit well, a heavy gold watch-chain showed at his waist-coat and his soft leather boots were highly polished. Anyone passing would place him immediately as a business man of some note in the town. Yet here was this normally confident man nervously turning his hat round and round in his hands.

Helen looked at him. What on earth was the matter with the man, she thought.

At last, after what seemed an eternity, Philip squared his shoulders, decision taken. 'Would ye ever consider marrying me,' he said.

Helen stood stock still in amazement. All the colour drained from her face. She could not believe what she had just heard. Then two red spots of anger appeared high on her cheeks.

She found her voice. 'Marry ye, marry ye,' she cried. 'Are ye mad, with my Arthur hardly cold in the grave?'

She turned sharply to walk away, tears starting up in her eyes. His next words halted her.

'Ye are not alone in yer sorrow, Mistress. My own wife, Dorothy, is not yet six months gone from me. I miss her every day. She was my love, my helpmate, and the mother of my children. We were together for twenty-nine years. No, Mistress, ye are mistaken if ye think I do not understand your grief, I understand it only too well,' Philip said.

The innate dignity of the man impressed Helen. The anger drained out of her. How could she have forgotten Philip's recent loss! Hadn't she sat with Arthur in the very church they had just left at this man's wife's funeral mass.

Colour flooded Helen's face. She was ashamed that, enveloped in her sorrow, she had never once thought to enquire of Mr Boylan how he was coping with his own loss at any of their recent meetings.

Helen, impulsively, took both his hands in hers. 'Oh a'm sorry. A'm that sorry, how could a hiv been sae unkind?' she stammered.

'Ye have not to worry,' Philip released one hand and patted hers which was still holding the other. 'Sure, it's me own fault for after being so hasty. I meant no offence, it's just me way. I'm afraid when a feel a thing is right a jest go fer it. Will ye walk a little more and listen to what I am proposing?' he asked.

Helen filled with remorse and ashamed at how ill-mannered she must have appeared felt the need to make amends by hearing the man out.

Philip explained a little of his and Dorothy's life together. His pride in his achievements was obvious, and rightly so, but Helen was moved at how much he credited his wife with that success.

'It's been my experience that wi the right woman by a man's side he can do anything,' Philip explained. 'Ye know, of course, that she gave me six sons and two daughters,' he continued.

Again Helen felt the heat rise in her face. She had forgotten! How could she have forgotten? All of Philip and Dorothy's sons had died, one after the other, as children. Their daughter Agnes had lived only to her early twenties. Of their large family only their daughter Eleanor had lived to adulthood.

'Dorothy and meself sometimes felt we had a curse upon us,' Philip said, explaining their loss. 'It seemed we had everything we could ever want, except the very thing we wanted most, our bairns. I sometimes wonder if it was the grief that caused her to lose her grip on life.'

Helen felt a sob rise in her throat at the man's agony. She remembered now how sad she and Arthur had felt in days gone by, seeing the couple sitting in the pew that had once held their large family. Now Dorothy, too, was gone and Philip had sat alone at mass this morning, as he did now every Sunday.

For the first time Helen sensed the deep loneliness of the man now walking beside her.

'Ye will know, Mistress,' Philip continued, 'that I do not lack anything in the material sense but I lack a son to pass the business to when I am gone.'

'You still hae yer daughter, Eleanor, though,' Helen interjected.

Philip seemed to pause for a moment.

'Aye,' he continued, 'that's true. But Eleanor has no need of my money. I made sure a long time ago that she was well set up. Her own abilities and hard work have done the rest.'

Helen remembered Jane's comment that the part of the Old Town that was not owned by Philip was owned by his daughter. Indeed, Eleanor Boylan's property ownership extended outwith the Old Town and down into the Port of Leith. Here she lived in some style, in a large stone house in South Fort Street. She was not Eleanor Boylan now of course, having married John Lennon.

As if reading her mind Philip said, 'And besides, Eleanor is a married woman who no longer bears my family name.'

Helen couldn't help but feel that, from what she had heard of her, Eleanor Lennon was more like her father than any of his dead sons might have been.

Philip continued, 'It would pain me that after I am gone the Boylan name would no longer mean anything in this town.' He flushed a bit as he said this and turning to Helen said, 'Do ye think me guilty o' the sin o' pride?'

'No, no,' Helen hastened to assure him. She was remembering the pride Arthur had felt that their three sons would carry forward the Delaney name and she told Philip this.

Philip turned to her again. 'I know well the concern ye have for what is to become of yer fine sons. If ye would consider my proposal I promise that they would want for nothing. I would make sure they were well schooled and care for them as well as for any sons we might hiv thegether'.

The implications of this brought Helen rudely back to reality.

Her mind and her body rejected such an option. Share this old man's bed!

'A'm sorry, a'm sorry, a mean nae offence, but a cannae, a jist cannae,' she stammered.

Philip had not been successful without becoming an astute observer of men and women. He knew well that the physical aspect of any marriage with him was scaring Helen. If he had asked her to be his resident house-keeper Philip felt certain she would have accepted gladly. But it was only fair to Helen that she should know that his desire for the union rested on the possibility that Helen, who had produced three fine sons for Arthur, might be able to replace his own lost sons. He was saddened but not really surprised at her evident distress.

'Tell me ye will at least consider my offer,' Philip urged, 'there's no hurry.'

But Helen had turned and fled.

Philip let her go, then, glancing after her, walked on, hands behind his back, deep in thought.

Helen practically ran up the Middle Meadow Walk, only managing to outwardly compose herself when she reached the street.

She knew where she had to go and minutes later she stumbled through the gates of the Greyfriars churchyard.

Grass now grew on the mound of Arthur's grave and the jug containing the last bunch of wild-flowers she and the children had picked had toppled over in the wind. Deprived of water the flowers had withered and died.

Helen looked at them. Dead, like Arthur, she thought, he wasn't ever coming back. What was the point of anything anymore. She picked up the jug and emptied out the withered flowers. Now, dried to straw, they blew away on the wind.

The walk back to Sarah's house, across George IV Bridge and down the High Street, enabled Helen to compose herself.

It wouldn't do to appear distressed. Sarah knew her so well she would be sure to sense something was wrong and try and get to the bottom of it. Helen couldn't face that after all she had been through this morning.

She would pretend her discussion with Philip had been about the rent.

Helen approached St Giles Kirk just as the bells pealed out from its spire. The great grey hulk of the old church squatted in the midst of the surrounding buildings but its distinctive crown spire soared above them all. The Krames and Luckenbooths, stalls and buildings, which had once pressed hard against the walls of the church had long been swept away. But market stalls still lined the north side of the High Street as far as the North Bridge. Though deserted today, it being the Sabbath, normally the market was a hive of activity its stalls heaped high with fruit and vegetables.

The Protestant services took place later on a Sunday than the Catholic mass. Helen had heard tell that sometimes the sermons in St Giles lasted two hours! Since the clock on the Tron Kirk further down the road had just chimed for one o'clock perhaps it was true!

As Helen passed, respectable looking people, in dark clothes, were filing out through the great west door and shaking hands with the minister.

She had once teased Father Rigg by asking him if he thought the Catholics in the town would ever have such a braw church as St Giles. He had explained to her that before the Protestant Reformation destroyed the old Faith in Scotland Catholics had actually worshipped in the splendour of St Giles. Helen now wondered if that was the source of the hostility expressed by the Protestants in the town towards the Irish. Maybe they were afraid we would take our church back!

Helen's musings had helped distract her mind from the incident with Philip but now she hastened her steps as the realisation of the time struck home. Sarah would be wondering where on earth she was!

She at last climbed the short stair that led from the Skiffington's grocer shop, at pavement level, to their home above the store at 92 High Street.

She pushed open the door and as she entered, Sarah, her face flushed from cooking on the range, lifted her face.

'Did he ask ye then?' she asked.

Helen stood as if turned to stone. Sarah knew! Helen began to feel anger rise up in her again. How dare Philip Boylan speak of the matter to Sarah, even before he had spoken to herself! But as quickly as it had flared her anger died. Of course he would, he was an honourable man. He would not have wanted to give offence to Arthur's sister. Of course he would seek Sarah's approval first. Helen realised now the significance of the nod her sister-in-law had given the old man outside the church.

Sarah had given her approval!

What could she have been thinking of, Helen thought, Arthur's own sister! She opened her mouth to protest but suddenly became aware of the others in the room looking up at her. John and the three younger children sat on the floor. They were playing with wee Arthur's collection of tin soldiers. They had lined them up in ranks in preparation for battle. Thomas and his brother John on one side, Arthur and his father on the other.

Seeing the expression on Helen's face John Skiffington suddenly announced, 'Let battle commence!' and the boys sprang into action.

Helen shook her head at Sarah, meaning she didn't want to discuss the matter now.

Taking the hint, Sarah said, 'We managed to save ye some of the ham, so sit yersel down and I'll make some eggs to go with it'.

Helen walked to the table by the window. Her eldest son, James, sat there. He was not part of the group on the floor or of the noisy battle that raged at his feet. He was drawing. He was always drawing. His father had once said he was sure his son had been born with a pencil in his hand. His sister reminded him that she had been present at the birth and had seen no sign of it!

Arthur had laughed, but had gone on, "Sure Sarah doesn't he just remind you of our Terry? Always drawing, drawing, drawing!"

Terry had been one of the brothers who had stayed home in Donagh. His job in the family business had been to carve the inscriptions on the tombstones, a source of work that was never likely to dry up in poor Ireland now.

Helen smiled at her son. 'Can a hae a look?' she asked.

James, shyly, slid the paper across the table.

As usual, his mother was taken aback at the skill of the drawing by one so young. He had drawn Sarah. It was only a rough sketch but he had caught her exactly, bending over the range, her hair escaping from its pins and falling across her face.

The subject of the work now laid a steaming plate of ham and eggs before Helen, who held up the drawing for her approval.

'Well now, is that not jest grand,' his aunt said, 'yer jest like yer uncle, back home, sure he has the same gift.'

James blushed at the praise.

The food was delicious, as it always was in the Skiffington household. Owning the grocer's shop below meant they never went hungry.

Helen had fasted, as was the custom, from the night before so that she could take the Blessed Sacrament at mass that morning. She had not eaten since but her appetite had deserted her. She could only pick at her meal but she cradled the mug of hot tea in her hands, feeling its warmth. She felt weak, as if she was in shock. She must have looked it, too, because Sarah looked at her sharply.

'Will ye have some spirits in that?' she enquired, indicating the mug.

Helen looked up. 'The tea's jist fine,' she said.

Later, the meal finished, and the kitchen redded up, Sarah glanced out of the window.

'Would ye look at that,' she said, 'the sun's out and, by the look o that washin' o'er the road, that wind has dropped. Will we go for a stroll, Helen?'

Putting on their bonnets and leaving John with the boys the women left the house. Sarah led the way and turned left at the foot of the stair.

'Where are we headed?' Helen enquired.

'I thought we would take a wee daunder down to the ould Palace,' Sarah replied.

Away from the ears of the children the two were able to discuss what had happened. Helen was astonished, and angry, to hear Sarah encourage her to accept Philip's offer.

'How can ye, Sarah, a thought ye o a folk, would want to honour Arthur's memory,' she said.

Helen felt the tears, that never seemed far away these days, fill her eyes.

Even Sarah seemed affected by her retort and bit her lip. But then she got herself under control, thoughts of her dead brother's sons strengthening her resolve.

The women had left the High Street behind and crossed over St Mary's Wynd into the Canongate. Though just a continuation of the street, the Canongate was a separate small town. Had they not been so engrossed in conversation they could have glanced down the Wynd and seen a fragment of the old town wall. Known as the Flodden Wall it had once run the length of the Wynd and joined the town gate here at the crossroads. The wall cut off the old town of Edinburgh from its neighbouring town. The entry point had originally been through an impressive gate called the Netherbow. The gate no longer stood but the crossroads still bore the old name.

Helen and Sarah walked downhill but the Canongate had actually grown uphill to meet the old town at the Netherbow. It had its origins in the building of the, now ruined, Abbey of the Holyrood beside the old Palace. Over the long years of its construction stone-mason's houses, originally clustered around the site, gradually spread uphill. The Augustinian canons who had served the Abbey gave their name to this street down which the pair were now walking.

Folk in the Canongate considered themselves a race apart from the residents in the town above. They boasted that they still had their ancient Town Chambers in the picturesque building known as the Canongate Tollbooth, whereas Edinburgh had long ago lost theirs. They also had a fine Kirk to rival the old town's Greyfriars church. Its graveyard, too, held the 'great and the good' of bygone times. Even Doctor Gregory of the famous medicine was buried there. No home was without its bottle of Gregory's Mixture which was said to cure all known ills.

And there were plenty of ills to cure.

Regardless of their pride in the place, its residents suffered the same decrepit buildings, dirt and disease as those of the Grassmarket or the Cowgate. Like the latter echoes of the old grandeur of the place still survived. Its location, so near to the royal Court at the Palace, encouraged the nobility to build grand homes here. Helen and Sarah passed Moray House, formerly home of a countess, with its impressive gateway and ornate balcony on which, it was said, the Duke of Argyll stood and spat down on the cart that carried his enemy, the great Marquis of Montrose, to his execution.

Nearby stood the gabled frontage of Huntley House, known locally as the 'Speaking House', from the stone tablets with their Latin inscriptions which decorated the façade. Long ago it was said a member of the noble Huntley family had lodgings here.

His next door neighbour had even higher social status. He was Sir Archibald Acheson who became Secretary of State for Scotland under King Charles. He had built this grand stone house in the seventeenth century and surrounded it with a high stone wall to ensure privacy. Sir Archibald had married Dame

Margaret Hamilton who stood even higher on the noble tree of Scotland. His family had begun as humble salt-panners extracting salt from sea-water by heating it to the point of evaporation in huge pans on the sea-shore in nearby East Lothian. They had prospered and grown so rich that this member of their line came to hold the highest public office in the land but his wife's Hamilton name could have challenged the royal house of Stewart itself.

Past glory did nothing to protect the homes they had occupied.

Behind the crumbling frontage of Huntley House poor families now lived crowded into one room dwellings in appalling squalor. The fate of Acheson House was even worse. It was now a notorious brothel.

As they walked Helen related all that Philip had said and her own response.

They had been so deep in conversation that when Sarah suddenly stopped Helen took a moment to get her bearings.

They stood in front of the grandest house of all. The former mansion house of the Duke of Queensberry. When Helen first came to live in Edinburgh she had been surprised to see many of the older residents of the Canongate spit as they passed this building. She had asked Arthur why they did this and he had explained that the Duke who had lived there had been held responsible for the signing of an Act of Parliament that had united Scotland with England.

'And the folk didnae want it?' Helen had queried.

'No, the folk did not,' Arthur had replied. 'The mob marched on the house and the Duke and his cohorts had to flee from their rage and sign the Act in a cellar.'

'So it wasn't jist him?' she had asked.

'No, there were others,' he had explained.

"Do you know what Rabbie Burns called them?" he had continued. "'A parcel of rogues!'"

Arthur had been a great man for the reading. He had haunted the second-hand shops digging out any books he could find buried among the junk. It was one of those that Arthur had taken from the shelf to show Helen. *The Collected Poems of Robert Burns.*

Helen knew how the locals revered this poet. She had seen many poor homes where a print of his portrait hung on the wall and an impressive monument to the man stood on the slopes of the Calton Hill. She had always been puzzled, however, by her husband's admiration for the man. She had voiced this once and Arthur had explained.

'Burns,' he had said, 'didn't just speak for the Scots.'

'He's the brotherhood of man poet, Helen. Listen to this,' he had continued.

' "That man to man the world o'er will brithers be for a that." Now isn't that a grand idea, Helen?'

His eyes had shone with enthusiasm.

But she had not yet exhausted the topic of the union with England.

She had asked when that took place and when he said 1707, she had burst out, 'But that was so long ago! Why do they still spit?'

Arthur had looked at her.

'Sure, Cromwell was a long time ago too,' he had said.

Helen had been born in Scotland to Irish parents. She knew little of Scotland's history but she knew all about Cromwell in Ireland and she realised that the

Scots, too, must hear the ancestral voices every time they passed this house.

Lost in her reverie, it was some minutes before she realised that Sarah stood looking at her.

'Well,' she demanded, pointing, 'is that where ye want yourself and the laddies to end up?'

Queensberry House, once home to the notorious Duke, was now the Old Town's Poorhouse. Helen's blood turned to ice. She had never been inside the place but, like everyone else in the town, she knew all about it. The windows were barred but at some of them Helen thought she could see pale faces peering out. In spite of the warmth of the sun she shivered and drew her shawl around her.

Little was said as the women retraced their steps back up the Canongate to Sarah's house both deep in thought.

But at the foot of the stair, Helen suddenly said, in a small voice, 'He's auld, Sarah.'

At this her sister-in-law completely lost her temper. And Sarah in a temper was something that people tried to avoid.

She stopped, hands on hips, and blazed at Helen. 'Take a look at yerself,' she shouted, 'yer no longer a young colleen, yer thirty, he's fifty-five, so what? Have ye a mind to wait fer a younger fellow?'

Now it was Helen's turn to lose her temper. 'Of course no,' she said, 'a dinnae want any fellow, young or auld'.

Sarah's anger died as quickly as it had flared. She linked arms with her sister-in-law. 'A'm sorry, a'm sorry,' she said, 'a didn't mean it, sure yer a fine-lookin', dacent woman.'

This made Helen laugh, in spite of herself, and together they went upstairs.

Helen's youngest son was nearly asleep when they returned, and John carried him when he walked with Helen and the children back to their own home. The two older children ran ahead.

'Ye must forgive Sarah,' John Skiffington said, 'ye know how impetuous she is, she only wants what is best for you and the lads and ye know how stubborn she can be when her mind's made up! But ye are the one who will have to live with it,' he paused, before going on, 'for the rest of yer life. Think well on it Helen.'

His stubborn wife was soon to prove her husband right. Shortly after John returned from taking Helen and the children home, Sarah put her shawl over her head and walked round the corner to Philip Boylan's house. Her knock at the door was answered by his servant Bessie and Sarah was shown in to the parlour while the maid went to fetch Philip.

Sarah had sat in this room many times but she was always impressed by how grand it was. The furnishings would not have disgraced a room in the New Town. Dorothy, Philip's late wife, had had very good taste and he had indulged her every whim. The walls, painted a soft green were hung with paintings in heavy gilt frames. Above the open fireplace a large ornate mirror reflected back the array of fine china arranged on the carved oak mantlepiece. A low fire burned in the black leaded grate to help keep the chill off the room and a stand holding a brass coal-shovel and toasting fork gleamed in the firelight. The window which faced onto the street was screened by pure white heavy Brussels lace curtains and framed by dark green velour drapes. Well upholstered chairs and sofas were placed around the room and a large oak sideboard against one wall displayed an oriental-style vase holding peacock feathers.

But the most impressive thing in the room was a highly polished grand piano which stood in the bay of the window.

Sarah had often heard Dorothy play the instrument when family and friends had gathered for celebrations, like those at Hogmanay which began each New Year.

Philip broke into Sarah's reflections as he entered the room.

He was still dressed in his dark suit, but without the jacket, and his gold watch and chain hung from his waist coat. The only sign that he was relaxing in his own home was that the sleeves of his fine linen shirt were rolled up in a workman-like style.

Sarah rose from her seat by the fire but Philip urged her to stay at her ease.

After hearing Helen describe her encounter with Philip, Sarah had been concerned that he would have been put off the whole idea. She now tried to excuse Helen's behaviour to him explaining that her sister-in-law was over-wrought.

Philip's reply alarmed her even more.

'Do not be worrying yerself, Sarah,' he said. 'In a way it was the response I hoped I'd get.'

Sarah groaned inwardly, he must have thought better of it!

'Ye know, Sarah, that I'm worth a bit o' money now?'

Sarah nodded.

'I don't think I'm being too proud when a say that if I had made my offer to any other widow woman in the town, it would like to have been accepted on the spot in spite,' here Philip hesitated, then went on, 'in spite of my age.'

Sarah agreed.

'Helen's reaction was different,' he said, 'so I hope she will, in time, change her mind. I would like that fine.'

Sarah breathed a sigh of relief.

As Philip showed her out she confessed, 'A took her down to the Poorhoose the day.'

'That was cruel,' Philip said.

Sarah looked crestfallen.

'But wise,' he added, with a twinkle in his eye.

Edinburgh

18th August 1850

Helen Delaney stood in the centre of her living room while Sarah and Jane fussed around her buttoning up her soft cream kid boots and adjusting the lace collar on her dress.

After discussion it had been agreed that black was not suitable for a wedding gown but a light colour would have been inappropriate with Arthur only three months dead. Sarah and Jane settled on a rich purple velvet trimmed with creamy lace at the collar and cuffs.

Helen could not have cared less what she wore to her wedding but since the dress was a gift from Sarah and John she feigned enthusiasm.

Helen's hair was as black and lustrous as it had been when she was young and Jane had arranged it with little bunches of ringlets behind each ear. Helen looked lovely. She was of medium height and her slim girlish figure had matured over the years without growing heavy. The wide skirts of the gown flared out from a waist that was still slender in spite of her many pregnancies.

Sarah carefully placed the matching purple bonnet on Helen's head and tied the mauve satin ribbons under her chin trying not to notice that they matched the mauve shadows smudged under Helen's eyes. Sarah well knew the many sleepless nights that her sister-in-law had spent before finally agreeing to marry Philip Boylan.

Sarah was to be Helen's bridesmaid and she was dressed in shades of browns and russets while Jane wore a dark green gown which set off her red hair to perfection.

Glancing out of the window, Sarah cried, 'The carriage is here!'

She darted to the door and held it open for her sister-in-law.

Helen took one last, long, lingering look around the home she had shared with Arthur knowing she would never again stand here as Helen Delaney. Before her resolve could falter she picked up her soft kid gloves and walked through the open door.

Philip had sent a carriage to convey the women to the church and the driver jumped down when the women appeared and helped them climb into the horse-drawn vehicle.

Neighbours stood around on the pavement calling out – "good luck" and waving - as they set off at a steady pace. Jane threw pennies out of the carriage and swarms of bairns rolled in the dust to catch them.

The traditional 'poor oot' at a wedding was always an event for the local bairns and brought them running from streets around.

Helen sank back, wearily, against the plush upholstery and her sisters-in-law glanced at her anxiously.

The carriage passed Philip's house, where, the women knew, the preparations were underway for the wedding celebration that was to take place there later.

They turned at the corner of the Netherbow and set off up the High Street.

As they approached St Giles Cathedral its bells suddenly pealed out. Helen was instantly reminded of a story that Arthur had told her. When the hated Act of Union was finally signed the bells of St Giles had tolled the old tune – *Why should I be sad on my wedding day*. The tune today was different but Helen felt the old tune would have been more appropriate.

The carriage turned on to George IV Bridge and was making its way to St Patrick's church when Sarah suddenly burst into conversation.

'Sure it's a right bonnie day, and not a breath of wind,' she prattled on breathlessly.

But her efforts were in vain.

Helen could not stop her head from turning instinctively towards the open gates to the Greyfriars Kirk through which she could see Arthur's grave.

Sarah went quiet as all three women struggled to contain their emotions but suddenly they were there!

The carriage came to a halt outside St Patrick's Chapel, on Lothian Street, the door of the cab opened and the driver helped the women descend.

Jane went ahead to warn Fr Grant that the bride had arrived.

Helen had hoped that when she and Philip had gone to see the priest about their intentions to marry that Fr Grant would have forbidden it. After all, she thought, didn't the Church teach that marriage was a Holy Sacrament not to be entered into lightly, and only by those who truly loved each other. She was sure that knowing that both their spouses were so recently dead that the priest would be scandalised and at least suggest they delay the nuptials. But Fr Grant had long ministered to his people in the Old Town. He had seen the desperate state of too many children left fatherless, or indeed motherless, to be concerned with any such niceties and gave his warm approval.

Helen and Sarah climbed the fine carved oak staircase. St Patrick's was unusual in that the church was on the first floor of the building. The lower part was used for the school and for meeting rooms.

The women paused outside the door on the top landing. Sarah inspected Helen and adjusted her bonnet then, after kissing her tenderly on the cheek, she opened the door and they entered the church.

The church they entered was gloomy and panelled totally in varnished oak. Tall windows ran down one side but they let in little daylight being blocked by even taller buildings on the other side of the road. The only light came from the candles that flickered in front of statues of the Virgin and of St Patrick himself.

There was no central aisle so Helen started slowly down the left-hand aisle followed by Sarah.

Philip stood by the altar wearing his Sunday suit but with a white flower in his lapel. His best man stood beside him.

A small group of family and friends clustered in the pews near the front. Helen's sons James, Thomas and John sat in the front row looking unnaturally tidy with their hair slicked back and faces well scrubbed.

Helen kept her eyes fixed on her children as she walked towards the altar.

Had she looked at Philip she would have seen what Sarah walking behind her saw. Philip's face registered admiration, and, what was it, Sarah wondered? Hope, she decided, that was it. Philip suddenly looked younger and full of hope.

Helen finally looked at Philip as she came to a halt beside him and, looking, saw only kindness there.

A smiling Fr Grant led them through the service, Philip slipped a ring on her now bare, wedding finger, and Helen Boylan walked out of the church on her new husband's arm, leaving Helen Delaney behind in the brown shadows of the church.

Given the circumstances, Philip and Helen had decided on a small gathering of family and close friends back at Philip's house. Bessie, and Philip's cook, Bridget, had done them proud. The house was gleaming, fresh flowers stood in vases on every surface, and the table in the dining-room groaned with a variety of food and drink. No expense had been spared.

As day turned to evening the celebration was still in full swing. Regardless of the intentions of the couple the Irish in the Old Town knew how to enjoy themselves. Wake or wedding it made no difference to them! Jackets came off, collars were loosened, and, with drink taken, lively step-dancing took place on the stone slabs of the kitchen floor to the tune of a fiddle.

Sarah, clapping her hands to the rhythm of the music, looked around at all the flushed happy faces and then her eyes alighted on someone who was not smiling, whose hands were not clapping.

Eleanor, Philip's surviving daughter, sat bolt upright in her chair.

Her face was flushed with anger and she glared at the dancers on the floor.

Sarah knew that Eleanor had been devoted to her mother, Dorothy. Indeed she had named her grand mansion house in South Fort Street, in Leith, Warrick House, after her mother.

Her husband, John Lennon, sat beside his glowering wife his foot tapping to the music. As Sarah watched one of the Collin's girls tried to drag John on to the dance floor but one glance from his formidable wife caused him to laughingly decline.

How in God's name did those two ever come to marry, Sarah wondered.

Eleanor was twenty-two years old and she could never be described as bonnie, her face was too strong for that. Perhaps handsome was the word that best described her. She was heavily pregnant but, as usual, was beautifully dressed in the latest London fashions which she was well able to afford given the profits from her many business interests. Today, though, she was clad in black from head to foot.

Her husband was tall and slim and, Sarah thought, probably the best-looking man in the room. He was also full of fun, loved to dance, had a fine singing voice and never a penny to his name until he married Eleanor.

Perhaps that was the answer, Sarah thought.

What Eleanor wanted she usually got. She had inherited her father's talent for business but she was much more ruthless than Philip. Sarah knew that Eleanor went personally to collect the rent from all her many tenants, trusting no one else.

As Sarah watched, Eleanor's face took on an expression of particular malice. Looking round she saw that it was Helen who had entered the room. Anxiety clutched at Sarah's heart but she forced herself to smile as Helen sat down beside her.

'Everyone's having a grand time,' Sarah said, 'but where are the bairns, I don't remember seeing them for a while?'

'They are upstairs, and your Arthur with them,' Helen replied.

After the meal was over, the cake had been cut and the toasts had been drunk, Philip had asked Helen to bring her sons and follow him upstairs. A large attic room ran the whole width of the house and as Philip had opened the door Helen had seen that it was laid out as a bedroom and playroom for the three boys. Boxes of toys were stacked around the room and a large rocking horse, with flowing mane and tail, stood in the window space.

Thomas and John immediately had run towards it and had asked to be lifted on. Philip had obliged and as he had done so Helen, looking round, had realised that these must have been Philip's dead sons' toys. He had certainly indulged them, the room looked like a toy shop!

James had stayed close to his mother. He had been very quiet since Helen had told her sons that she was to marry Mr Boylan and she could never be sure just what her ten year old son was thinking.

Philip had turned to him, 'Come and see what I have for ye,' he said, and led James to the far corner of the room.

A desk had been set up under the eaves and on it had sat a large drawing-board. Philip had reached under the desk and had drawn out a large gift-wrapped box. Handing it to James he had asked, 'Will ye manage to open it?'

Another boy might have torn at the wrapping, but James had undone the string and had carefully unwrapped the gift, smoothing out the paper. Opening the lid he had gasped at the array of colourful paints, crayons, pencils and brushes it contained.

Helen had seen her son's face light up for the first time in months.

'Is this a fer me?' he had stammered.

'It is indeed,' Philip had replied, 'and there is plenty of paper in the drawer in the desk.'

James had smiled at his mother in delight then going to stand in front of Philip he had said, 'A thank ye, Papa.'

Helen had breathed a sigh of relief. Papa had been the name they had decided her sons would call Philip, to distinguish him from their own father, and she was glad the name had come so naturally to James's lips.

'Ye are most welcome,' Philip had responded, 'and a look forward to the fine drawings ye will do – yer mother tells me ye do right good work.'

Philip had then turned to the other two boys who were still rocking happily by the window. 'A have something for ye both, too,' he had said.

He had lifted the two younger children down and then had taken another parcel from a chest of drawers and had handed it to them. Unlike their brother, the boys had torn at the wrapper in anticipation and had revealed a wooden train set complete with engine, carriages and track. Helen had seen from the box that it was a fine set, made in Germany.

'Can we set it up now,' Thomas had asked, jumping up and down with excitement, 'and can Arthur come and see?'

Philip had knelt on the floor, in his good suit trousers, and with James's help, had started to lay out the track.

Looking over his shoulder at Helen, Philip had said, 'Would ye like to send wee Arthur up, Mistress?'

Helen had described the scene in the attic to Sarah. 'He's right kind Sarah,' Helen said.

'He is that,' Sarah replied. Then taking Helen's hand she tried to reassure her. 'It's going to be alright, Helen, ye made the right decision.'

A shadow flitted across Helen's face but she smiled wanly at Sarah and agreed.

Sarah, John, and a reluctant wee Arthur were the last to leave that night.

Bessie had gone upstairs to settle the three boys for the night and Helen and Philip stood on the doorstep to make their farewells. The two men shook hands and Sarah warmly embraced Helen but when she stood back and looked deep into Helen's eyes the pain she saw there caused her to take a sharp intake of breath and she turned away hastily.

Helen and Philip waved until the family turned the corner, out of sight, then turned back into the house with Philip bolting the door behind them.

Sarah made it as far as their own home before bursting into tears. Throwing herself into her husband's arms she wailed, 'What hiv a done, what hiv a done!'

Back in St Mary's Wynd Philip went into the parlour while Helen climbed to the attic to say goodnight to her sons. The boys exhausted by the long day and the excitement of their new toys were already fast asleep. She stood looking down at the three, now tousled heads, of her sons tucked up safe and warm in their snug beds.

She sent up a prayer. 'Blessed Virgin, please grant that I have made the right decision.'

When she returned to the parlour Philip was sitting by the fire, and she took the seat on the other side of the fireplace, painfully aware that this was where Dorothy probably used to sit. She felt like an intruder.

They discussed the events of the day and Helen again thanked Philip for his kindness to her sons.

'It's what I promised ye, Mistress, and I try never to break a promise,' Philip said. 'But ye must be tired, why don't ye go off to bed? I'll jist stay here a bit and hiv a wee glass o spirits.'

Helen entered the room that Philip had shared with Dorothy, but she was surprised to see that all the bed-linen and furnishings had been changed since Philip had showed her round the house on her accepting his proposal. Philip had asked her if she wanted to bring any of her own furniture with her but Helen had declined. Apart from the fact that her things would have looked out of place in this grand house, she felt she could not bear to see anything that reminded her of her life with Arthur. She didn't think she would be able to cope with that.

A fine fire burned brightly in the grate and Helen saw that Bessie had unpacked her small bag and laid her new night gown across the bed. Helen undressed and struggled quickly into it. She hung her wedding dress in the closet which she was relieved to see contained only Philip's clothes and the few items of clothing she had brought with her. Dorothy's clothes had all been cleared away.

A china basin and water ewer, decorated with large pink cabbage roses, stood on the hearth and Helen washed her hands and face in the warm water. She loosed her hair from the pins that held her ringlets in place and brushed out her long hair, then she climbed into the high bed.

The clean white linen sheets felt cold and Helen shivered as she lay there waiting for Philip.

Sheer exhaustion must have caused her to drift off to sleep but she was awakened by Philip climbing in beside her.

She went rigid but Philip simply reached over and tucked the quilt in around her shoulders.

His lips brushed her forehead and he said, 'It's alright, Helen, let's jist get to know each other a bit first will we?' And turning on his side away from her Philip settled down to sleep.

Helen felt her whole body relax and as she drifted off to sleep she realised that it was the first time he had called her by her name.

HELEN'S STORY

PART TWO

Chapter 1

Edinburgh

31st December 1854

Helen Boylan stood at the window of her house at 17 St Mary's Wynd. It was Hogmanay and the street was still busy with folk making sure they had food and their Ne'erday bottle in for the New Year.

She had been married to Philip Boylan now for almost five years.

To Philip's great joy a son, Luke, had been born to them in August 1851.

When he was baptised in St Patrick's Church, in Lothian Street, Sarah Delaney and her husband John Skiffington had proudly stood as his god-parents. Luke was a sturdy, robust bairn who had survived all the dangers of early childhood in the Old Town and was now approaching four years old. He was a serious, calm, child who appeared wise beyond his years. Even in the rough and tumble of play with his older stepbrothers, James, Thomas and John Delaney, Luke always emerged clean, tidy and with not a hair out of place.

His father, Philip, doted on him, seeing in the bairn the realisation of all his hopes for the family name continuing. The loss of all his sons to his first wife, Dorothy, had been a hard blow to him. Luke followed his father around everywhere, hands behind his back, showing his father great respect. Learning the tools of the trade Philip joked.

But it was his mother, Helen, that Luke loved with all his heart.

Helen knew that Philip would only feel secure when he had another son but two years had elapsed before Helen became pregnant again. She knew Philip had been disappointed, though he never said anything, but Helen felt as though she was not keeping her part of the agreement. She was relieved, therefore, when she gave birth to another son, whom they named Philip, in 1854. His father was delighted at another male child to carry the family line.

His brother, Luke, was not so delighted. He resented sharing his mother's attention with the newcomer. Helen would sometimes come into the room and see Luke glowering down at the baby in the cradle.

Helen rested her head on the cool glass of the window feeling suddenly weary. She was now thirty-five years old and from her two marriages she had given birth to seven children. Helen wondered how many more times she would be brought to child-bed. She had hoped that after the birth of a second son, Philip would have been content that she had fulfilled her purpose. This proved not to be the case.

Almost as soon as she thought it Helen felt guilty.

She should be grateful so many of her children had survived. Only her twins to Arthur, Mary and Rosanna, had died after birth. She remembered anew her heartbreak at the death of her daughters, as first one then the other, sickened and died. She looked instinctively across the street to where she had mourned their loss in the house she had shared with Arthur.

She felt ungrateful, too.

Philip had more than kept his side of the agreement. He treated his Delaney stepsons as well as he treated their own sons. James was now fifteen, Thomas twelve and John seven years old. They wanted for nothing. They lived in comfort in this big house in St Mary's Wynd. They were well fed and very well dressed. Philip, a master tailor, made all their clothes himself. He had paid for them to have the best education possible. But, most of all, he showed them care and affection. Helen was in no doubt that her three sons returned that affection and showed Philip great respect. Over the years any resentment that they might have felt that he was not their own father had long gone.

What on earth would have happened to them if she had not agreed to marry Philip, Helen thought. Her mind flew back to the day she stood in front of the Queensberry Poorhouse, in the Canongate, with Arthur's sister Sarah Skiffington.

'Well,' Sarah had demanded, 'is that where you want your sons to end up?'

As if she had conjured her up the door of the room opened and Bessie, the maid, showed Sarah into the room.

'Is it a dream ye are in?' exclaimed Sarah. 'Sure, did ye not see me waving up to ye from the street?'

'A was miles away,' Helen replied, as she turned from the window.

Sarah Skiffington missed nothing – she took in the view that Helen had been looking at – the house where Helen and Sarah's brother, Arthur, had lived.

She marched forward and pulled the lace curtain back across the window.

Taking Helen by the hand she led her to a chair beside the fire and pushed her into it.

'Yer tired tis all,' she said.

'Aye, yer right,' Helen agreed.

'Yer not doing too much wi' all the preparations are ye?' Sarah demanded.

'No. no,' Helen responded. 'Bessie and Bridget have it all in hand. In fact a'm totally useless.'

Sarah knew that Helen found it hard to be the lady of leisure that marriage to Philip had entailed. Philip had always had servants and when Helen married him he had employed another to attend to the needs of Helen's sons. When their own sons were born Philip had also employed a Nanny for them. Philip required only that she attend his many business and social functions with him and act as hostess when he entertained. Apart from that he wanted her to devote her full attention to his sons. With a household of five laddies Sarah thought that was demanding enough, even with help.

As if reading Sarah's mind Helen suddenly burst out –

'A was jest thinking that now he has two sons will Philip be content? What dae ye think?'

Sarah shook her head. 'A dinnae ken, Helen,' she replied.

Sarah knew what the agreement had been from the beginning – that on their marriage Helen would replace Philip's lost sons – so she didn't pretend not to understand Helen's meaning.

Helen suddenly sat up straight in her chair.

'A'm an ungrateful besom, so a am – a don't know what's got intae me,' she cried.

Changing the subject, she asked, 'An how is Jane? Did her wedding gown fitting go well?'

'It did indeed, she looks jest lovely,' Sarah replied. 'John Murray is a lucky man tae get as bonnie a colleen as my sister. I have given the gown tae Bessie tae lay out in yer room.'

The preparations that Sarah had previously mentioned referred to the fact that not only was it the eve of the New Year, but that on the morrow, the first day of January 1855 Jane Delaney was to marry John Murray.

John was from Letterkenny, in Ireland, and, although only twenty-two years old, was a successful clothier and broker in the Old Town.

The wedding was to take place here, in Helen and Philip's house, and it was to be a grand affair.

Sarah, and her husband, John Skiffington, had provided the wedding gown and her dowry. Philip had insisted that he pay for everything else that the wedding celebrations entailed.

Over the previous week the entire house had been cleaned from top to bottom, though it was already spotless as far as Helen could see. Philip's cook, Bridget, had been given extra help in the kitchen to prepare the food for the wedding breakfast. She had been cooking and baking for days and storing it in the cold larder in the offshoot from the kitchen. Philip had also arranged for a large delivery of ale and spirits to accompany the celebrations.

Fr O'Donnell had agreed to come to the house in the morning to perform the marriage ceremony. He had explained that a new law had been passed which meant that John Murray would have to register the marriage afterwards at the local Registry Office. The priest explained that from the first of January 1855, all births, marriages and deaths would have to be recorded by the Civil Authorities. He had teased Jane that perhaps she would make history by being the first bride to appear in the new Registers in Edinburgh!

Sarah took her leave of Helen and returned to her own house at 105 High Street to dress for the celebrations. They would all return to Helen and Philip's house in time for the bells at midnight.

Helen sat on staring into the fire then rose, reluctantly, and went to supervise the preparations.

After being reassured by Bessie and Bridget that all was in hand, Helen climbed the stair to the room being used as the nursery. Jenny, the Nanny, sat at the fire knitting. Luke lay in his small bed, his chubby arms behind his head. Baby Philip lay in the cot in the corner. Looking down at him Helen was amazed at the difference between the brothers. This bairn was thin and had a fuzz of downy black hair, a little pixie face and a pointed chin. He must be a throw back to some long ago Boylan she thought. Both the bairns were fast asleep. Helen then climbed the stair to the large attic bedroom that her three older sons still shared. Thomas and John were asleep in their beds but James lay on top of his reading a book. They had been told that they could get up and join in the celebrations at midnight, and then stay up for their Auntie Jane's wedding. This was on condition that they had gone off to bed early to get in some rest. After exchanging a few quiet words with James Helen returned to her own bedroom to get changed.

Entering the room she saw that Bessie had laid Jane's wedding gown, carefully encased in tissue paper, on the large bed. The accessories lay alongside them.

Helen resisted the temptation to have a quick peek at the gown.

She slipped out of her day dress, unloosed her long hair from its pins and stood in her lacy underclothing. She picked up the jug of warm water from the hearth and poured it into the rose-patterned china basin.

The door opened and Philip entered the room.

Helen jumped and had to resist the temptation to cover herself with the towel.

Philip was already dressed in his best suit complete with fine linen shirt and cravat. His heavy gold watch and chain hung at his waistcoat. He still had a full head of silvery hair and looked every inch the prosperous business man that he was.

'I'm sorry Helen, did I startle thee? I just came to see if thee were ready,' he said. His Irish lilt remained as strong as when he had left Monaghan thirty-five years before.

'A'm almost ready,' Helen stammered as Philip crossed the room.

'So this is the famous bridal gown, is it?' Philip said looking down at the froth of lace escaping the tissue paper on their bed.

While his back was turned, Helen reached into the large oak wardrobe and removed her new gown, slipping it quickly over her head. It was Philip's choice. He had chosen the crimson satin and the black velvet trimmings. The most skilled dress-maker in his business had made it and it was a perfect fit.

As she struggled to fasten the cloth-covered buttons Philip turned to her.

'Let me help ye with those,' he offered.

He deftly fastened the buttons then touched his lips to each of her bare shoulders in turn.

Helen felt a flush spreading from her face down over her neck.

'Ye will even outshine the bride in that gown,' he said, admiringly.

'A don't think so,' said Helen, 'Jane is a bonnie, young lassie. Just go down, Philip,' Helen urged. 'A'll be down in a minute, a have jest tae put ma hair up.'

'Leave it, Helen, it looks grand just as it is,' Philip said.

Helen sat down at the mirror and pulled the brush through her hair. It was still plentiful with only a few silver hairs threading their way through her black curls.

She could see in the mirror Philip watching her, and as he stepped towards her she turned round on her dressing table stool.

'I have a gift for ye,' he said, drawing a small box from his jacket pocket. He opened it and let the gold chain run through his fingers. A large ruby flashed in the lamplight. 'Let me fasten it for ye.' He fastened the chain then turned her back round towards him. His fingers touched her bare flesh as he adjusted the ruby so that it hung straight over her décolletage.

'It's beautiful,' Helen said, turning to look at her reflection in the mirror, 'but ye shouldnae have. Ye have been good enough tae me already.'

'I wanted tae thank ye for the fine sons ye have given me,' Philip responded. 'Maybe, in this New Year, if God blesses us, we will have another son.'

Helen felt her heart sink.

Just then the doorbell chimed and Helen and Philip descended the stairs to greet the first of their guests.

Well before midnight the rest of their guests had assembled. Now they all stood, whisky glass in hand, waiting. The large oak sideboard in the parlour groaned with baskets of Irish soda bread, trays of cheese and plates of Madeira cake. As a gesture towards the traditions of their Scottish friends there were also plates of buttery Scottish shortbread and slices of the dried fruit encased in pastry that in Scotland they called Black Bun.

Just before midnight all the windows and the front door were thrown open to welcome in the New Year and to better hear the bells. On the stroke of midnight every church in town set its bells pealing. Ringing out the old, ringing in the new. On this still clear night they could even hear the boats down in the Port of Leith sounding their ship's horns.

There was an outbreak of kissing and warm handshakes all round.

Philip swept Helen into his arms and kissed her full on the mouth.

'Happy New Year, my dear,' he said.

Once the bells had stopped, as many guests as possible crowded into the hallway to see who the First Foot would be.

There were strict conditions attached to who should be a First Foot (that is the first person to step over the doorway after midnight). It had to be a male. For some reason women were regarded as unlucky. He had to have dark hair. Fair or red-haired men were not welcome on your doorstep. The tradition was said to date back to the days, long ago, when the Vikings invaded Scotland. The last person you would want to see on your doorstep was a man with flowing fair hair or red beard! The First Foot had to bear certain gifts, shortbread, whisky and a lump of black coal. These blessed the home with food, drink and heat in the year to come.

Luckily, tonight, the First Foot was the groom-to-be, John Murray, and since he was tall dark and handsome and carried the appropriate gifts he was warmly welcomed in.

Jane Delaney did not arrive until after the bells.

It was considered unlucky for the groom to see the bride on the night *before* their wedding day. However, there was no way Jane was going to miss the Hogmanay celebrations! It was therefore decided that since New Years Day began after midnight it was in fact the *next* day so she was free to attend. She was not yet in her wedding apparel though that would come later.

The Irish community in the Old Town knew how to celebrate a wedding, and the Scots friends they had made knew how to celebrate Hogmanay, so the hours flew by with drinking, eating, dancing and singing.

There was as much noise outside the house as in.

The Edinburgh Hogmanay tradition was to gather around the Tron Kirk on the High Street to welcome in the bells. The celebrations then spilled out into the surrounding streets. Every door stood open. Everyone carried their Ne'erday bottle – always whisky - and this was passed from mouth to mouth among friends and strangers alike. The result was many sore heads the next day as well as some broken ones as the inevitable drink-fuelled fights broke out.

But inside 17 St Mary's Wynd, only fun and friendship reigned, though the amount of spirits consumed was considerable.

Towards morning Sarah and Helen found themselves seated together watching the lively dancing. Sarah was reminded of that other time when she and Helen sat like this at another wedding, the wedding of Helen herself, to Philip, five years ago.

As the memory returned, Sarah glanced across the room to where Philip's daughter, Eleanor, sat. Her husband, John Lennon, sat at her side now as he had then all those years ago. Eleanor and John now had two sons. Philip Lennon was six years old and his brother John was only four. They had been left at home in the care of Eleanor's many servants in their opulent house in South Fort Street in Leith.

Eleanor, though only twenty-six, was an astute business woman. She had built up a considerable property empire by buying houses, sub-dividing them and renting them out. In this she was following in her father's footsteps but Eleanor not only had property in the Old Town she had expanded down into the Port of Leith.

John's foot was tapping in time to the music, he was obviously keen to join in the dancing, but Eleanor in the parlance of the Old Town, had 'two left feet' so it was unlikely her husband would be permitted to join in!

Eleanor was not averse to reminding her husband that even the clothes on his back were paid for by her. Sarah wondered how much longer John would be prepared to put up with such treatment. Sarah had heard rumours about John that had disturbed her. It was suggested that he was a bit of a ladies man. Though how he ever got away from Eleanor's vigilant eyes she was at a loss to know.

Sarah was unaware that she had been staring at Eleanor throughout these musings but her scrutiny had obviously caught Eleanor's attention. She rose and crossed to where the two women were sitting.

'Sarah,' Eleanor said, and acknowledged her with a nod of the head.

Then her attention turned to Helen. Her eyes swept over Helen's crimson dress and loose hair.

'Dae ye no think the colour is a bit inappropriate for a woman of your years?' Eleanor enquired.

Helen's face flushed as crimson as her dress and even Sarah was rendered speechless for a moment.

'I suppose ma faither gave you that bauble,' Eleanor continued, stabbing her finger towards the ruby on Helen's breast. 'Ye were a lucky woman when ye managed tae snare a rich old man,' she sneered.

Sarah leapt to her feet, her temper rising, but in a flash John Lennon was at his wife's side.

'Will ye dance, Eleanor?' he pleaded, and attempted to lead his wife on to the floor.

She pushed his encircling arm away.

'If a wanted to dance, a wid tell ye,' she snarled but she returned to her seat and sat down still glaring in Helen's direction.

Helen was now pale and shaking but she managed to pull Sarah down into her seat.

'Leave her be, Sarah, ye ken how she feels about me and her faither,' Helen said.

Sarah could barely restrain her temper. She glared across the room at Eleanor with such venom that even that formidable woman took fright and retreated through to another room.

Luckily, at that moment, Jane, oblivious to the drama, came to fetch her sister to prepare her for her wedding. Jane was wearing a dress of green velvet which set off her red hair and porcelain-white skin to advantage. She and John had been joining in the New Year festivities but now it was time to withdraw to Helen's bedroom to don her wedding attire.

'Jesus, Mary and Joseph, would ye look at the state of ye!' Sarah exclaimed.

Jane's damp ringlets were half up and half down as a result of all the dancing. Two bright pink spots gleamed on her cheeks.

Suitably distracted Sarah bustled away pushing her giggling sister in front of her.

Helen breathed a sigh of relief.

John Lennon rose from his chair and came and stood in front of her.

'A'm right sorry, Helen,' he said. He spread his hands wide, 'A can do nothing with her when she's like that – it's as if a devil takes hold of her.'

'It's a right, John,' Helen said, 'it's no yer fault.'

'Ye'll no tell her faither, will ye?' he pleaded.

Helen assured him that Philip would not be told.

She remembered too well the time when Philip had overhead Eleanor being rude to her step-mother. Philip had given his daughter to understand that she would no longer be welcome in his house unless Helen received an apology.

Eleanor, previously the apple of her father's eye, had been shocked. She apologised forthwith but it was obvious the two women would never be friends. Helen had never been invited to Eleanor's grand house in Leith.

Reassured, John burst out laughing.

'Mind ye,' he said, 'her faither might be the least of her worries. My wife should maybe be careful when collecting her rents in any High Street closes lest she meet Sarah Skiffington one dark night!'

Helen joined in with his laughter and felt some of the tension leave her.

Over John's shoulder she saw Philip enter the room and look around for her. She rose and caught his attention.

'There ye are, Helen, the priest has arrived,' he explained.

Helen and Philip stood chatting to Fr O'Donnell in the front drawing room while Bessie moved a small table into the bay of the window. She covered it with a pure white Irish linen cloth and carefully placed on it a large vase of white, mop-headed chrysanthemums. Helen knew that Philip had ordered them in a high-class florist in the New Town. They had to be imported from Holland and Helen could only imagine how much they had cost. It was typical of the generosity of the man, she thought.

John Murray and his best man, his brother Charles, took up their positions to the side of the table. The priest stood in front of it and John Lennon sat himself down in front of the grand piano that had belonged to Philip's first wife, Dorothy. As many guests as possible crowded into the room. The double doors that led through to the small parlour behind had been opened and more guests took up their positions there.

Sarah appeared in the doorway and nodded to John at the piano, who struck up a bridal march.

As Sarah stepped to one side her sister Jane stood framed in the doorway. A big sigh of appreciation ran round the room and John Murray's smile grew even wider.

Jane was a vision of loveliness. Her tall slender figure showed off to perfection the creamy lace bridal gown which was gathered up in a small bustle behind. The neckline was high and ended in a collar studded with tiny seed pearls. Sarah had managed to rescue Jane's hair and had piled it up in thick coils and encircled them with a ring of pearls attached to a short veil of cobweb fine lace. The veil covered Jane's face as far as her mouth. Her feet were encased in soft cream leather buttoned boots. In her lace-gloved hands Jane carried the white rosary beads that had been given to her by her Ma and Da on her First Communion Day all those years ago in the little chapel in Donagh, in Monaghan.

Helen felt the tears start in her eyes at the sight of her sister-in-law.

Arthur should have been here to give his sister away, she thought.

Sarah and John had spared no expense on Jane's outfit. James Delaney and Mary Hughes would have been so proud to see their two daughters this day but they were both too old and frail to make the voyage from Ireland.

Jane started to walk slowly towards the priest, her bridesmaid, Mary McLachlan, following behind in a dress of palest pink silk. As the last chords of the music died away Mary lifted the veil from Jane's face, took the rosary beads from her hands, and stepped back.

Jane turned to face her admiring groom.

When Fr O'Donnell concluded the marriage ceremony by declaring them man and wife the cheers and applause almost lifted the rafters of the roof!

The long night of dancing had given the guests an appetite and led by the newly-wed couple they streamed through to the kitchen to partake of the wedding breakfast. When they saw the array of food laid out on groaning trestle tables three cheers were called for Bridget and Bessie and a protesting Philip was lifted high on the shoulders of the groom and his brother!

After the meal the guests called for the fiddler to return and Jane and her new husband led off the last dance. It was a waltz and after a few turns on their own they were joined by their bridesmaid, Mary, and best man Charles. The assembled guests then called for Philip and Helen to take the floor.

Philip approached his wife. 'Will ye do me the honour?' he said, bowing slightly in his old fashioned way.

Sarah watched as the three couples circled the floor.

She was so proud of her lovely sister and was sure John would make her happy.

After following them with her eyes for a while Sarah's attention shifted to Philip and Helen.

As she watched, Sarah saw Philip look down at Helen. There was no doubting his expression. Then he stooped and kissed the top of his wife's head.

Sarah stood rooted to the spot.

Philip was in love with Helen! How had she never seen it before?

What had started for Philip as an agreement to replace his lost sons had been replaced by a deep passion. If Philip wanted more children from Helen it was no longer to secure that aim. Philip desired Helen for herself.

But what of Helen, Sarah wondered. Had her feelings changed? She knew Helen was fond of her husband and appreciated his kindness. But love?

As Sarah stood watching and wondering the dance came to an end. Sarah saw a friend of Philip, John Anderson, a Scotsman, approach John Lennon and say something to him. John rose and went to the piano again. The opening bars of the old Scots song, Auld Lang Syne, filled the room. John Lennon had a fine singing voice and people gathered around the piano to listen to the words of Robert Burns.

Her brother Arthur had always admired the Scottish poet. Many a time Sarah had heard him sing this song. She glanced across the room to where Helen stood beside the fire.

Philip had his arm around her waist but the tears were streaming down her cheeks.

Sarah had her answer.

For Helen there would only ever be Arthur.

HELEN'S STORY

PART THREE

CHAPTER 1

Edinburgh

31st December 1860

Helen stood looking out of her window onto St Mary's Wynd. As usual, on Hogmanay, the street was thronged with people making their way to the Tron Kirk to see in the New Year.

Helen was waiting for the first of their guests to arrive for the Boylan's traditional Hogmanay party. Philip had gone through to the kitchen to supervise the setting up of the large barrel of ale that would keep their guests going through the night.

Helen's mind wandered back over the year that was passing. It had been an eventful one. Her son James's wife, Ann, had given birth to Helen's first grandchild here in this house on the 20 March. The couple had named the child Arthur Philip after James's own father and his step-father. Helen remembered how touched Philip had been at the gesture and when James and Ann asked him to be their son's god-father in St Patrick's new chapel, in the Cowgate, his pride was evident to all.

The christening had been a grand affair.

A fine new church had been purchased in 1856 to house the growing congregation in the Old Town. The old St Patrick's was now used as the school and so the name was transferred to the new chapel. It wasn't a new building, however, as it had previously been a Protestant place of worship. But the Kirk had been perfectly happy to sell it to Bishop Gillis for the huge sum of £4,000.

After some work had been done on it to adapt it to the Catholic form of worship it was officially opened on 3 August 1856 by Bishop Gillis in front of a packed congregation of over 2,600 people. Even the semi-circular gallery that ran around three sides of the upper walls of the church were packed.

The main altar was placed in the apse on the wall to the east. It was surrounded by the most beautiful stained glass windows. Since these had belonged to the original parish they contained no religious images as such would have been regarded as sacrilegious in the Protestant tradition. Instead, the windows were elaborately patterned, the glass in jewel bright colours, mainly of blue and red.

On the morning of young Arthur's baptism the sun had streamed through these windows creating pools of colour on the stone floor.

The baby wore a Brussels lace christening gown and a tiny satin cap edged in swansdown. He was wrapped in a pure white wool shawl as fine as a cobweb. Philip had asked an old lady, he knew, to knit it. The lady had come originally from the Shetland Isles and she was famous for her knitting. She had told Philip that there the tradition was that a christening shawl should be fine enough to pass through a wedding ring.

Philip stood proudly beside the font holding his new god-son in his arms.

Helen couldn't help but feel that Philip had been more forgiving towards the couple than she herself felt.

Philip had made sure that James had received a good education and had even funded him to go to an Art College. That James was a gifted artist was never in doubt but that Philip had indulged her son rather than insisting he be apprenticed in a more secure trade had surprised Helen.

Little thanks he got for his generosity, Helen thought, bitterly.

Helen loved her son and they had always been close, but when he eloped to Dunfermline with Ann Maloney his mother had been more hurt than she could have imagined. The couple had been married on the 8th August 1859 by a Fr Stuart in Viewfield House, the priest's home in Dunfermline, since the town did not yet have a Catholic church. They had lied about their ages. James had said he was twenty-one when in fact he was only nineteen and Ann had declared she was nineteen when she was actually only seventeen.

When they returned and her shamefaced son announced they were married and that Ann was pregnant Helen had been furious. But Philip had taken it all in his stride. He had insisted they stay here at home until the baby was born. It was generous of him, and sensible, since they had little money to set up home on their own.

Would she have been more accepting if she had actually liked Ann, Helen wondered. Perhaps that was why they eloped. Her son was sensitive and intuitive. He must have sensed her dislike and realised his mother would never have given her approval to a marriage with Ann.

Helen had watched as her son fell under Ann's spell.

What on earth did he see in her Helen wondered?

Ann was not conventionally pretty. She was short with a full figure but a fine boned face and masses of red hair. She was new to the Old Town having only recently arrived from Ireland with her father Patrick Maloney. Her mother, Catran Gorman, was dead. Helen had to admit that what Ann lacked in looks she more than made up for in personality. She was quick-witted with a wicked sense of humour and a ready laugh. Whenever you heard that laugh you could be sure to see Ann surrounded by an admiring circle of lads.

Helen had watched as her quiet, shy son had stood in just such a circle his eyes never leaving Ann's face.

Helen had tried to reassure herself that it was just a passing infatuation but one day James dropped an art case he was carrying and a sheaf of drawings of Ann fell out. As Helen helped her blushing son pick up the sketches she saw in them the Ann that James saw and her concern increased.

She had confided her worries to Sarah but like Philip her sister-in-law could not understand her concern.

'Sure, it would be the same no matter what colleen stole the heart of your first-born,' Sarah joked.

But Helen didn't think so. They were so ill-matched Helen could never see how they could be happy together.

Once they had moved in Helen did her best to make her daughter-in-law feel welcome. But she watched, in amazement, as even her normally wise husband roared with laughter at one of Ann's quips.

James had been working as an artist and he also picked up some work making designs for the linen industry but it was a precarious existence.

One night Helen had heard her son and Philip discussing how fewer people were asking for drawings of themselves to be made and choosing to have photographs taken instead. Previously a luxury for the well off more and more ordinary folk were flocking to the new studios in town to have their image captured in this fashion.

'Perhaps it's something you could consider yourself, James,' Philip had said. 'It seems to be a growing trade and you have a good eye – you could do well.'

James had explained that photography was an expensive business to start. Apart from a camera, of course, you also needed plates, chemicals, paper and all manner of equipment as well as premises.

'Well a'm sure a could help wi a that,' his step-father had replied.

Helen was alarmed at this and later when they were alone in their bedroom had expressed her concerns to Philip.

'This could cost a lot of money – ye shouldnae feel ye must do this. Ye have done so much for my sons already,' Helen had argued.

Philip had come and sat on the edge of the bed where Helen lay propped up on pillows. He had laid his hand gently on Helen's hugely swollen stomach.

'A think ye have mair than kept yer side o our agreement, do ye not?' he had asked.

Helen had looked down to where his hand was resting. Her tenth pregnancy and she was now forty years old!

Helen flushed as she remembered walking by their stables at the Netherbow heavily pregnant again. Two of the stable lads doffed their caps as she passed but as she rounded the corner out of their sight they imagined her to be out of sound to.

'A,' said one of them, 'sure there's life in the old dog yet!' This was followed by a burst of ribald laughter.

Helen was mortified. No wonder they were laughing. What must people be thinking? Her, pregnant again at her age and Philip now sixty-five years old.

Since Jane Delaney's wedding Helen had given birth to two more bairns to Philip. Their daughter Mary was born in 1857. Helen had thought that Philip would have been disappointed that it was a lassie but Philip seemed genuinely delighted at the birth of a daughter.

Helen had discussed it with Sarah.

'A thought the point o the agreement was to produce sons to carry on the Boylan name,' Helen had said, 'but he's carrying her around showing her off to all and sundry, for all the world as if she was another laddie!'

Helen thought that Sarah had looked at her strangely and was about to say something but she thought better of it.

When a year later another son, whom they named James, was born Philip was pleased but it seemed that it was wee Mary looking so like her mother, with that mop of black curls, that Philip still doted on.

Surely, three sons would be enough of a reassurance that his name would continue, Helen had hoped. But no, looking at her swollen stomach Helen had fervently prayed that this bairn would be another laddie and perhaps that would be an end to it.

Perhaps being pregnant at the same time as her daughter-in-law had also affected Helen's attitude towards Ann she sometimes thought. The fact of being pregnant again at forty when she was already a grandmother had caused Helen some mortification.

Philip though had shown no such embarrassment. Helen had seen him blush when one of his friends had teased him on his continuing prowess but he had still seemed pleased.

As she stood there Helen was overwhelmed with sadness.

When their fourth son, John, was born on 12 April 1860 it was obvious there was something amiss. It had been a difficult labour and the baby had struggled to come into the world. They called his condition 'water on the brain' and he just sickened and died five months later.

Helen had been consumed with guilt. She felt sure that it was because she had not wanted another bairn that her wee son had died. She was being punished by God.

Philip had been saddened by the loss of his son and Helen wondered what he was thinking when he laid the baby to rest in the Boylan family plot in the Canongate Churchyard beside his other lost sons.

But he had tried to comfort Helen saying they should be thankful that their other bairns were all strong and healthy.

Helen, lost in thought, jumped when their door bell chimed.

She heard Bessie go to answer it.

The first of their guests had arrived.

Helen came downstairs and the evening was set to unfold as had all the Hogmanays they had celebrated during the ten years of their married life together.

But this year's festivities were to be different in one dramatic way.

The windows and front door had been opened, as usual, to welcome in the New Year. The church bells had chimed and the ships' horns had hooted down in Leith. Kisses and handshakes had been exchanged all round and then they had all crowded out into the hallway to await the First Foot.

This year, Philip, had arranged for Helen's son, James, to fill this role. He had orders to wait outside the door until the bells stopped pealing.

However, before James could step over the threshold his wife, Ann, oblivious of the old Scots custom, stepped in front of him.

James, his hands full of whisky, shortbread and coal was powerless to stop her.

There was a collective intake of breath as those gathered realised the significance of her action.

A woman, a red-haired woman, became the First-Foot of the year 1861!

Even Philip looked shocked. However, always the most courteous of men, he quickly regained his composure and welcomed Ann in with a kiss.

As James handed the traditional gifts to Philip he whispered, 'A'm sorry, Papa.'

'Ye are not tae worry,' Philip reassured him, taking the gifts. Then shaking his stepson by the hand, he added, 'It's jist an auld superstition.'

Helen sincerely hoped he was right.

The music started up, the dancing got under way and the food was as lavish as ever but she couldn't help sensing that an undercurrent of unease affected the whole gathering.

'What would the year 1861 bring?' she wondered.

She hoped the incident with Ann was not a bad omen of things to come.

Chapter 2

24th November 1861

Helen and Philip lay in bed. It was a dreich, dark morning and neither was keen to rise until the fire that Bessie had just lit in the grate had time to catch and burn and release some warmth into the chill of the room.

Suddenly, there came a hammering on their front door and a voice from the street called –

'Maister Boylan, Maister Boylan, ye had better come quick.'

Philip leapt from the bed and was still struggling with the braces of his trousers when Bessie burst back into the room.

'Maister Boylan, it's Mistress Sarah's hoose …a hale building has jist collapsed,' she gasped.

Philip ran from the room.

'Wait!' Helen called after him, 'a'm coming wi ye.'

'No, ye stay here,' he shouted over his shoulder.

But Helen was already up and pulling on her clothes.

A cold, wet haar engulfed Helen as she stepped into St Mary's Wynd and she drew her shawl closer around her. The street was deserted but as she turned the corner into the High Street she saw crowds of people up ahead. All the house windows in the High Street were open and above her head people were leaning on their windowsills craning to see.

Helen could feel the panic rising in her throat. Please dear Lord let Sarah, John and wee Arthur be alright, she prayed. She broke into a run. What would she do if anything happened to them? They had always been there for her. They had supported her all through those dreadful days after Arthur's death. Sarah had been her confidant all through the years of her marriage to Philip. Only Sarah truly appreciated her predicament and she doubted if she could have survived without her. As she approached 105 High Street her vision was obscured. It was still dark and gloomy with the haar, but also from the clouds of dust that hung in the air.

Helen tried to peer through the gloom and as she got nearer she was filled with horror. The building behind Sarah's house had just disappeared. There was just a space were once it had stood.

The noise was deafening. People were shouting and Helen could hear screams of pain from the pile of rubble that was all that remained of the tall tenement that had stood there. She closed her eyes and covered her ears against the horror of it all. People were trapped in there!

When she opened her eyes again she saw Sarah stumbling towards her across the rubble strewn High Street. She had wee Arthur by the hand. Sarah was as pale as death and her red hair tumbled across her shoulders. She collapsed into Helen's arms and sobbed her heart out.

'The noise, Helen, ye would not believe the noise when it fell,' she wept.

She was in deep shock.

Helen was so relieved to see them that it was a few moments before she thought to ask if John was safe.

'John, Sarah, where's John?' Helen cried.

Sarah had no breath to answer wracked as she was with sobs. She pointed, wordlessly.

Following the direction of Sarah's shaking finger Helen looked and saw John clambering up on a pile of rubble at the side of their house. Their building was still intact but a gas pipe jutting from the side of their house had fractured.

Helen learned later that John had turned off the gas supply as soon as he realised the danger. However, it was so dark that the rescuers couldn't see so it dawned on John that lighting the escaping gas would illuminate the scene. He had arranged that when he reached the fractured pipe word would be passed down the line to his neighbours. They would turn on and light the gas in the Skiffington's shop and house.

John carried a lit oil lamp and a taper.

As soon as the gas started to escape again he lit the taper from the lamp then applied the taper to the escaping gas.

By this time, realising the danger he was in, Sarah was in hysterics and wee Arthur was weeping and rubbing his eyes.

Helen watched, her heart in her mouth. When the gas took it didn't explode but flared up and illuminated the whole scene.

A rousing cheer greeted his heroism and willing hands helped him scramble down off the rubble.

Sarah ran forward and threw her arms around her husband then led him back to where Helen stood holding wee Arthur by the hand.

'God Bless ye, John,' Helen sobbed, as John lifted his son into his arms.

The four stood for a moment in a huddle, their heads touching, then John straightened up.

'A have tae go and help, the Lord only knows how many poor folk are trapped in there', he said. 'Take Sarah and the bairn back tae yer hoose, Helen'.

However, Sarah had recovered somewhat and her old spirit had returned.

'A'm going nowhere, John Skiffington,' she shouted after him, 'a'm staying right here!'

John didn't argue he returned to where the men were digging in the ruins with their bare hands.

Some people had escaped from the building as it began to collapse and dressed only in their night clothes they were digging frantically looking for family and neighbours.

Looking at the scene it seemed to Helen that every able bodied man in the Old Town had come to help in the search.

She looked for Philip and saw that he had organised a chain of men who were passing large stones from hand to hand and laying them to one side so as not to impede the search. Efficient, as always, Helen thought. Glancing along the chain she saw that John Skiffington had joined the chain with her son James, and John and Charles Murray. A real family affair she thought with pride.

An old man had joined Helen and Sarah as they stood there.

'They're brave lads so they are,' he said. He pointed to where a tall section of a wall still stood. 'If they are no careful that bit o wa could come doon on top o them.'

It took all Helen's courage not to run forward and demand that her family leave at once.

The scene had been noisy but a sudden silence descended when an old woman was pulled from the rubble.

A doctor stood nearby, a stethoscope round his neck. The woman was carried to him and he bent over her. Straightening up he shook his head. A sheet was place over her and a collective groan escaped from the watching crowd. But the diggers returned to their task with renewed vigour determined to save who they could.

Their efforts were to be largely in vain.

While Sarah and Helen stood there thirty-six more dead bodies were removed from the rubble.

The dead were laid out in rows and Fr Marshall and Fr Hannan from St Patrick's chapel moved along the rows. If they recognised one of their flock they knelt and anointed them, administering the Last Rites.

People who had lost loved ones knelt beside the corpses their wails renting the air. The old Irish women among them began the traditional keening that had greeted death in the old country. Helen had never heard it before and the sound made the hairs stand up on the back of her neck.

The early morning gloom had faded and a wan sun was trying to pierce the haar as the day wore on. It was now easier to see the full extent of the devastation and it was truly horrible. An entire ancient tenement had collapsed in just a few moments. It had fallen forward blocking Paisley Close. It was a miracle that it had avoided Sarah and John's house and shop as it fell. Apart from the fractured gas pipe the building had escaped unscathed.

As the bodies were removed the men kept on working shifting rubble.

Helen called to Philip and begged him to come home and have a bite to eat. He was grey with exhaustion and looked every day of his sixty-six years, but Philip refused.

'There might still be some poor soul in there – a can't leave til we're sure,' he explained, but he was obviously touched at her concern.

Suddenly, there was a shout from the top of the diminishing pile of rubble. Helen and Philip looked up and saw her son, James, waving to his step-father. Philip ran and scrambled up the rubble to join him. When he reached him James said something to Philip who turned to the assembled crowd and shouted.

'Could we hae a bit quiet now – me laddie thought he heard something!'

Gradually the onlookers fell silent and Helen saw her son drop to his knees his head pressed to the rubble. He turned to look at his step-father and then they both began scrabbling at the fallen stones.

Then they all heard it.

A young male voice shouting, 'Heave awa lads a'm no deid yet!'

The other rescuers gathered round and carefully removed the rubble that entombed him.

A twelve year old laddie, Joseph McIver, was hauled out and carried to safety.

All the rescuers followed and gathered round the laddie as he was laid in the road. His clothes were filthy and torn to ribbons. He couldn't see as his eyes were caked with dust but he was alive!

The crowd was cheering loudly and the tired, dusty rescuers wore broad smiles.

Joseph McIver was the only person they had dug out alive that terrible day and everyone rejoiced at his escape.

Suddenly, there was an ominous rumble and turning in horror everyone saw the remaining section of wall come crashing down. The hole they had dug to rescue Joseph and the area were the rescuers had been digging was now completely covered in a fresh pile of rubble.

The crowd fell silent, many of the St Pat's folk crossed themselves as the enormity of what might have befallen the rescuers struck home.

It was all too much for Helen. The realisation of what she might have lost was sinking in. She felt herself growing faint. Philip's arms came round her just before she sank to the ground.

When Helen came to herself she found that she was lying in her own bed. Looking up she saw a cluster of concerned faces surrounding her. Philip, her son James, Sarah and John all loomed over her. When she opened her eyes Philip's stricken face registered relief.

'There ye are then,' said Sarah, 'giving us a fright like that. What were ye thinking off standing oot there a day in the chill wi no a bit o breakfast inside ye?'

The three men turned to look at her.

'What? What?' Sarah said. Then she had the grace to blush as she realised that she had done exactly the same thing herself!

The city authorities had now got themselves organised and had employed men to clear the rubble. It was obvious that all the bodies had been removed so Philip and the other men felt free to leave.

Bridget had prepared a late breakfast for them, but James said he had better get back to his wife, Ann, and the bairns. They now had two bairns as a daughter, Ellen, had been born to them a year after their son Arthur.

As Helen and Philip sat with them at the table John and Sarah explained how the tragedy had unfolded.

They were still in bed when they were woken by a loud rumble.

'Tae tell the truth,' John said, 'me first thought was we were in for a bad thunderstorm.'

But then there was a horrendous crash followed by screaming and shouting. They had leapt from bed, grabbed wee Arthur, and had run out into the street.

The sight that met their eyes would never leave them as long as they lived.

People in their night clothes were running from Paisley Close yelling that the building behind them was falling.

John said, 'A didnae want tae take Sarah and the bairn back into the hoose – a didnae ken how safe it would be if the building behind was crashing doon so we moved as far across the High Street as we could.'

'An then,' Sarah interjected, 'the roof o the close fell in and what seemed like an avalanche of stones caught the escaping folk. It swept them along. Some struggled and got free but others – she started to sob – others jist got buried!'

John took his wife's hand as she struggled to compose herself. He explained that once the close roof fell in they could see the collapsing building behind.

'It was terrible, terrible', John covered his eyes as if to blot out the sight. 'The whole front of the tenement had been ripped off. We could see families standing in their living rooms, their furniture still in place. They seemed frozen with fear. And then, and then….'

It all became too much for John. He laid his head on the table and sobbed as if his heart would break.

Sarah had composed herself and stroking her husbands bowed head she continued….. 'An then the floors collapsed and people jist fell through the air, bairns as well, Helen, down and down they came from ten stories up, and landed in the courtyard below...an then, an then...her composure broke.... the building jist fell on top o them,' she sobbed.

The horror of the image they had conjured up was too much for Helen and she dissolved in a storm of weeping.

Philip, too, was visibly moved but he tried to comfort the others, patting them on their backs.

'There, there,' he said. 'let the tears oot, ye need tae let it oot.'

Later when they had recovered they sat on talking.

Helen could see that Philip was more angry than she had ever seen him.

Why anger as a response to this tragedy she wondered? Anger at whom?

At last Philip burst out. 'A should hae kent this would happen,' he raged. 'Gavin Greenshields wis right. A telt him tae report it and a ken he did. They didn't listen tae him. A should hae backed him up!'

The other three round the table were mystified.

What was Philip on about?

Helen knew that Gavin Greenshields was a carpenter who often did work for Philip on his various properties. Philip regarded him as a careful, reliable workman but what was the collapse of Paisley Close to do with him?

Philip explained that weeks ago Gavin Greenshields had been sent to the Close to adjust doors in several of the houses in the tenement which were repeatedly jamming. 'Gavin had been puzzled by this but he became really alarmed in October, which was when he spoke to me,' Philip said. 'He told me that one day he had been wheeling a barrow down through Paisley Close when it had stuck under the arch where it had never stuck before. When he looked closely he saw that there was a bulge in the wall of the old tenement that formed part of the close. He measured the gap and then reported his concern to the factor of the building, who dismissed Gavin's concern as havering.

'But Gavin Greenshields was worried, so after that he made a point of going into the close and measuring it every day for three weeks. He found that the wall was bulging more each day. The gap was getting narrower and narrower.

'He telt me aboot it one day when he was doing some work for me and a advised him to tell the appropriate people,' Philip said.

'Gavin again raised his concerns with all who would listen, including some of the folk who lived in the tenement but they just laughed. He went to the home of the owner of one of the flats who lived on the south side of the city and told him of the danger. The man had been contemptuous of Gavin's opinion and asked how he was qualified to make such a statement. He dismissed him and warned him not to go spreading alarm.

'Then,' said Philip, 'just yesterday, a large piece of masonry fell into the Close. Gavin became really alarmed and went and reported this to his boss – only to be threatened with dismissal if he mentioned the matter again.

'A spoke to his boss at the site the day and asked him why he hadn't taken Gavin's warning seriously, and dae ye ken what he said? He said that he hadn't because – "Gavin was a peculiar man, always speaking nonsense!"'

Philip suddenly banged his fist on the table.

'A should hae gone and looked meself – a should hae backed him up – but a was busy an a let it go – an now look what has happened!' he exclaimed.

They tried to persuade him not to blame himself but they knew, as well as Philip did, that the opinion of a man of Philip's standing in the Old Town would have carried more weight.

Chapter 4

John and Sarah had been advised not to return to their home by the City Surveyor until it had been ascertained that no unseen structural damage had been done to it, so they moved in to stay with Helen and Philip. Helen's sons were delighted to have their cousin staying and the house was bedlam with six noisy bairns charging around.

The collapse of the building and the huge loss of life had been reported in newspapers throughout the land. The London Illustrated News had even sent an artist to draw the scene and it was later printed in the paper. Even the famous writer, Charles Dickens, who was visiting in the town, had gone to inspect the collapse and had expressed concern at the appalling overcrowding in the building and the tragic loss of life.

They were all sitting down to breakfast next day when John Skiffington stormed into the room looking very flushed in the face. He carried a rolled-up copy of their local newspaper, The Scotsman, in his hand.

'Listen to this,' he said, in a furious tone of voice.

He opened it and read aloud the report of the tragedy which included the detail of the fractured gas pipe on the Skiffington's property being used to illuminate the scene. The reporter then went on the criticise the dilapidated condition of the two hundred year old tenement which had fallen. It also demanded action on overcrowding in the Old Town after it was discovered that over a hundred people had been crowded into the tenement when it collapsed.

'So why are ye sae angry,' Sarah asked.

'Dae ye no see,' John exploded, 'the way it's worded it makes it sound like oor building is also in a dilapidated state! A'm jist going down tae their office to demand they print an apology!'

John was a mild-mannered man but when he got the bit between his teeth he could be thrawn. He valued the reputation he had as a shop-keeper and landlord in the town. He was particularly proud of the new building they had moved into further up the High Street from their original home. It housed their home and business at 105 the High Street.

Sarah and Helen exchanged amused glances as John stomped off.

Next day John was out bright and early in the morning and returned waving a copy of The Scotsman. He read out the correction they had published making clear that Mr Skiffington's home and business premises were indeed housed in a new building.

After the collapse of the tenement, Philip and John had become concerned for the welfare of the folk who had escaped the fallen building, but been left with only the clothes they stood up in. They decided to start a Disaster Fund to aid the stricken people now left destitute. They spoke to their friends in the business community and all agreed to donate to such a good cause.

The day that John and Sarah returned to their own home Helen walked up in the afternoon to see if she could lend a hand with anything.

The labourers were still removing cart-loads of rubble from the site and it was pathetic to see the remains of folk's possessions in among it.

Helen climbed the stair to the house above their shop, knocked the door and was invited to enter.

A curious sight met her eyes.

John, Sarah and wee Arthur all sat on the floor in a circle. In the centre sat a wee mongrel dog. A bowl of food and a bowl of water sat beside it. The dog dipped its head alternately in each of the bowls.

Helen was mystified. John and Sarah didn't own a dog, nor had she ever heard them express any desire to do so.

The three looked up as Helen entered and wee Arthur said gleefully, 'Dae ye like oor new dug, Auntie Helen?'

Helen looked again at the dog.

Its hair was matted and it was covered in dust. Indeed it was one of the scruffiest dogs she had ever seen!

Not wanting to hurt wee Arthur's feelings however she responded, 'It's a very nice wee dug.'

This obvious fib sent the family into peals of laughter.

At last, Sarah took pity on Helen and led her to a chair, still wiping the tears of laughter from her eyes.

'Sure, it's a terrible liar ye would make,' Sarah exclaimed.

Over a cup of tea Helen heard the whole story.

On their return to the house John had gone out the back door of the shop to survey the scene behind. Rubble still lay several feet deep with wooden floorboards pro-truding from the fallen stones. As John stood surveying the scene he suddenly heard a whimpering noise nearby.

'Sure, a nearly jumped out o me skin. A thought a bairn still lay buried there.' John explained.

He called to two labourers working on the site and together they located where the sound was coming from. They carefully lifted aside fallen stones and floor boards and buried in a little air pocket they found this wee mongrel dog.

'A recognised it right away,' John said. 'It was auld Mistress McLuskie's dug.'

The three of them fell silent remembering the first old lady who had been pulled dead from the rubble.

'It had been buried there for three days without food or water and it was shivering with fright and covered in dust, as you can see. Isn't that an amazing survival story?' he demanded.

Helen agreed that it was and although she was happy enough that the wee dog had survived it seemed small consolation when so many people had died.

John seeing her lack of enthusiasm tried to explain.

'Ye see, Helen, ye are looking at a wee gold mine here,' he said.

Helen's eyes widened and she looked again at the dog - still engrossed in its meal on the floor – it looked just as dirty and unappealing as before.

She shook her head.

'A dinnae ken what yer talking aboot,' Helen protested.

Then John explained his plan.

Sarah was going to clean up the wee dog and they were going to auction it for the Disaster Fund!

'But surely,' Helen protested, 'ye are not going to tae get much for a scruffy wee dog like that!'

As if understanding what she said the dog turned its head and looked up at Helen as if sorely hurt.

This set them all off again into fits of laughter.

'Now Helen,' John coaxed, 'ye must agree that the wee dug has great novelty value having survived the collapse of the building.'

Helen admitted that this was so.

'And ye ken that there are some folk care more aboot their wee dugs than they do about people,' John continued.

Helen had to agree that this also was true.

'Can ye no see the headline?' John proclaimed -

"SMALL DOG SURVIVES THE COLLAPSE OF THE BUILDING IN PAISLEY CLOSE!"

'Aye,' said Helen, 'but who would print it?'

'Well,' answered John, pulling on his cap, 'a'm jist away back doon tae the Scotsman office. A think they owe me a favour, don't you?'

John was proved right.

Within days of the story appearing in the paper it seemed that every dog-lover in the town was beating a path to John and Sarah's door.

The wee black and white dog, suitably scrubbed and wearing a nice tartan collar, sat on a cushion holding court and even Helen had to admit he looked reasonably appealing!

The bids rose and rose until finally he was awarded to a lady in the New Town for the princely sum of twenty pounds!

'What did a tell thee, Helen,' John said, 'a wee gold mine that dug!'

'It certainly boosted the coffers of the Disaster Relief Fund,' she conceded.

HELEN'S STORY

PART FOUR

CHAPTER 1

Edinburgh 1875

The Canongate Churchyard was thronged with people. The old burial ground stretched back from the main street of the old town of the Canongate and was overlooked by the great bulk of Calton Hill behind.

Impressive iron gates led into it and the Canongate Kirk itself reared up beyond its paved entrance courtyard. It was a large church designed in the Dutch style with a graceful shaped gable adorned with decorative plaques. As the parish church for the area of Holyrood Palace its pews were often graced by members of royalty and the aristocracy.

Many famous people were buried in the graveyard that surrounded the kirk on three sides. There was even a tradition that David Rizzio, Mary Queen of Scot's Secretary, who had been brutally murdered in the old Palace, had later been buried here.

A handsome tomb enclosure to the left of the main gate held the remains of the great Adam Smith, the Philosopher and Economist.

The famous beauty, Agnes MacElhose's grave lay to the right of the gates. The poet, Robert Burns, called her

'Clarinda' and it was to her that Burns wrote that lovely Scots love song, *Ae Fond Kiss*.

Scientists, medical men and artists also rested here. But the burial ground also held the remains of more lowly people, indeed, even of paupers.

The great Edinburgh poet, Robert Ferguson, had died in the lunatic asylum, Bedlam, when he was only twenty-three and had been laid to rest here in a pauper's grave. When the poet, Robert Burns, had come to pay homage to Ferguson, his inspiration for writing poetry in Scots, he had discovered that he lay in an unmarked grave. Burns was horrified. He immediately arranged to have a handsome headstone erected on the plot and there it still stood. Helen Boylan could have seen the headstone from were she stood on the Boylan's large plot in the graveyard had she glanced over.

She stood beside an open grave in which her second husband, Philip Boylan, was soon to be laid. She looked around at the gathering of mourners and reflected on how different it was compared to when she had laid her beloved Arthur to rest in the old Greyfriars churchyard, twenty-five years before. She could remember it as if it was yesterday. Then, only family and close friends had been in attendance, but here were many representatives of the business community and even some town councillors.

Philip was eighty years old and had led a long, productive life. He had been a prominent and well-respected member of Edinburgh's merchant community and in his later years had been drawn into active support for Home Rule for Ireland.

Helen, dressed in mourning black with a long velvet cloak around her shoulders and a matching velvet bonnet trimmed with black satin ribbons, looked at the close family members gathered here beside the open grave.

Her eyes rested first on Sarah Skiffington who had supported her through all the sad and difficult times of her life. She hoped that she had been as much comfort to Sarah but she knew that her sister-in-law was not, could never again be, the spirited, laughing Sarah of earlier times. Her husband, John, had died during an epileptic fit two days after Christmas in 1863. Just four years later, on 2 February 1867, Sarah and John's twenty-four year old son, Arthur, had died of bronchitis and tuberculoses. Sarah was now fifty-nine years old but she looked older. Her red hair had faded to a sandy grey, her skin sallow and her face puffy. Helen realised that Sarah drank more than she should, but knowing her deep sorrow she couldn't find it in her heart to blame her, or deny her the solace it brought.

As usual, standing beside her, holding her arm, was Sarah's niece, Ellen Murray named after Helen herself. She remembered the joyous occasion of Jane Delaney and John Murray's wedding in 17 St Mary's Wynd on New Years day 1855 and young Ellen's birth there the following year.

Jane and John had asked Philip and Sarah to be the baby's godparents. It was fitting that Ellen should be here as she was so fond of Philip and he of her.

Young Ellen was doted on by her parents because after her birth Jane did not conceive again for many years.

Jane stood on the other side of Sarah beside the grave. The couple had later been blessed with six more children but, tragically, John Murray had died in May 1874, of dropsy, aged just forty years. Jane was bringing up the younger children alone. They were too young to attend a funeral.

After the death of Sarah's son, Arthur, her sister, Jane, had been so alarmed at how Sarah's health had declined that it was decided that young Ellen would go and live with her aunt to keep her company.

Since the expanding Murray family filled their house at 6 High Street. the arrangement had worked really well.

Ellen was a lovely, gentle lassie whom Sarah doted on. She openly admitted that caring for the lass had saved her sanity. Ellen still lived with Sarah above the shop at 105 High Street.

Another of Philip's god-children stood beside the Murray family. Arthur Delaney was Helen's grandson, her son James's first-born. He was fifteen years old, of slim build with dark curly hair. Helen could see her son in him. He did not resemble his mother Ann in any way. Helen looked for Ann in the crowd but couldn't see her, but Arthur's sister, Nellie, stood beside him. Helen was saddened, but not surprised, by Ann's absence. Since her husband, James, had walked out on his family, five years ago, Ann had tended to avoid family gatherings. Still, Helen thought, she might have come to bid farewell to Philip since he had been unfailingly kind to her since she had first married James. He had set them up in their first house and had stood as god-father to their son, Arthur.

Then Helen remembered something that made her realise why Ann was not here. In 1863 James and Ann had had a third child, a daughter, but three years later she had died of croup at the Royal Infirmary. After the bairn's death, Philip had arranged to have her buried here, in the Boylan plot, in the Canongate.

No wonder Ann hadn't been able to face it, but had stayed home with their second son, James, who was only ten years old.

Helen felt ashamed of herself. She, of all people should have understood. For she had forgotten that she, too, had a bairn lying here in this same plot.

She and Philip's son, John, was only five months old, when he died but how could she have forgotten him! Guilt overwhelmed her.

Why did she always think the worse of Ann? She had doubted if her son and Ann were suited right from the start. But since they had eloped she had been powerless to prevent their marriage. But James had made his vows and he should have honoured them instead of abandoning Ann and his bairns.

She had telegraphed him to tell him of Philip's death, but he had replied that he would not manage to come to the funeral as things were not going well with him in England, where he was still working as a photographer. Helen resisted the temptation to think, serve him right, he was still her son after all and she loved him in spite of everything.

The fact remained, none the less, that Ann had been left to bring up the family alone though James did send money when he could.

Philip had tried to help. He felt especially responsible for his god-son, young Arthur. He had paid for his schooling and then when he was ten enrolled him in an Industrial School, paying for his lodgings and his apprenticeship fees.

Arthur had inherited his father's artistic talent and was in training as a crystal engraver at a glassworks in Abbeyhill.

Arthur had come to 17 St Mary's Wynd as soon as he had heard of his god-father's death. He was genuinely upset as he appreciated just how much Philip had done for him and the kindness and interest he had shown him in the absence of a father.

Helen worried about him. She knew Philip had meant well but she had been concerned at a ten year old laddie with an absent father being sent into a boarding house for apprentices separate from his mother. She knew it was a great chance for young Arthur to have a trade and she knew it was a help to Ann. One less to clothe and feed and yet...

Looking at him now, across the grave, his face sad, he seemed lonely. How would it all go for him, she worried. His sister Nellie was very close to her mother and did not cause Helen such concern. But she felt a laddie needed his father's influence.

Helen was glad that young Arthur got on so well with his Uncle Thomas. Indeed Thomas stood beside him now. She knew that Thomas gave his young nephew the affection he needed but she was not sure her middle son was the best example for him to follow.

Thomas Delaney, Helen's second son, was a happy go lucky sort, very handsome and popular with the lassies. Philip had apprenticed him in the brass-foundry so he had a good job and money in his pocket.

Helen remembered the shock she had felt when the young McIntosh lassie's mother had come to the house in 1868 and informed them that Thomas had made her daughter pregnant. Philip had insisted that Thomas marry the lassie but her son flatly refused. Helen had rarely seen Philip so angry but Thomas had dug his heels in – he would not marry. Philip had to be content with settling a sum of money on the lassie. When the bairn was born he was called James and Philip insisted that Thomas pay the lassie a shilling a week from his wages to maintain the bairn.

Within a few months it became clear why Thomas refused to marry, when young Margaret McGuire announced she too was pregnant with Thomas's bairn! This time Philip would brook no refusal and Thomas and Margaret were married on 2 August 1869. Exactly three months later Margaret gave birth to a daughter whom they named Mary Helen. Margaret had proved as fertile as Helen herself as the couple were now the parents of four more children. Even Thomas's good job in the brass-foundry did not provide enough of an income for so large a family, so Philip had turned over the running of his Boot and Shoe Emporium, on St Mary's Wynd, to his step-son.

On the other side of Thomas stood his brother, John Delaney, Helen's third son. Philip had apprenticed his step-son in the printing trade. Printing was one of Edinburgh's biggest industries and as it provided secure life-time employment demand for apprenticeships was high. However, Philip, as usual, had contacts and John trained as a compositor in the trade.

He was a natural charmer, a born mimic, and fond of clowning around. His young half-brothers and the Murray bairns adored him. At work he became friendly with his boss' son, Robert Pillans. Both lads joined St Patrick's Young Catholic Men's Association. Canon Hannan, a priest at St Patrick's was anxious to keep the young lads away from the temptations of the Old Town. He arranged many activities in the new Church Halls on St Mary's Street. These included an Amateur Dramatic Club and before long John and young Pillans were enthusiastic members. John had real comic talent and usually had the audience rocking with laughter at every performance.

But John was not laughing today. He was only four years old when his father, Arthur Delaney, died and his mother married Philip Boylan. He never really remembered his own father and was devoted to Philip.

Helen turned to her son, Luke, who stood close beside her. This was the first son Helen had given Philip and he had loved his father dearly. He was a respectable business-man in his own right. A real credit to his father. Luke was trying to be dignified and supportive of his mother but she could feel him gripping her arm tightly and when she looked into his face his eyes were bright with unshed tears.

Helen's right hand grasped that of her daughter, Mary. Mary, just eighteen years old, who had been the joy of Philip's old age made no attempt to wipe away the tears that streamed down her cheeks. Her brothers, Philip and James, stood beside her, their heads bowed.

At the head of the grave, in the most prominent position, stood Eleanor Lennon, daughter and only surviving child of Philip's first marriage. By her side stood her surviving son, John. His older brother, Philip, had died as a child. Eleanor was dressed in deep mourning in a fine black wool coat, her face obscured by a heavy black lace mantilla. She looked elegant as always but her son outshone even his mother in the elegance stakes. John was tall and slender. He wore fine wool trousers, a black wool jacket cut in the latest fashion, a stiff white linen shirt with a black silk cravat held in place with an ostentatious gold and jet tie pin and carried a cane with a heavily engraved silver handle. John was every inch the dandy, even in mourning clothes. He was twenty-six years old and he had never done a days work in his life. He lived at home with his doting mother in their large house in South Fort Street. If ever anyone asked Eleanor her son's occupation she replied that since he had no need to work he could best be described as a gentleman.

Eleanor's husband, John Lennon, had finally had enough of his wife's domineering ways. One day he failed to return to the palatial mansion in South Fort Street. Eleanor searched all his usual haunts in the Port of Leith and questioned all his friends. All denied knowing his whereabouts. The next day Eleanor received a telegram from John informing her that he had set sail for Australia and had no intention of ever returning. Eleanor was furious and never got over the humiliation of it all. She threw herself even more into building up her property business and only ever showed affection to her young son.

Philip had been heartbroken for his daughter but all his attempts to comfort her were met with a rebuff. To Helen she was barely civil.

When Philip died all restraint towards Helen went. She informed Helen that she intended to bury her father beside her own mother in the Canongate churchyard and that when the time came there would be no place for Helen in the Boylan plot.

Helen, grief-stricken at the death of the kindly man who had shared her life for twenty-five years, was too upset to argue. She insisted only that her son Luke should make the arrangements with Eleanor and this was agreed.

Now Helen stood beside the open grave and watched as Eleanor behaved as though her marriage to Philip had never existed. But Luke, in spite of being slightly intimidated by his older, domineering half-sister, had stood firm. He insisted that he, his brothers and his step-brothers would be cord bearers for the coffin.

There was a sudden stirring in the crowd and Fr Hannan from St Patrick's, his black vestments blowing in the wind, appeared, followed by the undertaker and his assistants as they carried Philip's coffin to the newly dug grave.

The coffin was placed reverently on the wooden planks across the grave. The undertaker held a bundle of cards in his gloved hand, a breeze blew the black plume on his hat as he began to call out the names of the cord bearers.

John Lennon's name was called first and he stepped forward to the head of the coffin. Luke's name came next and he took up position at the foot. His brothers Philip and James stood on one side and his half-brothers Thomas and John on the other.

Fr Hannan began the Latin prayers for the dead and as the grave-diggers slid away the planks the six men gently lowered the coffin into the grave.

Beside her Helen heard her daughter, Mary, begin to sob and she put a comforting arm around her.

When he had finished the priest stooped, picked up a handful of earth and sprinkled it down on the coffin. Then, changing to English, he intoned, 'ashes to ashes, dust to dust'.

Eleanor stepped forward and picking up a handful of earth sprinkled it down on the coffin. Helen, still supporting her daughter, bent forward and did the same and then one by one, in time-honoured tradition, his sons and Philip's friends followed suit.

Once they had all finished the grave-diggers replaced the planks across the grave and the undertaker's assistants began bringing the wreaths forward. There were many large ornate displays and none more so than Eleanor's.

Luke took the family wreath, a simple sheath of white lilies, and laid it carefully down. Then he took his mother's tribute from the man and handed it to her.

She bent and placed a single white rose amid all the flowery splendour.

The attached card read simply – "To Philip, with love and gratitude – Helen."

CHAPTER 2

Edinburgh 1877

Helen Boylan stood at the window of 17 St Mary's Street for the very last time.

The view across the street was much changed from when she had first stood here after her marriage to Philip in 1850.

After the collapse of the building in Paisley Close in 1861 there had been a public enquiry into the dangerous and unhealthy conditions in much of the Old Town.

As a result Edinburgh had appointed a Medical Officer of Health – the first city in the United Kingdom to create such a position. The man appointed was Dr Henry Littlejohn a compassionate and highly energetic character. It was his good fortune that the Lord Provost of Edinburgh at that time was William Chambers. The two men shared a reforming zeal to better the state of the Old Town and the conditions for its poorer inhabitants. One of their first achievements was an Act of Improvement passed in 1867. This resulted in a plan to systematically demolish some of the narrow wynds and closes, widening the streets and opening them up to fresh air and light. One of the first streets to be improved was old St Mary's Wynd.

Helen recalled how she and Philip had watched as one side of the Wynd was reduced to rubble. One of Philip's newer tenements where Helen had lived with Arthur stood in the way of the plan. This was compulsory- purchased from Philip, by the city, with handsome compensation paid. Though the building was in good condition the aim was to widen the street and since the tenement stood in the way it had to go. So Helen had watched as her last link to her life with Arthur crashed to the ground.

Helen shuddered as she remembered how the rats had swarmed out of the demolished buildings and sought refuge in those still standing on their side of the street. They were overrun with vermin and it seemed that Philip had the rat-catcher in continuous attendance in their home.

Eventually things settled, the rubble was cleared from the site, the rats were cleared from their house and gradually new buildings rose across the street.

In spite of her sadness at the loss of her old home Helen loved the new buildings that rose on the site.

Philip had told her that Lord Provost Chambers and Dr Littlejohn were determined that all new buildings were to be of top quality and so no expense was spared in the materials or construction. They even hired prominent architects, David Cousin and John Lessels, for the designs. The street on the corner with the Canongate rose to five storeys! It had a two-storey oriel and a crow-stepped gable. A turret, dormers and a further crow-stepped gable decorated the range of buildings downhill. Helen thought the buildings grand enough for a palace but here they stood in their old street!

Helen's favourite part of the street was St Mary's Hall. She loved the way the sun sparkled on the large mullioned windows at the first floor level of this building.

The Hall was now very familiar to her. Canon Hannan, at St Patrick's Church, had seized the opportunity of building a grand new Parish Institute on one of the plots to house the Catholic Young Men's Society.

Helen remembered the foundation stone being laid by William Chambers, the Lord Provost on the 2 April, 1869.

In his address to the congregation, gathered at the site that day, the Lord Provost had declared -

"Through my whole life I have never taken part in any proceedings calculated to exalt one sect above another. My wish is to see fair-play and toleration to all, and since I have the honour to be raised to the Magistracy of this city I have studiously, and in a particular manner, adhered to that line of conduct..... From the enquiries which I have latterly made, I find conclusive evidence that the Catholic Young Men's Society is one worthy of support. It began about four years ago and has done much good. Its particular object, I am told, is to raise the moral and intellectual status of its members, who now amount to about 800 in number.....We are told that up to the present time the society has exerted a remarkable beneficial influence over its members. Youths, formerly degraded and intemperate, have been reclaimed. Those who were once ragged and dissolute are decently clothed and now a creditable part of society. Through the energetic effort of the society a very conspicuous improvement has been effected in the Cowgate."

Helen remembered how his listeners had cheered the Lord Provost's words feeling that, at last, here was someone, in authority, who recognised that the poor Irish were also citizens of the town.

None of this would have been possible without the commitment and energy of young Fr Hannan. When completed, the building he commissioned was a warren of meeting rooms upstairs, but the lower level consisted of a large Hall able to accommodate over a thousand people. It had a proper raised stage and with the addition of curtains was used for productions by the Amateur Dramatic group. The Hall served the parish well with ample space for a wide range of activities to enhance the social life of St Patrick's congregation.

Helen's familiarity with the Hall was because of its use by the Dramatic Association of Edinburgh Catholic Young Men's Society of which her son John was an enthusiastic member! Helen smiled at the memory of John's part as the character, Gaiters, in his first performance in the Hall in 1870. He had donned a kilt for this comic part and even the critic of the Scotsman newspaper had applauded his performance.

That production had been in aid of the Building Fund for the Institute. Philip had bought a whole row of the best reserved seats at 2s.6d. each. The whole family sat together and how they had laughed and cheered John's appearance!

Helen had been happy for her son to appear in these amateur productions but when, within a year of his first appearance in St Mary's Hall, John had decided to give up his safe job in the printing trade and become a professional actor she was dismayed. Again, to her surprise, Philip had given his consent.

"Let the laddie try," he had said. "If it doesn't work out he always has a good trade to fall back on and who knows he might make a success of it. Think how proud ye will be if ye go to see him in the Theatre Royal!"

Helen had remained unconvinced but Philip had been proved right.

He bought tickets for every production that his stepson appeared in. He and Helen would dress up in all their evening finery. Philip would call a horse-drawn cab and they would drive across the North Bridge and down Leith Street to the grand Theatre Royal that stood cheek by jowl with St Mary's R.C. Cathedral, there to take their place in the best seats in the house.

John had continued to have success as a comic actor on the Edinburgh stage and he had recently been invited to join a touring company. He was filled with enthusiasm and set off touring around Britain. He sent his mother press cuttings of all his reviews from newspapers and she proudly pasted them into a scrap-book.

He also sent her postcards from all the towns he appeared in. One had come from Wigan, where John wrote he had met up with his older brother, James, who was now working as a photographer in the town.

Helen turned from the window and looked around the bedroom she had shared with Philip.

So many memories, she thought.

All the furniture had been removed, including their marriage bed, where their bairns had been born and where Philip had died.

Philip had retained much of his vigour into old age but then he had developed bronchitis. Many nights he had fought for breath in this room as Helen had applied hot bread poultices to his heaving chest.

After each attack he fought back but after five years of suffering and at the age of eighty there was no more fight left in him.

When the end came Helen and the ever-faithful Sarah had been at his bedside. It was a peaceful end for a good and generous man and as Sarah had closed his eyes Helen had bent and kissed him gently on the forehead.

'Ye ken he loved ye,' Sarah had said.

'Aye, a ken,' Helen had replied.

The two women had lain their heads on the bed and sobbed their hearts out.

Helen moved quickly out of the bedroom trying to dispel the sad memory and climbed the stair to the big attic room. She remembered her wedding day and how Philip had knelt on the floor and laid out the train set for her sons. He had promised her sons would want for nothing and he had more than kept that promise.

Helen felt the tears start in her eyes as she turned and descended the stairs. On the ground floor she wandered through the main rooms. She thought she could almost hear the fiddle music as memories of weddings, Hogmanay parties, and other celebrations came back to her, filling the rooms with people, some long departed, others still part of her life, like dear Sarah.

Would those dear friendly ghosts still linger here when other families came to live in these rooms, she wondered.

Her son, Luke, was now twenty-five years old and as his father's oldest son he had inherited all his properties. He put one of his father's oldest employees in to manage the tailoring business but his half-brother, Thomas Delaney, continued to run the Boot and Shoe Emporium.

He had sold most of the rental properties to his half-sister, Eleanor Lennon.

This made him a wealthy young man but Helen knew, as his father had done, that he could be trusted to look after his brothers and sister.

Luke had decided that this house at 17 St Mary's Street was too big for them now his father was dead and his brothers had their own homes. He had decided to divide the house into flats and rent them out.

His brother, Philip, had married an English lassie, Catherine, after his father had died and now had a bairn of his own whom he named after her mother. The family lived in a house at 45 Blackfriar's Street.

His other brother, James, had married his childhood sweetheart, Jessie Sharpe, when she was just sixteen and he was eighteen. James worked for Luke in his auctioneer's business and the couple were living in the Potterow. However, Luke had promised them one of the flats he intended to create out of this house.

The fact that one of her sons would still be living here brought Helen some consolation though she wondered how she would feel visiting them. She was just glad that Philip had not lived to see this day.

Most of their furniture had been moved to the handsome flat that Luke had bought, beside his pawn-broker's business, at 2 Chessel's Court in the Canongate.

Helen's daughter, Mary, was still living with them but judging from the frequent visits of a young man named, John McGill, Helen didn't think it would be long before Mary, too, was wed.

Helen took a last look around the kitchen where Bridget and Bessie had served so faithfully for all those years. Bridget was dead now but Bessie had moved with them to Chessel's Court.

She walked into the hallway were they had waited for the traditional First Foot every Hogmanay.

She put her hand on the doorknob to open the front door and then she heard the piano. She turned startled and moved towards the parlour but then she remembered that the piano too had gone – but then a voice sounded in her head – it was John Lennon's voice – "For auld lang syne", he sang.

CHAPTER 3

The move to 2 Chessel's Court was accomplished with Luke's usual efficiency. There were not enough rooms to hold all the furniture from their old house but Helen and Luke had chosen some of the best pieces and now that they were installed in the new flat it began to feel like home. The grand piano was placed beside the large window in the parlour with the view over the garden square and soon looked as if it had always been there.

Luke had allowed his brother, James, to use the horse and cart that he usually drove as a porter in Luke's auctioneer's business to remove the rest of the furniture from 17 St Mary's Street.

Luke's pawnbroker's business always had unredeemed furniture and so he had a store-house behind his pawn shop. Once enough furniture had accumulated Luke would hold an auction and sell off the unredeemed items.

Some of the furniture was very fine. Not only the poor used Luke's pawnbroker's, he had quite a number of clients in the New Town. Some of these were men who had gambling debts to pay, but some were genteel widows who had fallen on hard times. They perhaps needed financial assistance to see them over a difficult patch. Luke was always very discreet and so his business flourished.

Luke allowed James to store the excess furniture from 17 St Mary's Street in this store until his flat was ready there, then he and Jessie could move in and furnish their new home with Philip and Helen's old furnishings.

Helen had offered to help Luke in the business but he was scandalised at the idea. In any case he had taken on Helen's grand-daughter, Nellie Delaney, as an assistant and she was proving very capable.

With Bessie to look after them Helen was often at a loose end.

She spent a lot of time up at Sarah's house as her sister-in-law was often confined to bed in poor health.

When Sarah's husband, John, had died she had come to rely more and more on her sister Jane's husband, John Murray, to run the Skiffington's business.

Sarah was still able to collect the rents from the properties they owned in the Old Town but the rest of the business was run by John and Jane.

The china merchant's shop, below the flat at 105 High Street, was managed by Jane, helped by her daughter, Ellen, while John was in charge of the rag merchant's warehouse at 109 High Street.

The rag-trade was particularly lucrative. The rags were sorted, baled and sent by the cart-load to the mills, there to be turned into paper. Sarah did not just supply the mills at Colinton in Edinburgh but also at Penicuik, across in Fife, and as far down as Yorkshire in England.

When John Murray died of dropsy in 1874, the year before Philip died, he was only forty years old. Sarah had given the use, rent-free, of one of her flats at 6 High Street to her sister and that is where John had died. He had been unwell for a few months and unable to work but when he died it was a shock to the whole family.

Jane was devastated. Her daughter, Ellen, was nineteen and still living with her aunt Sarah at the time but Jane still had six other children at home, ranging in age from fifteen to three years old.

John was buried close to John Skiffington in the Grange Cemetery with a simple obelisk marking his grave.

Soon after his funeral Sarah had insisted that Jane came back to work.

Helen had thought at the time that Sarah was being very harsh and told her so. Sarah had said that moping would not help.

'Sure, didn't a do that meself after my John died and look what it did to me,' she said.

Helen knew that Sarah was referring to her heavy drinking which she still found difficult to control.

So Jane came back to work bringing her youngest bairn, three year old Janey, with her.

Sarah took on extra workers and employed Patrick Delaney, a cousin newly arrived from Ireland, as the cart-driver.

Sarah herself helped when she could but her bad periods began to outweigh the good ones. Sometimes when Sarah was feverish Helen would sit beside her bathing her face which was now puffy and yellow tinged. No sign now of the lovely spirited woman she had been when Helen first knew her. Sarah would be restless turning her head this way and that on the pillow. More and more she would talk of the old days back in Co. Monaghan.

'A Helen if only ye could have seen it,' she would say, 'it's so green, not like this dull, dreary toon. What would a not give to walk down the fine main street in Emyvale and stand on the Blue Bridge over the river. We would wait for me brothers there when they brought in the hay and jump up on the cart for a ride back home.

There is a field beside the bridge. We called it the fairy field. Late one night me and Arthur crept out of the house. He had told me that we could see the fairies dancing in the field if we stayed very quiet. We waited for ages, until the dawn came up, but the devil a fairy we saw!

'Before going off to bed we would all kneel around the turf fire – sure a can still smell that fire to this day – and Mammy would lead us all in the Rosary. Then she would dampen down the fire and ask St Brigid to keep it alight to the morning. Now a wonder if the family are still doing that?'

Helen hadn't the heart to remind her that there were none of her family left in Emyvale. All were dead or had emigrated to Prince Edward Island.

Jane was grateful for Helen's care of her sister because she had her hands full running the business. She now had a staff of seven workers in the warehouse as well as her cousin, Patrick Delaney. Her son, John, now seventeen, was her right hand man. Her daughter, young Sally, worked in the shop. She was only fourteen but was a really sensible lassie. Jane could no longer depend on her eldest daughter, Ellen, because just a few months ago she had married, Joseph Tregilgas, and was now living in a grand house in the New Town.

When Sarah was having one of her better days, she loved to reminisce about the old days and the happy times they had shared, but her favourite topic was the recent wedding of her dear niece, Ellen Murray.

Ellen had been courted by a young man who was the nephew and heir of a high-class draper with premises on Princes Street, in the New Town of Edinburgh. When the wedding was being planned Sarah was determined that old man Tregilgas would have no cause to think that in marrying Ellen, his nephew was marrying beneath him. Sarah took all the expense of the wedding on herself and money was no object. She booked one of the top hotels in the New Town for the wedding breakfast and invited not only her family and friends but many of the Skiffington's well-to-do business associates.

'Sure,' she would later say, 'twas the Society wedding of the year, so it was!'

Ellen and Joseph were married in St Patrick's Church. Candles were ablaze on every surface and vases of white flowers adorned every altar. Luke had supplied a rich Turkish red runner which was laid in front of the high altar where the couple were to kneel.

When Ellen entered, on the arm of her brother John, who was to give her away, a gasp ran round the packed congregation.

Ellen Murray was a beautiful lassie but since her face was covered with a fine lace veil it was not her beauty which stunned the gathering but her wedding dress.

It had been made by the most famous dress-maker in the New Town and it fitted Ellen perfectly. The material was white satin but it was encrusted with hundreds of pearls and crystals which sparkled in the candlelight. From her shoulders a heavy train of pure white Brussels lace spread out behind her as she walked. The short veil over her face was held in place by a band of heavily embroidered satin. She held a huge bouquet of white roses in her lace-gloved hands.

Helen was sitting beside Sarah in the church and as Ellen drew abreast of them she turned her head slightly towards them and under the veil Helen saw her wink at her aunt.

Afterwards, Sarah used to recall time and again.

'Sure, did you see the look on old Tregilgas's face? A tell ye it was worth the hundred pounds jist to see the look on his face!' she proclaimed.

The first time she said it Helen had been stunned.

'Ye didn't pay a hundred pounds for the dress, Sarah, tell me ye didn't?' she exclaimed.

'Sure a did and it was worth every penny,' and she cackled with laughter.

Helen was shocked. A working man would be lucky to earn a pound a week to keep his whole family in these times.

She knew that Ellen, who had lived with her aunt since John Skiffington had died, was like a daughter to her and of course Sarah had no surviving bairns of her own. But Sarah was such an astute business woman and it seemed out of character.

Sarah saw Helen was perplexed.

'A, Helen, ye know as a do that a won't be much longer for this world. Would ye deny me a wee bit indulgence after all the years of hard work?' she pleaded.

Helen had tried to reassure her that she would outlive them all but they both knew it wasn't true.

'Are ye thinkin it's maybe no fair on the other bairns?' Sarah continued. 'Dinnae worry, Helen, Ellen was in on all me plans. She knew it was important that she impress old man Tregilgas, sure hasn't he got pound signs where his eyeballs should be!'

Now Helen understood the wink that Ellen had given her aunt in church.

'She also kens,' Sarah went on, 'that when a die ma will states that any share she is entitled to at such time will have one hundred pounds removed from it first.'

Helen was ashamed of herself. She knew that Sarah cared for all her sister's bairns very much.

'Speakin' o ma will,' Sarah said, 'a want to confide in you something else. A'm no keen on that Seamus O'Brien that's always hanging around Jane. He has her blushing and giggling like a young colleen and her forty-three years old! A'm sure it's me money he is after.'

'A hiv made a new will and am going to tell Jane tonight. The condition is, that if she marries again, then my will states that she is to be treated as if she is dead for inheritance purposes, and a ma estate will revert to her bairns.'

Helen was shocked. It seemed a bit harsh considering how much work Jane had put into the business during the past few years. But then she thought of Seamus O'Brien. Sarah was an astute judge of character and as far as O'Brien was concerned Helen couldn't but agree with her. He was ten years younger than Jane, darkly handsome with a touch of the blarney about him but he had a reputation as a bit of a ladies man. Helen couldn't see him making Jane happy.

As she left Sarah that day Helen was so preoccupied that she nearly bumped into her grandson, Arthur Delaney.

He saw that she was leaving Sarah's house and asked how she was. Helen told him that she was not too well and he promised to go in and see her later.

Helen asked how his bairn was. Arthur blushed but said with pride – that his son was a fine big laddie.

'Have ye decided on a name for him yet?' Helen enquired.

'We are going tae call him, James, after ma Faither,' he replied.

Helen was moved that young Arthur was keeping the family naming tradition going.

Helen had always had a soft spot for her grandson as he was named after her own beloved Arthur. But since his father, James, had deserted him when he was young Helen wouldn't have blamed the laddie if he had refused to give his son his name.

'And how is Mary?' Helen asked.

Again the blush but his eyes lit up at the mention of her name.

'O, she's jist grand. A'm away up to see them now. Thank thee for the shawl ye sent, it was right guid o ye, Grandma,' Arthur said.

'A hope tae see them both soon,' Helen said, 'once Mary is past her lying-in time.'

'Aye, that would be grand,' Arthur replied.

Helen turned and watched him as he disappeared into Morrison's Close.

She felt heart sorry for him. He was just seventeen and Mary Mowat, his bairn's mother, a year older. She was a nice lassie and Arthur wanted to marry her but her father, Robert Mowat, forbade her to marry a "papist".

Helen shook her head – what difference did it make, surely when a bairn was involved it was better they were wed.

Helen felt that young Arthur had always been looking for warmth and affection. She knew that Arthur and his mother had never been close. Helen worried about him and had always had a sense that his life would not be an easy one.

She still found it hard to forgive her son for abandoning his family and going off to England.

CHAPTER 4

Hogmanay 1877

With their move to Chessel's Court the tradition of the grand Hogmanay party ended. In the smaller house it became more a family affair. Looking around the room Helen was saddened to see how few that family now consisted of.

Sarah was there, of course, and Jane, both widows now, like herself. Jane's family, John, Sally, Mary, Arthur, James and wee Janey were clustered around the piano singing as Luke played.

Helen's sons, Philip and James, could not be here as they both had new bairns and were spending Hogmanay in their own homes. Her son, Thomas, also had a large family of bairns too young to bring. Her daughter, Mary, sat beside her. She had married John McGill and was now nursing her first bairn, John. She wondered what her other sons, James and John Delaney, were doing at this moment. They were both down in England so perhaps they were not celebrating at all.

Helen had heard that Hogmanay was not a big occasion down there. John had told her that the English made more of Christmas with decorated trees and meals of turkey and rich puddings being served. Everyone got a holiday on Christmas Day. Helen found that strange, because Christmas Day was just an ordinary working day in Scotland with all the shops open as usual.

Then Helen remembered that John had written he would be working on Hogmanay in the Music Hall.

John's career was going from strength to strength in the Music Halls.

The same could not be said for his brother James. He wrote to Helen from time to time. He was still in Wigan but reading between the lines she did not think he was making much of a living as a photographer. Times were hard with a lot of unemployment, especially in the industrial towns.

Helen smiled up at her grand-daughter, Nellie Delaney, who bent over her offering a plate of cakes.

Her brother, Arthur, was now in the group around the piano. He had his arm around Mary Mowat's waist and Helen had never seen him look so happy. Their baby son, James, was being cared for by Mary's sister, Betsy Newall, back in Morrison's Close.

Helen had invited her daughter-in-law, Ann Delaney, to the party but young Nellie had explained that her mother no longer celebrated Hogmanay. She preferred to be in bed before 'the bells'. Helen was sorry but understood Ann's feelings – life had not been good to her.

Nellie had brought her younger brother, James, with her though. He was now twelve years old and tall for his age. He was standing beside Luke at the piano accompanying him on the penny whistle. Helen was amazed at the sound he got out of it!

About four o'clock in the morning Luke returned to the piano and Helen heard the familiar introduction to *Auld Lang Syne*. They all stood, arms entwined, and began to sing the old song that they had sung every Hogmanay since Helen could remember.

After the last of the family left Helen suddenly felt very old and very tired. Luke noticed and told her to get off to bed. He would help Bessie clear up here. As Helen lay in bed she felt unbearably sad. She reflected on how Hogmanay could be such a joyous celebration for some, but such a sad time of remembrance of absent friends for others.

As she drifted off to sleep she wondered what the year 1878 would bring.

CHAPTER 5

1878

It brought the death of Sarah Skiffington.

Sarah's health had continued to deteriorate and now Helen was spending every day with her. As her illness progressed Sarah was remembering less and less about the happy times, the good old days, and dwelling more and more on her losses of her husband, sons, and her dear brother Arthur.

One afternoon, Helen noticed a change in Sarah as she bathed her face. Fear clutched at her heart and she went to the door and called down to Jane working in the shop below. Closing the door quietly behind her Helen told Jane she thought her sister was nearing her end. The colour drained from Jane's face but she called to Patrick Delaney stacking bales of rags by the cart.

As Helen returned to Sarah's room she glanced out the window and saw Patrick whipping the horse into a fast gallop. She knew that he was going to get young Ellen from her house in the New Town. She also saw young John disappearing down South Gray's Close, gone to fetch the priest from St Patrick's Church.

Minutes later a tear-stained Jane showed Fr Hannan into the room. The priest knelt beside Sarah and anointed her with oil in the Sacrament of Extreme Unction. He stood and made the sign of the cross over her.

'Goodbye, Sarah, daughter of Ireland,' he said.

They heard hurried footsteps on the stair and a distraught, Ellen, ran into the room.

After the priest had left, the three women knelt around Sarah's bed. Her eyes were closed but as Helen mopped her brow she suddenly opened them and smiled around at the kneeling women.

Then fixing her eyes over their shoulders she suddenly said – 'John' - and held up her arms.

Startled, the three women looked behind them, but there was no one there. When they looked back Sarah was gone.

Helen, Jane and Ellen began to weep uncontrollably, but eventually Helen composed herself and gently closed Sarah's eyes. As she did so something amazing happened. The young Sarah came back! The puffiness left her face, the yellow drained from her skin leaving it porcelain white as it had been in her youth. Even her hair seemed to regain some of its vibrant colour.

Jane and Helen washed Sarah and dressed her in her favourite gown.

The word spread quickly and all day family, friends and business associates called to pay their respects.

Sarah had been a great character and had lived in the Old Town for more than forty years. She was well known and greatly respected. For a woman who had never been taught to read or write she had run a highly successful business even after the death of her husband.

Helen and Jane were kept busy preparing food and arranging drink for the wake, which kept their minds off their grief for a while, but young Ellen was inconsolable. She lay huddled in a chair in the back shop refusing to go back to her own home even when Joseph came with the carriage for her.

CHAPTER 6

Once again Helen stood beside an open grave.

With the death of Sarah, Helen felt an era was passing away. She had been the last link with those long ago days when Helen had first come to Edinburgh as Arthur's bride. There was no one left to share those memories. Sarah had been a constant presence during the happy years of her marriage to dear Arthur and a constant support for her and her sons after his death. Standing there she recalled her anger at Sarah's support for a marriage to Philip Boylan. Looking back now she gave thanks for Sarah's wisdom. What would have happened to her sons if she hadn't married Philip?

Helen glanced up at the large Celtic Cross that marked the grave where Sarah was soon to be laid. The inscription said –

In loving memory of
My Beloved Husband
John Skiffington
Merchant of Edinburgh.

Dear John, Helen thought. She owed him, too, a debt of gratitude for all his care over the years.

The Grange Cemetery was packed with mourners. The horses pulling the black lacquered carriage bearing

Sarah's coffin stamped their hoofs and snorted. Their breath was visible in the cold morning air.

Sarah's two sons having died before her the coffin was now being carried, shoulder high, by other male members of the family.

Fr Hannan walked ahead of them accompanied by Fr Corcoran.

The pall-bearers were led by Sarah's nephew, Thomas, her brother Arthur's son. Helen's other Delaney sons had been unable to come up from England but James's son, young Arthur, took his father's place. The other coffin bearers were Luke, Philip and James Boylan. Young John Murray, now eighteen years old, represented his mother Jane.

They laid Sarah's coffin on the planks across the grave then the undertaker handed each of the men a cord. As the planks were removed the coffin was lowered reverently into the grave.

Fr Hannan, his cassock blowing in the wind, said the prayers for the dead and turning to Fr Corcoran, who held the vessel with the holy water, he removed the brush and sprinkled the coffin.

Helen held the hands of Jane and young Ellen and as Sarah was finally laid to rest the two women began to sob.

Helen remained composed because she could not mourn Sarah's passing. She, more than anyone, knew that since losing John, Sarah had never been truly happy. Helen could not grudge Sarah being re-united with her beloved husband.

As she bent, in turn, to scatter earth on Sarah's coffin Helen's eyes remained dry but she knew that part of her had died with Sarah.

Her life would never be the same again.

HELEN'S STORY

PART FIVE

CHAPTER 1

Edinburgh

Hogmanay 1881

Helen sat gazing into the fire of her new home at 22 George IV Bridge. Bessie bustled in and out, laying whisky and shortbread on the sideboard or banking up the fire where Helen sat. Helen wasn't expecting many visitors but tradition demanded you were prepared just in case.

She thought that Luke and his new wife, Patricia Campsie, might come by since this was her first Hogmanay on her own.

In truth Helen was in no heart for Hogmanay. It had never been the same since Sarah had died and then last Hogmanay her son Philip's bairn had died on the morning of the 31 December. He had been named Philip after his grandfather and he was nearly two years old. The whole family had abandoned their plans for celebrating that New Year. Catherine, Philip's wife, had been distraught, and his four year old daughter, wee Cathy, tear-stained, when Helen had arrived at their house at 35 Blackfriar's Street on hearing the news.

The birth of her wee grandson in February 1879 had been such a boost to Helen after the loss of Sarah

Skiffington the year before. Helen had gone often to the house to help Catherine recover from the birth and look after wee Cathy.

She had been happy to help as she was at a complete loss after the death of Sarah.

Once Catherine was back on her feet and able to cope herself Luke had decided that Helen needed something to occupy her. He bought a wee shop in the Canongate and set her up selling newspapers and sweeties. Helen was surprised at how much she enjoyed it. She didn't need the earnings as Philip had left her a generous annuity to provide for all her needs but she enjoyed hearing all the gossip from the Old Town.

She particularly enjoyed the bairns coming in to spend their pennies on bonbons. It reminded her of when her own sons had run gleefully to Ma Casey's sweetie shop in St Mary's Wynd, when their Auntie Sarah had given them pennies for a treat. Her grandson, Arthur, often came into the shop with his two older bairns, James and Annie, for a poke of sweeties. Helen loved to fill the paper pokes to the brim with all their favourites.

Arthur had married Mary Mowat on 10 May 1878, in St Patrick's Church. When Mary's father, Robert, had discovered she was pregnant again he had withdrawn his opposition to a marriage with Arthur. The couple had gone immediately to see Fr Hannan, and he had arranged for them to be married quietly in the church. Mary's bridesmaid had been her sister, Robina, and Arthur's mate, Thomas Robertson was the best man. Helen was there, and Arthur's mother and sister, Nellie, but Mary's father had refused to attend.

Two months later Mary had given birth to their daughter, Annie, on 27 July 1878 at 2 Morrison's Close.

It had been a difficult labour and the howdie, Maggie Clark, who had delivered the bairn had confided to Helen that she had doubted the bairn would survive. However, she had, and although delicate looking and inclined to be breathless Annie seemed to be doing fine.

Though resigned to the marriage, Mary's father had insisted that no grand-bairns of his would be raised as papists. Not wishing to distress her father further Mary and Arthur had agreed not to have the bairns baptised. Arthur's mother, Ann, was furious and Helen knew that Fr Hannan was angry. It was a requirement of permission being given for a marriage to a non-Catholic that the bairns were raised in the Faith.

However, Arthur held firm. Mary would be heart-broken if her father refused to have anything to do with her, as he had threatened. Her mother had died when she was young and she had been raised by her father.

Arthur refused to have his Mary upset further.

Helen had secretly agreed with her grandson but had said nothing for fear of angering her daughter-in-law, Ann.

However, Robert Mowat died the following year on the 10 April at his house at 17 New Street in the Canongate. A few days later on 22 April, James and Annie were baptised in St Patrick's church by a relieved Fr Hannan. Their god-mother was, Maggie Clark, who had brought Annie into the world.

Less than two months later Mary had given birth to their third bairn, another daughter, Robina. She was born on 17 June at 17 St Mary's Street where her own father had been born all those years before.

The doorbell ringing brought Helen out of her reverie and she heard Bessie going along the hall to answer it.

The parlour door opened and Luke entered and strode towards the fireplace where Helen sat. He bent and planted a kiss on the top of her head. He was followed in by, Patricia, his wife of four months.

It had been the biggest surprise of Helen's life when Luke had come into their flat at 2 Chessel's Court and announced that he had asked Patricia Campsie to marry him!

Luke was twenty-six years old and had never shown any interest in any lassie before, as far as Helen knew. Indeed she used to worry in case he felt he needed to devote himself to her. But when she urged him to look for a wife for himself Luke always laughed saying she was the only woman in his life!

So his announcement was welcome, as well as surprising.

Helen knew Patricia by sight, of course, as her father, James Campsie, had been a spirit dealer in St Mary's Street. He was dead now but the pub was still run by his wife. "Campsie's", was the pub most frequented by Luke and his brothers but since respectable women did not enter pubs, it being strictly men only, Helen did not know the lassie well.

The first thought that came to her after Luke's announcement was that surely Patricia was too young to marry yet. Seeing her in the street Helen thought her still a bairn. When she tentatively raised Patricia's age with her son he had said that she was sixteen but they would marry in a few months when she turned seventeen.

Helen felt she could hardly make any comment given that she had married Luke's father, Philip, who had been twenty-five years older than her. Still, Helen thought, she had been a widow of thirty, not a young lassie.

Her next thought was that Patricia was expecting. As the months had gone by this proved not to be the case.

Luke married Patricia in an elaborate wedding in St Patrick's Church on 28 August 1881.

Patricia looked stunning. Her wedding gown may not have been as expensive as young Ellen's had been but her mother had done her proud. In the Irish ghetto of the Old Town where black or red-haired lassies were the norm Patricia stood out. She had a cascade of golden hair that reached down to her waist. She was tiny, not even up to Luke's shoulder, and slender with it. Her dress disguised the slightness of her figure as it consisted of layer upon layer of organza material in the skirt. The bodice of the dress had long lace sleeves and was topped off by a short satin cape. Her head-dress was a small skull cap studded with pearls and she wore no veil so that her amazing hair was revealed in all it's glory.

Luke's best man was John Murray, Jane's son, and Patricia's bridesmaid was his sister, Sally Murray. Luke and the Murray bairns had always been close. Helen wondered if Patricia had had any choice in her bridesmaid. She surely must have had friends of her own she would have preferred?

Jane Murray stood in the pew beside Helen and as Patricia made her way down the aisle, Jane whispered, 'Ah, Helen, he might have taken his time about it but, sure, he picked a beauty.'

Helen nodded, in agreement, but could not suppress a feeling of unease about this marriage.

The wedding reception had been a grand affair in the top hotel in the New Town. Helen knew that Luke had paid for the whole wedding himself, since Patricia's mother was a widow. Looking round Helen had seen that as well as family and friends Luke had invited what seemed like the whole of the Liberal Party in Edinburgh. Luke had become committed to the Party because of their support for Home Rule for Ireland. He was now the Chairman of the Party in the Old Town and very active in local politics at Council level.

Looking up at him now as he stood over her Helen was aware of how handsome her son was. He was also extremely well dressed – every inch the prosperous business-man.

Patricia now came forward to greet Helen and it was just as well she was sitting down or the lassie would have had to stand on tip toe to kiss her.

Helen smiled at them both. 'A'm right pleased tae see ye both, a thought ye might hae stayed in yer ain hoose til after the Bells,' she said.

'No, not at all,' Luke replied, 'we both wanted to be with you for your first Hogmanay in your new home.'

Patricia nodded, smiling her agreement, but Helen was aware that it was the lassie's first Hogmanay in her own new home and wondered what she really thought.

After their marriage, Luke had bought them a large flat in Marchmont and had furnished it in the best of taste. Helen wondered how much say Patricia had had in the choice of furnishing, not much she suspected.

Luke had also bought his mother this flat in George IV Bridge.

He had wanted Helen to move with them to the big house in Marchmont but Helen had flatly refused. The couple needed to start their married life alone in their own home she felt.

This flat on George IV Bridge was in a handsome stone building with views over the bustling street.

Helen loved it because from the back windows she could look over the huge wall in Candlemaker Row into the Greyfriars graveyard. She never told Luke but since moving to this house she went every day to visit her first husband Arthur's grave in the Greyfriars churchyard.

Luke continued, 'After the Bells we will go down and see Patricia's mother then we will take a cab down to see Eleanor in Leith.'

'That would be right guid o ye,' Helen responded.

Luke's half-sister, Eleanor Lennon, had suffered the grievous loss of her only son, John, on 2nd June this year. He was only thirty years old when he died.

Eleanor had been so distraught that she had even allowed Luke to make the funeral arrangements for her and since then the two had become close.

Helen had gone to the funeral but she kept well in the background aware that her presence would not be welcome by her step-daughter. Helen had felt she had to go for dear Philip's sake. John was, after all, his grandson.

Since the death of her father Eleanor had commissioned a large impressive monument for the Boylan plot in the Canongate Graveyard. It took the form of a stone base with a large white marble pyramid, ornately carved, rising up from it. Symbols of the saints were carved at each point of the pyramid.

The stone base bore the inscription –

Erected by Eleanor Dorothy Warrick Lennon
of Leith

The marble pyramid had four panels and Eleanor had had engraved on one of them –

In affectionate remembrance of her parents
PHILIP BOYLAN
who died 22 February 1875
aged 61

and his spouse

DOROTHY WARRICK
Who died 3 March 1850

Aged 31

R.I.P.

Helen realised that Eleanor had got her father's age wrong but that was not surprising given that Philip was quite sensitive about his age and the fact that Helen was so much younger. He was actually 81 when he died.

Helen had often visited Philip's grave when she lived in the Canongate but since young John Lennon had died and she had moved here she had gone less frequently.

She knew Eleanor went often to place flowers on his grave and she had recently had her son's name added to one of the other panels on the monument. The inscription read

In memory of

JOHN ALOYSIUS LENNON

only and beloved son of

ELEANOR D.W. LENNON

who died 2 June 1881

Age 30 years

R.I.P.

Eleanor had made no mention of her son's father, but that was not surprising, given that he had deserted her and their son and gone to Australia, but Helen was surprised that Eleanor had not included their other son, Philip. He had died as a baby and was, in fact, buried in this plot. So the inscription was wrong John was not her only son.

Knowing Eleanor visited the grave so often Helen was reluctant to go in case they should meet.

Eleanor had made it very clear that there would be no place for Helen in the Boylan plot. Helen knew in her heart of hearts that she didn't really care where she would lie. Greyfriars churchyard had long been closed for new burials on the orders of Sir Henry Littlejohn, Edinburgh's Medical Officer of Health. He had feared the old graveyard was so overcrowded that it was a health hazard to the town. So if she couldn't lie beside her beloved, Arthur, she didn't care where she went when her time came. Perhaps, Luke would lay her beside dear Sarah and John in the Grange Cemetery.

She was so lost in thought that she didn't hear Patricia ask her what she wanted to drink for the New Year Toast and the lassie had to repeat herself.

'Sorry, lass, a was miles away,' Helen replied, 'a wee sherry would be jist grand.'

Helen saw that Patricia had already poured a large whisky into a crystal glass for Luke. The crystal glasses had been a gift from her grandson, Arthur. Helen took real pleasure in the fact that Arthur himself had engraved them.

After serving Helen the lassie returned to the sideboard and poured herself an equally large whisky. Though she was shocked, Helen reminded herself that since Patricia had been brought up in a pub she supposed the lassie was used to being around strong spirits.

The carriage clock on the carved wooden mantelpiece struck midnight and the bells of the Greyfriars Kirk behind the flat and the Augustine Bristo Church across the road pealed out.

'Happy New Year, Mother,' Luke said, wrapping his arms around her and kissing her on the cheek.

Turning to his wife he kissed her also on the cheek.

As the bells pealed Bessie had entered the room and Luke picked her up and swung her around before kissing her fondly and replacing her on the ground. Bessie was now an elderly woman but she had been part of Luke's life as long as he could remember.

'Pit me doon, Maister Luke,' Bessie was protesting, but her face flushed with pleasure – Luke had always been her favourite.

When kisses had been exchanged all round and the Toast drunk Bessie bustled out to bring in more food and not long afterwards the doorbell rang again.

When Bessie opened it young John Murray entered - the proud First Foot, bearing coal, whisky and shortbread – followed by his mother and his younger brothers and sisters.

Much merriment ensued until Luke and Patricia reluctantly took their leave to go to her mother's house.

'Mind how ye go when passing the Tron,' Helen called after them, 'ye ken how rough it can get doon there.'

As the door closed behind them Jane nodded at it and said, 'Any news yet?'

Helen knew Jane was referring to a possible pregnancy.

'Gie them time,' Helen protested, they've only been married four months!'

'How long dae they need,' Jane retorted. 'Sure, he's no his faither's son if he doesnae hae a ween o bairns,' and she dug a blushing Helen in the ribs!

Not long after Luke and Patricia had left the doorbell rang again and Bessie showed young Arthur into the room.

After kisses and hand-shakes all round, Arthur came and sat beside his grand-mother.

'A cannae stay long but a wanted tae wish ye guid luck in yer new hoose,' he explained.

'A'm right pleased tae see ye,' Helen replied, 'and how is Mary?'

'That's another reason a came,' Arthur responded, 'we wanted ye tae ken that Mary's expectin' again!'

Helen offered him her congratulations.

Unlike many men in the Old Town, Arthur took real pleasure in his bairns and was often to be seen out and about with them. Still, Helen thought, the lassie was only –what?- twenty three?- and had already had three bairns.

'A'm trying tae keep up wi ma Uncle Thomas,' Arthur joked.

Helen's son, Thomas Delaney, and his wife, Margaret McGuire, already had four bairns and Margaret was now expecting their fifth.

When Arthur extended his news to the assembled family there were more handshakes and back-slapping all round.

'Tank the Good Lord fer that,' declared Jane, 'sure a wis beginning tae think that haein bairns was going oot o fashion in this family.'

After everyone had gone Helen helped Bessie clear up then sat on by the fire.

She was remembering how anxious Philip had been that the Boylan name in the Old Town should continue after he was gone. Indeed, that was why he had married her in the first place. Helen had given him three sons but with the death of young Philip's bairn last year no further laddies had been born to those sons.

Philip had a daughter, wee Cathy, and James had a daughter, Ellen. So far there was no sign of a bairn for Luke, though it was early days for him.

Helen wondered what the New Year of 1882 would bring.

It was to bring another death.

ARTHUR'S STORY

PART ONE

Chapter 1

Edinburgh

17th June 1882

Arthur's seat! I had aye had a feeling for the place, ever since I was a wee laddie and my faither told me it was named after me. He was joking, of course, but for a long time after that I believed him.

The hill was a refuge, a place to come when the stink and noise of the auld toon below became too much to bear or if I was in trouble after some scrape or other!

Auld Mowat, the bairns' grandfaither, used to come here too. Its green spaces, with sheep grazing, reminded him of the lands of the north he'd been forced to leave all those years ago.

'Mind what yer daein, Jamsie! Come doon frae that rock before ye fa and split yer heid.'

What a laddie that was, aye climbing and feart o nothing. He was a wee tearaway but he had his mother twisted roon his wee pinkie.

"Leave him alane," she would say, when I was giving him a row for some mischief or other. "Dinnae break his spirit. He'll need every ounce o it if he's to survive what this life has in store for him."

Looking up at Jamsie, I was reminded again of how like his mother he was. His hair was bright red. Today, with the sun behind him it glowed like a halo. He was pale skinned which made the freckles stand out on his face. His green eyes danced with devilment.

Annie, too, looked like her mother but she lacked the sheer energy of Jamsie. As I looked down at her as she sat making some buttercups and daisies into a wee bunch I felt a pang of anxiety. She had a lovely wee face but she was delicate looking and painfully thin, not robust, like Jamsie. She frowned and her little pink tongue poked out of the corner of her mouth as she concentrated hard on the task. Catching me looking at her she held up the wee bunch of flowers.

'It's for ma Ma,' she said.

I felt a sharp tug on my hair and glancing up saw my other daughter, Robina, looking down at me from her perch high on my shoulders. She was so different from her brother and sister you would hardly think she came from the same family. She bore a striking resemblance to my grandmother, Helen, who, in her youth, had been regarded as a great beauty. Though she was not yet two she had a mop of jet black curls which fell into her deep blue eyes as she leant forward demanding my attention. She pointed down to where the water sparkled on St Margaret's Loch below.

'Ducks,' she said.

Once I had assured her that she was a clever wee lassie she settled happily back on her high perch, content to survey the surrounding scene like the queen of the castle.

Aye, Mary had given me three bonnie bairns and soon, very soon, there would be another. Laddie or lassie, I didna care, either would be welcome.

At the thought of Mary the unease I had felt all day returned. Why had Maggie Clark, the howdie, suggested I take the bairns up the hill? When Annie and Robina were being born I had waited in the kitchen.

Not with Jamsie though. Arthur frowned as he remembered how auld Mowat had reacted when he had learned Mary was in the family way. Even though he had wanted to marry her straight away.

Ach, forget it, that's all in the past, Arthur thought.

"It's a bonnie day, Arthur," Maggie had said. "Mary will be a wee while yet, why no take the bairnies up the hill?"

And it was a bonnie day. Down below the auld grey Palace lay bathed in sunshine. It looked so peaceful but the ruined Abbey beside it, roofless and windowless, reminded folk of less peaceful times. But nothing spoiled the scene today. From my high vantage point I could see the waters of the Firth of Forth sparkling in the sunlight. The dark shape of Inchkeith Island lay like a great whale in the middle of the river and beyond the lands of Fife were spread out as far as the eye could see like a great green patchwork quilt. To the east the river lapped the sands of Portobello with its pier reaching out like a long finger into the sea – a favourite haunt when I was a laddie. Further down the coast lay Musselburgh from whence came the fisher lassies with their creels of fish and fresh mussels to sell around the toon. It was so clear I could even make out the odd shaped rock that folk said was called Berwick Law. I had never been down that far myself though.

Aye, "Auld Reekie" was in a fine situation right enough. It was home, even though I got the name of "Paddy". Born in the auld toon I had spent all my days here, aye, and my faither before me. I spoke as they spoke, and yet it was always "Paddy" – how long before that would change? –a long, long time, I suspect.

Ah well, perhaps it was only to be expected with the toon full of Irish folk. Their rich brogue was heard on every corner. The old stories of the dear green land they had lost being told and retold down through the generations, the old songs sung. The memories of oppression and famine still red in their memories. Little wonder that the Grassmarket and the area of the Cowgate and High Street enclosing the chapel of St Patrick was known as 'Little Ireland". Little wonder that when you bore a name like Delaney you were regarded as forever, "Irish".

Stupid of me though, to rise to the bait, on a Saturday night, when I had drink taken. A chance remark in a pub was excuse enough to set Scots against "Irish", then the fists would fly. Last time that had cost me a night in a cell in the Police Station in the High Street and a fine on the morrow for breach of the peace. Next time I'd keep my temper in check and my fists in my pockets.

Even the bairns followed our lead. On St Patrick's Day, they would divide into Scots or "Irish" and set about each other with paper balls attached to string. They would chase each other up and doon stairs and in and oot o closes yelling patriotic war cries at the top of their voices all the day long. Never mind that the "Irish" bairns had been born in the auld toon and that neither side understood what on earth it was all about. Their favourite chant was -

> "I was born in Edinburgh city
> And I cannot this forget
> But I always loved old Ireland
> Though I've never seen it yet."

But it wasn't just Scots and Irish who fought. Never trust a Donegal man my faither was fond of saying (his own family having come originally from Co. Monaghan) and in the absence of any handy Scots opponent, the Irish were just as happy to fight among themselves!

But the Irish were not the only incomers to the auld toon. Mary's own ancestors had been Highlanders, driven from the Clearance lands in the north and forced to seek a new life here. They were held in as much contempt by the locals as the Irish were.

Wouldn't you think that poverty would have been enough of a bond to unite poor folk? What did it matter if it was sheep or the blight that turned your potatoes to sludge, that had driven you from your homeland?

Aye, and neither minister nor priest had been able to prevent that.

But it didn't work out like that.

Mary's faither had been furious when she said she had wanted to marry me - a Papist. He had forbidden it.

Her faither was an embittered man. He had belonged to a strict religious sect in the Highlands. When the landowners and clan chiefs began to clear their lands of clansmen to make way for the more profitable sheep runs many members of the sect had sailed with their minister first to Canada and then to New Zealand. Mary's faither, a schoolmaster's son, had been raised on tales of this community and their epic voyages to find the "promised land". From childhood he had resolved to save enough to leave the deprivation of his Highland home behind and sail to join them. Instead, when things grew even more desperate in their crofting township, he came to the capital seeking work.

After the peace and fresh air of the north, the auld toon stifled him. It was overcrowded and squalid and his soul sickened at the drunkenness and debauchery that surrounded him. But here he had met and married Mary Brown. They had a family of three daughters and a son but his wife died young. He had to bring up his younger bairns, Mary and Robina, on his own and he never reached that "promised land".

Eventually, his daughter, Mary, and I were married anyway in St Patrick's Church.

Not that I had cared myself where we married but my mother had insisted on it, and Mary, always gentle, and unable to cope with any further family disapproval, from my side this time, had agreed.

Mary's faither never came to the wedding and my own mother never really accepted it either. Afterwards, we had a blazing row and it was not until after Annie had been born to us that that an uneasy reconciliation took place.

Arthur's mind had wandered and suddenly he felt chilled.

Looking up he saw the sun had disappeared and a cool breeze had sprung up. The "Windy City" indeed, he thought, the toon well deserved the name, few days went by without a stiff breeze or a full-blown gale.

Looking down he became anxious again – I hope Annie hasn't caught a chill, he thought, Mary would never forgive me.

The wee one suffered badly with her chest and Mary was terrified that any night another attack of the croup would leave Annie gasping for breath, sure each breath would be her last. She would hold Annie on her knee, rocking her to and fro, singing the Gaelic songs that

Annie loved to hear. Meanwhile I would be filling every pot and pan with water and placing them on the fire to boil until, at last, the blessed relieving steam poured out. Eventually, the walls would be running with rivulets of condensation, the blanket round Annie damp with moisture, and Mary's red curls stuck to her pale worried face. Gradually, however, the steam would work it's magic. The terrible rasping noise would stop and Annie's head would droop on her mother's breast and she would sleep. There would be no sleep for Mary or him. They would lie awake, afraid to move, Annie between them, watching their gentle wee daughter until morning broke and another crisis had passed.

He removed Robina from his shoulders and called to Jamsie to come and take her hand.

'You can toddle for a wee bit – ye wee toe-rag - it will do you no harm,' he said.

Bending down to Annie he lifted her on to his back.

'Come on ma wee lamb and I'll give you a coalie buckie,' he said.

To still his anxiety for her he burst into song –

> "The wind, the wind, the wind blows high,
> The snaw comes falling from the sky,
> Jamsie Delaney says he'll die
> For want o the Windy City."

The bairns joined in and in this way the little family made their way down the path and back to the auld grey toon huddled at the foot of the hill, its chimneys belching smoke.

CHAPTER 2

The town which Arthur and the children approached
had, outwardly, changed little in more than a hundred
years. Inside the buildings though things were very
different. Grand houses were partitioned and subdivided. Whereas previously, they had housed one
noble family, they were now homes for sometimes fifty
poor people.

As they reached the foul burn Arthur removed Annie
from his back and called to Jamsie to bring Robina.

'Mind how you go,' Arthur called, as Jamsie ran on
ahead.

Then taking both the girls by the hand he walked
them carefully over the planks across this open sewer
which ran through the Abbey district of the town. Care
was needed because this area was notorious for its high
rate of infant deaths and the townsfolk didn't need
Littlejohn, their Medical Officer of Health, to tell them
that living and playing on the banks of this polluted
burn was part of the reason. However, farmers at
Lochend used the burn as a means of fertilising their
fields, damming it at points to encourage the raw
sewage to flood over their land. So, despite Littlejohn's
best endeavours, the burn remained un-drained, and
mainly uncovered, for most of its course and children
continued to sicken and die.

Jamsie waited at the foot of the Canongate for his father and sisters to catch up with them and they began the climb up the street that led to their home.

The street was known as the "Royal Mile" but little of its former grandeur remained.

Arthur kept a tight grip on Robina's hand in case she was tempted to dart into the middle of the road. It was late afternoon and the horse-drawn brewery drays still rumbled over the setts of the roadway creating a terrific din.

The town was famous for brewing and many of the breweries were located here served by a chain of natural wells that stretched up the Canongate, the smell of hops always on the air.

They passed Queensberry House, the district's Poorhouse, and glancing up Arthur could see pale faces pressed to the window glass. Poor souls, he thought, for it was the dread of every poor person in the old town that they would be forced through destitution to apply for Parish relief. The result was usually incarceration in this building, their lives so regulated that they might as well be prisoners in the Calton Jail. Little wonder families chose to huddle together in one room hovels, hungry and cold, but free, rather than seek Parish help.

Not for the first time Arthur felt grateful that he had a skilled trade as a glass-cutter with John Ford's company.

Arthur glanced up to check the time on the Canongate Tollbooth clock. It was just on five o'clock.

'Faither, faither,' Annie called, tugging at Arthur's jacket, 'can we get some mussels?'

Looking ahead Arthur could see the fishwife sitting at her usual pitch under the balcony of Moray House.

Although he was impatient now to get back and see Mary, he could never refuse Annie anything. As well Jamsie knew. A glance at his son confirmed Arthur's suspicion that Jamsie had been the one to put his sister up to the asking!

'Alright lass, ye can hae a wee treat,' he said.

'I'll hae three saucers please Jeanie,' Arthur told the fish-wife.

Arthur stood back as Jeanie Hosie reached into the bucket of water by her stool and lifting out three china saucers shook them free of soap suds. She settled them on the lid of her wicker creel, which sat on the ground beside her, and reaching into the creel she spooned out the mussels for which her native village of Fisherrow was famous. A portion was placed in each saucer, though Arthur noticed, that after a quick glance at Annie's pinched face, she added a few more to her portion.

'Here ye are ma wee pet,' she said.

The three children sat on the kerb with their feet in the gutter and balanced their saucers on their laps.

Arthur offered to help Robina but she refused, pushing his hand away.

'Me, me,' she said.

While the children ate Arthur chatted to Jeanie.

Ever since he could remember she had sat here, in this same spot, wearing the fisher lassies costume of a blue and white striped kirtle over a long underskirt, a black knitted shawl crossed over her chest and a fringed headscarf covering her hair. A deep weal across her forehead gave her a permanent frown. This was caused by the strap of her fish creel, which carried on her back was held in place by a broad leather band. She must be a good age now, Arthur thought, but she still walked the six miles from

Fisherrow into Edinburgh every day, except the Sabbath, with a laden creel on her back and made the return journey, in the evening, hopefully with a lighter load.

Aye, Arthur thought, they were a hardy race the fisher-lassies. They were up at dawn to greet their men returning with the catch, which the lassies would gut, before loading their creels and setting out on the road. Then after their days work was done they still had to run their homes, mend any torn nets, and bait them for their man's next fishing trip. The fisher-folk formed a small tight community where marriage with an outsider was frowned upon. How could any incoming lassie master the ways of a sea-faring family that she hadn't been bred to, and the loss of a fisher-lassies talents was a loss to the whole community should she marry outside the village.

Arthur minded how one of his neighbours, Willie Coyle, had married a lass, Peggy, from Newhaven, another fishing-community, amid great disapproval from the fishing folk. When she died in childbirth it was seen by some in that superstitious community as divine retribution. Willie's childless sister, Mary, was now bringing up the wee lass in her house at Greenside because Willie, unable to come to terms with his loss, had decided to try his luck in Australia.

Was there ever a town so divided Arthur thought, as he stood back to let Jeanie serve another customer.

Fisher-folk against townies, Presbyterians against Papists, Highlander against Irish and the gentry looking down with disgust from high on the South Bridge to the low-life residents of the Cowgate below.

What was it in human nature, Arthur wondered, that folk could only feel happy with themselves if they had someone else below their feet?

The bairns finished their mussels, Jeanie dunked the saucers back in the soapy water and, still licking their fingers, they followed Arthur up the steep street.

Once beyond Moray House, the Canongate, on either side, was lined with small shops, pubs, old clothes dealers and rag merchants.

Irish names were prominent above many doors.

It was the custom for hawkers to make their way around the doors in the better class districts, begging for cast-off clothes, offering wooden pegs in return for rags. Any donations were thrown into the centre of a large tartan shawl which was then bundled up and carried to the nearest dealer in the old town. Here loud, ferocious, haggling took place from which the hawkers always came off worse. Any gains were usually quickly spent in the pub next door, very often owned by the same dealer.

Most of the shops were small being only one room of a house at pavement level. The dealers extended their display area by hanging clothes from the doorway or window lintels or on hooks set in the outside wall for the purpose. Wooden tables on the pavement were piled high with odd cups or plates, or blackened and battered pots and kettles. Old shoes were thrown in to baskets underneath. Most shoes were beyond any further wear but parts of them could be used to repair worn shoes. Few children of the poor could afford shoes. Most ran barefoot summer and winter. Now and then the outgrown shoes of some New Town child were found in the jumble and a poor bairn wearing them would strut about like a prince, lording it over his peers, until the shoes, quite literally, fell apart on his feet.

So all-encroaching were the shops and stalls that progress was slow for Arthur and the bairns.

To add to the problem the street was crowded with people. It was a warm June evening and such was the overcrowding within the homes, with families of six children or more crowded into one-roomed houses, that most people lived their lives on the street. Women stood gossiping on the pavements or sat in doorways smoking clay pipes. Men stood outside pubs, a beer glass in their hands. Children played in the gutters or risked life and limb chasing each other between horse-drawn carts, often jumping on the back for a free ride until threatened by the driver with an upraised whip!

The public well outside John Knox House was a favourite meeting place, a hubbub of gossip and activity.

Though most buildings boasted a sink, and sometimes a water closet on each landing, these were a shared facility for all the people in the houses. Since they were often shared by up to fifty people they were usually filthy and many people still preferred to use the old street wells for their water needs.

Things had at least improved from the times when the town's inhabitants had emptied their slops into the gutters below from their high windows with a warning cry of 'Gardyloo' – mind the water. It would have been bad enough had it just been water but all sorts of nasties were thrown into the street below at the sound of the ten o'clock drum. Or from the times when the "Wha needs me" man, carrying a tall chamber pot and wearing a long overcoat to cover folks modesty, called out his trade in the streets of the old town.

Dr Littlejohn made sure that public conveniences were erected throughout the town in areas where adding water closets to each home in decrepit buildings would have caused more problems than it solved.

It was as they made their way through the crowd that clustered around the well that Arthur spotted his wife's sister, Bina, running down the road towards him, her long skirt held up to speed her progress.

'Arthur, Arthur,' she shouted, 'it's Mary, the bairn......' She pointed back up the street.

One look at her tear-stained face and Arthur didn't wait to hear any more. Putting Robina, her namesake, into her aunt's arms he took to his heels and ran through the throng, pushing, shoving and being met with loud curses, until he reached Morrison's Close. His heart in his mouth he leapt the stairs two at a time and pushed open the door of his house.

CHAPTER 3

The house that Arthur entered consisted of two large rooms with windows overlooking the High Street.

As Arthur burst through the door Maggie Clark straightened up from the fire in the kitchen and he saw that she was burning the blood-stained newspapers used to protect the mattress during childbirth.

She took a step towards him but he pushed past her to the room beyond.

Arthur's wife, Mary, lay in bed, her red hair with it's damp curls spread out across the pillow. Her skin always pale looked like marble. As Arthur took a step towards the bed a floorboard creaked and Mary's eyes flew open.

She reached out her hands to him.

'Arthur,' she said, 'we have another laddie.'

Arthur sank to his knees beside the bed. In truth, he doubted his legs would have held him a moment longer. He had feared the worst and so great was his relief that it overcame him. He laid Mary gently down on the pillow.

'You're my clever, bonnie lassie,' he said.

As his head sank on the pillow beside her he strove to control his racing heart, which his run and the fright had caused, she demanded –

'Are ye no going to look at your bonnie son?'

Arthur rose from his knees and turned towards the wooden kist. Placed on top of it was a kitchen table drawer which Maggie had lined with a soft white towel. The baby, wrapped in the shawl that Mary herself had knitted, lay inside it and only a loving mother could have thought him bonnie. He was the smallest baby Arthur had ever seen. His skin was waxy and his breathing was so shallow you had to stoop to hear it.

Maggie had come quietly into the room and stood looking down at the kist with her back to Mary.

Arthur lifted his head from examining his son. His eyes met Maggie's and what he saw there caused his heart to sink.

Mary called from the bed –

'Well, what dae you think of your son – is he still sleeping? A couldnae get him to suckle but Maggie says that's just cause he's a wee bitty early and he had an awful struggle to get into the world. He'll be fine though, once he's had a wee sleep,' she prattled on.

Arthur gathered his scattered wits.

'Aye, Mary, he's right bonnie,' he said.

'Who do you think he is like?' Mary continued. 'He's got your chin, I think, wi that dimple. We'll call him, Arthur, of course, after you. Won't Jamsie be happy. He'll have a wee pal. He's aye complaining about only having the lassies to play wi – where are the bairns, did you no bring them with you? They'll want to see their new brither.'

'I'll go and get them, Mary. They are doon the stair wi Bina – a didnae want them clattering in here in case you and the wee one were asleep. I'll go and get them now,' said Arthur.

Arthur left the room, followed by Maggie.

'What's wrong wi the bairn,' Arthur whispered, once they were in the kitchen.

'He just came too soon,' Maggie explained. 'I'm right sorry but I don't think he will see this night oot. He just cannae get enough breath, he hardly had the strength tae greet when I skelped him.'

'Oh God,' Arthur groaned, 'Mary, poor lass, she'll go daft, ye ken what she's like about her bairns, Maggie,' Arthur said.

'Aye a ken, Arthur,' Maggie replied. 'But you're going to have tae pull yerself thegether. Ye ken how chicken-hearted ye are, it will be nae help to Mary if you break doon tae.'

'Aye, yer right, Maggie. I'll dae ma best. I'll away and get the bairns now,' he said.

Arthur left the room and Maggie shook her head sadly as she looked after him. He was a soft-hearted man, Delaney – aw, useful enough wi his fists if the need arose and wi a quick temper, but he was fair daft on that lass that lay next door, and she on him. It had been that way since they set eyes on each other and a the opposition they had to face never changed that.

Maggie sighed and sank down on the chair beside the fire, suddenly tired. It had been a long hard delivery and, though she had helped bring many bairns into the world, she wasnae getting any younger herself and it fair took it out of a body. A that effort and yet that poor wee scrap next door wouldnae see this night out. Maggie was sure of that.

Down in the street Arthur made his way through the crowds of folk. It was still a fine June evening. The men were in shirt sleeves and the women had discarded their shawls but Arthur felt chilled. It was as if a dark cloud had overcast his world.

He knew, of course, that many couples lost their bairns in the auld toon. But this was the first time such sorrow had touched Mary and him. Poor Mary, he thought, lying there, after all the months of carrying the bairn and the struggle to gie it life. To lose it now would break her heart.

He found Bina sitting on the forestair outside Moubray House, Robina on her knee, watching as Jamsie and Annie joined in the horseplay around the street well.

Hugh, the Coyle's oldest laddie, had turned on the water and put his finger over the spout causing it to spurt water in different directions. He was trying to soak the other bairns who leaping about and squealing tried to avoid it.

Bina raised an anxious face as Arthur approached.

'How is he – how's the bairn?' she asked.

Arthur shot a warning glance at wee Robina.

'Just the same,' he replied.

The tears started to run down her cheeks again.

'Dinnae Bina,' he urged. 'If Mary sees you like this she'll ken there's something wrong. I'll no have her grieving the noo. Maybe Maggie's wrong.'

But Arthur knew that Bina had seen the bairn, too, and they both knew old Maggie was right.

'Come on now, dry your eyes, Mary wants to see the bairns,' he said.

He lifted Robina from her aunt's lap and shouted to Annie and Jamsie.

Annie came running immediately, her face alight.

'Auntie Bina said we've a new wee brither, can we see him now faither?' she asked.

'Aye,' Arthur replied.

'Jist a minute then,' she said, and going to where a worn stone held a pool of water she retrieved her bunch of wild flowers. 'A thought they would wilt if a didnae give them a wee drink,' she explained.

Jamsie was reluctant to leave the fun around the well and it took another shout from his father before he dragged himself away.

As they walked back up the street Arthur arranged with Bina that she should take the bairns back to her house in New Street to spend the night after their visit to their mother.

They climbed the stair of 2 Morrison's Close and Jamsie and Annie ran through to the back room.

Annie ran straight to the bed and presented her mother with the still dripping bunch of flowers and threw her arms round Mary's neck. Robina seeing this tried to struggle out of her father's arms and he had to sit her carefully on the high bed so that she too could give her mother a cuddle.

Jamsie went straight to the kist and stood looking down at the bairn.

The room went strangely quiet.

Mary broke the silence.

'Well,' she said, 'what do you think of your new pal?'

Jamsie frowned. 'He's awfy wee,' he said. 'A thought he would be bigger. A doubt it will be a long time before he kicks a fitba.'

Arthur felt a sob catch in his throat but Mary laughed.

'Ye wee ruffian,' she said. 'Ye were gie wee yerself when ye were born but look at ye now!'

Annie now left her mother's side and came to look at the bairn.

'He is wee, Ma,' she said. 'He looks like one o the dolls that the toff's bairns push in carriages round the park.'

And, in truth, Arthur thought, that is just what his poor wee son did look like, a wee wax doll.

Robina now clamoured to see and Arthur lifted her down from the bed and held her over the kist.

'A ba ba,' she lisped.

'Aye,' Jamsie said, 'an a hope he doesn't turn oot as much a pest as you!'

'That's enough of that,' Maggie said. 'This room is like the Waverley Station, so it is. Away ye all go and let yer mither and this wee yin get some rest.' Shooing them before her, like hens, she drove them from the room, though Annie turned at the door and waved.

'See ye the morn, Ma,' she said.

Arthur went with Bina and the bairns back to her own house. Wee Robina had been on the go all day and now she was too tired to walk and her aunt, being just a slip of a lass herself, could never have carried her even that distance.

Though it was still quite light outside, the house, when they entered, was dark. The kitchen was lit only by a small window which let in little light. Arthur went forward and lit the candle on the mantelpiece and then another on the dresser. There was gas light in the room but it ran away with the pennies and folk were careful how they used it.

The fire had burned low so Arthur raked the ashes and added some firewood and once that had caught added a few lumps of coal. Though it was June fires were always kept burning as that was where the cooking was done, on the big range. Arthur opened the oven door, at the side of the range, and felt the cast iron pot inside.

'It's still warm, Bina,' he said.

Mary had made the soup before going into labour, and Bina had brought it down earlier to have ready for the bairn's tea.

'Fine,' Bina said as she stood at the table slicing bread. 'Once I've mashed a pot of tea it will be just ready. Will you stay and have something yerself, Arthur?'

'Naw, thanks anyway, Bina, but a wid like tae get back to Mary, if you're sure you'll manage.'

Arthur hadn't eaten all day but he felt he couldn't have swallowed a bite. It would have stuck in his throat.

'I'll manage fine,' Bina said. 'Away ye go.'

Arthur was passing the pub on the corner of St Mary's Street when the door opened and big Mike Grady lurched out. 'Arthur, it's yerself,' he bellowed. 'How's yer bonnie lass. I heard her time had come. Has she dropped yer bairn yet?'

'Aye Mike,' Arthur replied, 'a laddie.'

'A laddie,' his workmate repeated, 'now that calls for a drink, or maybe two. Come away in.'

He attempted to drag Arthur back into premises he had just left.

'Naw, naw,' Arthur said, and attempted to pull himself free. 'A'm away back up to see Mary now.'

'Well, she'll keep man. She'll keep,' Mike shouted.

'Naw, a said,' Arthur protested, pushing Mike aside, his temper rising.

He knew Mike meant well but he was in no mood for drinking this night.

Mike's good natured face took on a hurt expression.

'Suit yer bloody self,' he swore, 'but a wis payin and ye'll no get an offer like that any night in this God-forsaken toon.'

But he was speaking to Arthur's retreating back as he had already turned the corner into the High Street.

CHAPTER 4

As Arthur made his way back up to Morrison's Close the street was still thronged with people. From the noise coming from the pubs it was obvious that a serious night's drinking was underway. Many men worked a six day week, the majority in heavy labouring jobs. They were paid on a Saturday night when they finished, and most men, and not a few women, made their way straight to the pubs. The alternative of returning to one roomed houses, dark and stifling, with many bairns underfoot, held little appeal.

Most sober wives had learned early in their married lives to make sure they waited outside their men's workplaces on pay night. In this way they could extract from him the week's rent and house-keeping money. Otherwise, it could easily disappear down their man's throat in one heavy drinking night.

However, some of the wives also sought solace for their miserable existence in the whisky or gin bottle. They joined their husbands on their journey to the pub and sat in the snug bar to drink their fill. Some couples prized drink above food and cared little that they, and their children, would go hungry that week because of this one night of oblivion.

It was their children who still played around the well, or sat pathetically in the gutter outside the pub, waiting until their parents staggered out late in the evening.

All the shops on the High Street remained opened till late on Saturday nights so that the fortunate women with money could do their shopping. Vegetable sellers and fish-wives did a brisk trade. Fish was more plentiful than meat and cheaper. Herring was the most popular choice and mackerel, being regarded as the scavenger of the sea, the least. Good cuts of meat never appeared on an old town table but the women would buy scrag ends of mutton to make soup. Tripe, offal and a sheep's head were bought from time to time. But no matter how careful the house-wife, the money only went so far and days before the next pay day many families were reduced to bread and dripping.

The women, clutching their baskets, their faces pinched and drawn in the flickering gas-lit streets, their children holding on to their skirts, made their way from stall to stall seeking the best bargains.

Many of them nodded or smiled to Arthur or asked after Mary as he made his way up the street.

When, at last, he pushed open the door of his house Arthur felt utterly exhausted.

Maggie was dozing by the fire and woke with a start as Arthur came in.

'How is she?' Arthur asked.

'She's fast asleep, lad, she's that worn out.' Maggie replied.

'And the bairn?'

Maggie shook her head. 'Just the same, he'll just sleep away I think.'

'I'll no go through and wake them then,' Arthur said.

'Aye, that's best,' Maggie responded. 'Now you're here, I'll away oot and get some messages for myself and Mary has given me some money to get a few things for her as well.'

'You're a good soul, Maggie, A dinnae ken what Mary and me would hae done withoot ye,' Arthur said.

Maggie flushed with pleasure but was embarrassed and replied, 'Away ye go, what are we here for but to help each other. It's the least a could dae for the lassie, her ain mother being deid an a.'

Maggie bustled out carrying her basket and Arthur sank into the chair she had just vacated.

He had been working that morning, then had the children up the hill in the afternoon and the strain of coming home to the worry of the new baby had drained him completely. His eyes grew heavy and his head began to nod in the heat from the fire. Soon he was fast asleep.

Some time later he was awakened by a blood-chilling scream which brought him leaping to his feet. Staggering in his sleep-induced stupor he ran through to the room. Mary, in her long white nightgown, stood over the drawer, screaming hysterically.

She turned as Arthur ran in. 'It's the bairn,' she wept, pointing, 'he's no breathing, he's deid. Arthur, he's deid.'

Arthur looked and saw that, as Maggie had predicted, his wee son had just slept away.

He tried to move Mary back to the bed but she was rigid and he just couldn't move her.

Just then the door opened and Maggie burst in.

She took in the scene at a glance and going up to Mary she slapped her hard in the face. The screaming stopped and Arthur felt Mary go limp in his arms. He felt his temper rising but in the silence he heard Maggie say, 'Get back in that bed, do you want to bleed to death?'

Arthur lifted Mary bodily and laid her back on the bed, covering her over with the quilt as she was now shivering with the shock of it all. She lay looking up at him, her face pale, her eyes so full of pain that Arthur could hardly bear to look at her.

'It's a right, Mary, it's a right,' he said, smoothing her hair back from her face and finding her skin clammy to the touch. 'We'll hae other bairns, there'll be another laddie...'

Mary pushed his hand away. 'It's no a right, a dinnae want another bairn, a want that bairn, how can you say it disnae matter, he's deid, my bonnie wee laddie's deid, and you dinnae care!' she sobbed.

Arthur felt the tears well up in his eyes. How could he have been so thoughtless.

'I'm sorry, Mary, a didnae mean it that way. It's just, it's just that I thought I was gonna lose you. A couldnae bear to lose you. It's no that a dinnae care aboot the bairn, it's just that a care mair aboot you....' his words trailed off.

He had never been good at expressing his feelings.

But Mary was weeping, not hysterically now but quietly, the tears running down her cheeks.

She reached for Arthur's hand, 'A ken, a ken,' she said, 'I'm sorry, a didnae mean it, a ken.'

Maggie came forward now.

'A'm sorry tae lass, sorry a had to slap you, and sorrier still aboot the bairn. It's a sore loss for you. But you've a man and other bairns to think aboot. You have to take care o yourself now,' she said.

Mary was calmer now. 'Aye, Maggie, a ken you're right.' But then she grew anxious again. 'Oh, Maggie, the bairn's no baptised, he'll go tae Limbo!'

'No, he'll no,' Maggie assured her. 'A baptised him myself when you were asleep. A kent he couldnae live long, he was too wee, lass, he came to soon. A went and got that wee bottle o holy water a keep handy and a sprinkled him. Now he is safe in the arms of Jesus and Mary.'

Arthur silently gave thanks for the wisdom of this old neighbour of theirs.

'Thanks Maggie,' Mary said. 'If the Virgin Mary's got him, he's a right then, she'll take care of him, she was a mother herself.'

'A'll away and make you a cup of tea, lass, and then you can try and get back to sleep,' Maggie said.

Arthur sat on the bed holding Maggie's hand and long before the kettle boiled she was fast asleep. Arthur tiptoed from the room and went to tell Maggie.

'Let her sleep, lad,' she said, 'sleep is the great healer.'

'What do we do aboot the bairn, Maggie,' Arthur asked.

'You'll have to get one o the medical men doon frae the Dispensary to confirm the death. I'm afraid it will cost you a half croon, and then he will give you a certificate to take to the Register Office,' she explained.

'What aboot the burial,' Arthur asked.

'Well if you havenae got a lair yourself then you can apply for a paupers burial, or the Medical man will take the bairn if you agree....'

She didn't continue with this but they both knew what that meant.

Arthur felt sickened but he knew they could not afford to buy a burial plot.

'Anyway, ye can do nothing tonight, it's too late. We'll keep the wee one through here so as not to distress Mary and in the morning you can go and make the arrangements,' Maggie said.

Maggie went across the landing to her own house for the night and Arthur dozed fitfully in the chair by the fire. Mary, totally exhausted, slept all night until Maggie took her some porridge in the morning.

Arthur went first to tell Bina about the bairn's death and then broke the news gently to Jamsie and Annie. Robina was too young to understand and Jamsie heard the news with a set face, determined not to greet like a lassie. Annie, however, burst into tears and threw herself into her father's arms.

'Dinnae greet, hen,' her father said, trying to console her. 'The bairns in heaven noo.'

He was amazed at how easily the words came to his lips. He had never been particularly religious himself, but he had seen how Maggie's words had comforted Mary and he just followed her lead.

After he left them, he walked up the road, past St Giles Cathedral. The bells were ringing and folk were making their way to the church. He climbed the stairs to the Dispensary for the Destitute Sick in Bank Street and asked for a doctor to come and certify the bairn's death. He paid the half crown and a young medical student was sent with Arthur back to Morrison's Close.

When they entered the house Mary's brother, George, stood talking with Maggie at the fireside.

The bairn lay, still wrapped in the shawl, in the drawer, stiff and cold.

The doctor made a quick examination.

'Prematurity,' he pronounced, confirming Maggie's diagnosis. 'I will give you a certificate for the Register Office.'

'What will you do with the child?' he asked, adding, 'I could dispose of it for you if you wish.'

Arthur spread his hands feeling helpless but before he could speak Mary's brother stepped forward.

'The bairn will lie wi its grandparents in the Canongate Kirkyard,' he replied curtly.

The doctor glanced at him and shrugged. 'As you wish,' he said. 'I will show myself out,' and handing Arthur the certificate on the way, he left.

'I thank ye for that,' Arthur said.

His brother-in-law brushed his thanks aside. 'No bairn should go under their knife,' he said. 'I will make the arrangements wi the Kirk and the undertaker, ye can leave it to me,' and he went out, putting his cap on his head as he left.

Later, Arthur could never remember how the rest of that Sunday had gone. Bina kept the bairns with her. Maggie was in and out attending to Mary, but the day seemed to pass in a blur and the night in uneasy sleep.

George Mowat was as good as his word. Early in the morning the undertakers arrived to coffin the bairn and said the arrangements had been made for the burial that afternoon.

Bina brought the bairns back as she had to go to work and Arthur left them in Maggie's care until he went to the workshop on Holyrood Road to tell his gaffer he would not be in for work that day.

He then made his way to the local Register Office.

A man came forward as Arthur approached a highly polished counter.

'A'm here to register a death,' Arthur said, handing over the certificate.

The man drew a heavy, leather-bound register towards him and began to take the details, writing it all down carefully with a fine copperplate hand.

'And the child's name?' he asked.

Arthur's mind went blank. He had never thought of the bairn by a name.

He remembered then that Mary had wanted him called, Arthur, after him. But something in Arthur, pride, tradition, call it what you will rose against the idea.

The tradition stretched right back to the Delaney family's origins in Ireland.

They had called their first son, James, after Arthur's father as custom demanded, and by rights this son should have taken the name, Arthur, after him by the same custom.

But Arthur didn't want to give his name to a dead son. He wanted it to continue, as it had done, down through the generations.

He was suddenly aware that the Registrar was looking at him, strangely, his pen poised above the Register.

Arthur looked around and noticed a brass plaque on the wall.

George MacDonald, Registrar, it read.

Mary's brother was called George.

'George,' he said, 'the bairn's name is George.'

As he made his way home Arthur felt disturbed. His conscience was troubling him. Mary would understand he tried to reassure himself. When she was better, he would explain, and they would have another son, and he would be named Arthur. But the uneasy feeling remained.

In the afternoon the undertaker returned for the coffin.

It had been decided that Maggie would keep the bairns with her and, of course, Mary was still in her lying-in period. So it was only Arthur that followed the small coffin, carried by the undertaker, down the Royal Mile. Men bared their heads and some women crossed themselves as they passed.

As they came through the gates of the Canongate Kirkyard a gravedigger stood beside a freshly dug grave. The gravestone at the head of the plot read –

In Memory of
Mary Brown
Beloved Wife of Robert Mowat
Died November 4th 1867 and
The above Robert Mowat
Died April 10th 1880

The gravedigger roped the small coffin and handed a cord to Arthur and held the other himself. Together they lowered it into the grave. As the small coffin descended Arthur knew at last the reason for his unease.

It wasn't Mary he had betrayed.

It was this little son of his, his own flesh and blood, and he hadn't cared enough to give him the name to which he was entitled. A sob broke from his throat. As the coffin settled, he dropped the cord, and, without even stopping to sprinkle a handful of earth on top of the coffin, as was the custom, he turned and ran from the graveyard.

CHAPTER 5

When Arthur felt more in control of himself he returned to the house and went in to see Mary.

She had been weeping again but obviously took comfort from the fact that the bairn was lying with her mother.

'A really miss her, Arthur,' Mary said. 'Maggie's a good soul, a dinnae ken what a would hiv done withoot her, but a wish ma ain mither was here. A've even been dreaming aboot her, a dinnae ken what it is, she seems really close somehow.'

Arthur felt apprehensive. "Dream of the dead and ye hear o the living", his own mother always said. It was considered a bad omen.

'Try and get some sleep, Mary,' Arthur said. 'I'll take the bairns oot frae under Maggie's feet and gie ye both a bit of peace.'

The bairns were restless having been kept in for most of the day and were delighted to get out of the house.

'Can we go tae Princes Street and look in the shop windaes, and see a the fine ladies in their bonnie dresses?' Annie asked.

Jamsie looked disgusted at this suggestion. 'Naw, a want to go somewhere a can climb,' he demanded.

'A tell ye what, we'll do both,' their father suggested.

'We'll walk along Princes Street and then come back through the gardens. Ye can hae a scramble on the castle rock. How about that?'

The bairns agreed to this compromise and with Robina again perched on her father's shoulders they set off. They made their way over the North Bridge and Arthur could see all the way down the coast of the Firth of Forth. Arthur's Seat shone green and gold in the light of the June day. The Calton Jail, perched on it's rocky outcrop on Calton Hill, looked more like a romantic castle than the grim place it was. Only the railway yard below struck an ugly note.

Arthur always took great pleasure in the beauty around him. His own father, James, was an artist and a photographer and he had inherited his eye and appreciation of the picturesque.

The little family waited while an open-topped, horse-drawn tram passed and then crossed the busy intersection in front of Register House.

'Whose the man on the horse?' Jamsie enquired.

'He's the Duke of Wellington,' Arthur answered.

'A thocht wellingtons were rubber boots,' his son responded.

'Aye, they are,' his father confirmed.

'They were named after him – see he's wearing a pair on this statue.'

Arthur and the children walked on.

Ladies promenaded along Princes Street or stood talking on corners. They wore long skirts caught up in a bustle behind, topped with a short cape, beribboned or lavishly fringed. Their hair was swept up and large hats trimmed with ribbons or flowers completed their costume. Most carried parasols to protect their complexions from the summer sun. Their feet were encased in narrow boots, fastened by rows of tiny buttons and kid or cotton gloves covered their hands.

Annie was entranced.

She constantly tugged at her father's jacket to draw his attention to some particular outfit that captured her fancy.

'When am big am gonnae dress up bonnie like that,' she declared.

Arthur doubted this very much but he said nothing. Let the bairn keep her dreams he thought.

James was unimpressed by all this high fashion but even he enjoyed pressing his nose to the lavish window displays or standing outside the high-class grocers. The smells that drifted out were delicious.

Tea shops were another big attraction for the bairns. Inside they could glimpse fine ladies taking afternoon tea. On tables set with starched white linen stood silver tea services and fine china cups and saucers. Silver cake stands stood in the centre of each table piled high with tiny sandwiches and little fancy cakes. Nearby, hovering attentively, stood the waitress in her long black dress, white apron and frilly cap.

The bairns' mouths watered at the sight of the cake stands. Such fare was never seen in the old town.

They reached the West End and, crossing carefully at this busy junction, made their way towards Princes Street Gardens.

By the gates stood a statue of James Young Simpson, the pioneer of chloroform. Arthur remembered, as a bairn of ten, being taken to see the funeral procession of this great medical man as it made its way to Warriston Cemetery. The newspaper at the time reported that the procession of mourners stretched for five miles and that the city streets had been lined by thousands of respectful citizens.

Arthur and the bairns descended the broad, stone stairway that led down into the gardens.

The valley in which the gardens were set had once been filled with water – the Nor Loch – where in olden times women accused of witchcraft were ducked prior to their death by burning at the stake on Castlehill. Here also, in times gone by, cattle were watered and the women of the old town did their washing. All this was swept away over a hundred years ago when the grand New Town was built in the eighteenth century. The loch was drained and the stinking swamp it had become was transformed into fine private gardens for those wealthy townsfolk who lived on Princes Street.

Now, though, the gardens were a public park, open to all.

They were laid out formally with stretches of grassy parkland, bright flower beds and trees which provided cool green shade on warm sunny days.

The Ross Fountain was, as usual, a great attraction for all the bairns. They splashed happily in its ornamental base and squealed when they were splashed with water from the overflowing bowl above.

Jamsie and Annie begged to be allowed to join in and Arthur sank gratefully onto the grass beside the fountain, glad of the rest.

Annie tucked her dress into her bloomers and, having done the same for Robina, lifted her bodily into the bowl. She kept a tight grip on her sister's hand in case she slipped or someone knocked her over.

Arthur thought, as he had often done, of how little poor bairns needed to be content. No dark shadows blighted their lives. They were happy to splash and play on a warm summer day with no thought of what lay ahead.

Long may they enjoy their carefree bairn-time since most could expect little but hard work and small reward to the end of their days, Arthur thought.

His heart grew sad again as he thought of his little son now lying in the cold earth. Never to feel the warm sun, never to leap and play with his brother and sisters. He rose, needing to shake off the feelings that again threatened to overwhelm him, and called the bairns to come.

They crossed over the railway lines by the little bridge and peered through the lattice work to watch for a train coming from Waverley Station.

Jamsie jumped up and down with excitement as one approached. He waved to the driver who, seeing him, let out a blast on the whistle causing Robina to jump with fright. As the train passed beneath them clouds of sooty smoke billowed up and engulfed the little family above.

They took the path which curved round the base of the castle rock.

Jamsie ran ahead and clambered up the rock by the ruins of the old well house.

'No too high, now,' Arthur warned him.

Annie, who always lacked the breath for climbing, contented herself with sitting on the grass making a long daisy-chain for Robina. When it was finished she made a crown, twining it through the wee one's dark curls.

'Doesn't she look bonnie, faither?' asked Annie.

'She does that,' Arthur replied.

It always touched him to see the pride that Annie took in this wee sister of hers and indeed Robina was a really bonnie bairn. Looking at her crowned with daisies, Arthur thought, she'll break a few hearts, that one, when she grows up.

'Time to go hame now,' Arthur shouted up to Jamsie, high on the rock above.

Turning to obey him, Jamsie lost his footing and rolled over and over down the grassy slope to land in a heap at their feet. He stood up, brushing dried grass from his clothes, and picking leaves from his hair.

Annie and Robina dissolved into helpless giggles at the sight of him.

Jamsie, his pride hurt, looked so affronted that Arthur felt the laughter burst from him and he laughed till the tears ran down his cheeks.

'It's no that bloody funny,' his son said, 'a hurt ma bahookie!'

This sent Arthur and his sisters into further fits of laughter and Arthur felt the build up of the tensions of the last few days ease.

He didn't even give Jamsie a row for the swear word.

As they came out at the gate on the Mound and began the steep climb up to the Royal Mile his spirits began to lift a little.

They would always remember their lost son, Arthur thought to himself, but they would put their sadness behind them.

Life would get back to normal once Mary was up and well again.

CHAPTER 6

Edinburgh

24th June 1882

But Mary showed no sign of getting well.

Instead she seemed to get weaker and weaker as each day passed.

Arthur couldn't understand it. With the other bairns Maggie had found it difficult to get her to stay in bed, so anxious was she to get back in charge of her own kitchen again. But now she was content just to lie there dozing on and off all day long.

At first Maggie thought she was just a bit down with losing the bairn but as the days passed she grew more concerned. The lassie was very pale and clammy to the touch. She was feverish and sweating, pushing the quilt away from herself one minute and shivering the next.

She was so disturbed at night that Arthur got little sleep and went off to work in the morning exhausted.

Maggie tried to hide her fears from Arthur but she had seen enough cases of childbed fever to know the lass was far from well. Finally, when Mary broke into a purplish rash, she said perhaps Arthur should get one of the doctors from the Dispensary to have a look at her.

When Arthur went to the Dispensary the next morning, on his way to work, none of the medics were in yet. An attendant promised to give the message and get them to call and see Mary that day.

Arthur was at his work bench engrossed in engraving an elaborate goblet when he became aware of his gaffer standing at his elbow. The glassworks was a noisy place and it took Arthur a moment to make out that someone was at the door to see him. He laid the goblet down and went in to the alleyway beside the workshop.

Jeanie Flynn, another neighbour from their stair, was standing there.

'Arthur, ye better come quick,' she said, 'Maggie said to tell you that Mary's far from well.'

Arthur didn't let her finish.

He set off at a run leaving Jeanie far behind.

He raced along Holyrood Road his heart thudding in his rib cage.

As he ran up South Grays Close, past St Patrick's Chapel, he found himself praying for the first time since he was a laddie. Dinnae let her die, Oh God, dinnae let her die. I'll come back to Mass, I'll come every Sunday, anything, only dinnae let her die.

He raced across the High Street, without looking, causing a horse to rear and nearly overturn it's cartload of coals. With the driver's curses ringing in his ears he ran into Morrison's Close and leapt the stairs to their house.

Mary lay in bed, barely conscious.

Maggie knelt beside her, ringing out a cloth and bathing her face. She looked up as Arthur burst in.

'Thank God you're here,' she said.

'Has the doctor no come?' Arthur gasped.

'No yet,' Maggie cried, 'and she's fading fast.'

Arthur groaned and sank to the floor beside the bed. He grabbed Mary's hand which was cold and moist. 'Mary, Mary,' he sobbed, 'dinnae leave me, dinnae leave me, a canny live withoot ye.'

At the sound of Arthur's voice Mary seemed to rouse and struggled to sit up. But the effort was too much for her and she sank back, panting, against the pillow.

'Arthur,' she gasped, 'the bairns, ye'll mind the bairns, ye'll no let anything happen to them?'

'It's aright, Mary,' he said, 'the doctor's on his way, he'll be here soon, you'll be aright.'

Now Mary moved her head restlessly and gripping his hand with her fast ebbing strength, she repeated. 'Promise me, promise me you'll look after the bairns.'

'A promise, a promise,' Arthur sobbed.

Mary gave a deep sigh and lapsed into unconsciousness.

Arthur never knew how long he knelt there.

Eventually he felt Maggie prising his fingers loose from Mary's hand.

'She's gone, lad, ye'll have tae let her go now,' Maggie sobbed.

'Naw, naw,' Arthur shouted, 'speak to me Mary, speak to me,' and he lifted her up from the pillow and cradled her in his arms.

There was a knock on the door and Maggie went to answer it.

A moment later she returned with the young medic Arthur had brought to the house just five days before.

At the sight of him Arthur leapt to his feet.

'Where the hell have you been,' he shouted, 'gripping the man by the lapels?'

Maggie pulled him away. 'Arthur,' she said, 'this'll no help, let the doctor look at the lass.'

Arthur's hands dropped to his sides and he stood back as the doctor examined Mary and questioned Maggie in a low voice.

At last he turned from the bed. 'I'm sorry,' he said, 'I understand your anger, but it would not have mattered when I got here. She has septicaemia. Her blood was poisoned. There is nothing we can do for it.'

Arthur barely heard him.

Great waves of grief and despair washed over him. He saw his Mary lying cold and still on the bed, her spirit fled. Never again would he hear her voice, never again would she laugh or sing. Never again would she hold him in her arms and comfort him for all life's ills. He saw years of emptiness and loneliness stretching ahead of him until he, too, could lay down the burdens of life and sink thankfully into his grave.

The doctor gave Maggie the death certificate and left.

Arthur never even saw him go. Shock and grief had taken him to a realm beyond all human contact.

He turned and fled the flat.

He never heard Maggie call after him.

He never knew where his feet took him.

When, at last, he came to himself he found he was again on Arthur's Seat.

The town below was settling down for the night. Street lights were coming on, one by one, as the lamplighter made his rounds. Lights sprang up on a ship moored out in the river. A train leaving the Waverley Station let out a long lonely whistle into the quiet of the night. Up on the hill all was silence apart from the odd rustle as the birds and creatures of the hill settled themselves for their rest.

Arthur sat on, scarcely aware of his surroundings.

His mind turned in on himself. Memories of Mary, of their first meeting, of her gentleness, of all she had brought to his life. Remorse at what he had given her in return, four bairns in five years and an early grave. All his fault, he would never forgive himself. Bitterness, he had prayed for her life and his prayers had been ignored. What sort of God was it that would let a bonnie young lassie, who had never done any harm, go to her death at twenty-three?

But over-riding all of these emotions, grief. The sense of loss overwhelming him, life without her, emptiness stretching on and on.

He started to sob and threw himself down on the grass his face pressed to the sweet smelling earth. He tried hard to find the comfort that the hill had always given him. Finding none he at last fell asleep, exhausted.

When he woke the morning light was breaking over the town.

He sat up, confused, and realised his clothes were wet with dew and that he felt chilled through. He stood up, brushed the grass from his trousers and took off his jacket and shook it. Replacing it he started back down the hill for the town.

Was it only a week ago, he thought, that he and the bairns had walked this path, filled with anticipation at the thought of the new bairn.

The bairns! He realised he had forgotten all about them.

He had promised Mary he would look after them and he had abandoned them without a thought. Wrapped up in his own sorrow he had forgotten theirs. He broke into a run. Mary was hardly cold and he had broken his promise to her.

When he reached Morrison's Close, Maggie was already up and had the kettle on the fire in his kitchen.

As he came through the door, she turned. 'Thank God, you're aright,' she cried, 'a was that worried!'

'A'm sorry, Maggie, am right sorry, a never thought. The bairns, where are the bairns?'

'They're with Bina,' Maggie said, 'we thought it better until Mary was coffined...' Her voice trailed off.

'Oh aye, the arrangements,' Arthur said, 'A'll have to make arrangements.'

He felt suddenly dizzy and swayed on his feet.

Maggie came forward and said, 'Are you aright?' – she took his arm – 'my God, yer soakin wet! Gies that jacket off and come away and sit at the fire till ye dry oot.'

She raked the fire till it flared up.

Soon, with a mug of tea in his hands, Arthur felt the warmth come back into his body.

'A'll make some porridge,' Maggie said, 'a don't suppose you've had anything tae eat since yesterday morning, hiv ye?'

Arthur shook his head.

After he had his breakfast and his jacket had dried out Arthur set out for Bina's to see the bairns.

Before he left Maggie asked him if he wanted to see Mary.

'A've laid her oot right nice, she looks bonnie,' Maggie said.

'A ken ye will have, Maggie, and I'm right grateful, but a canny bear to look at her deid. A've only got ma memories now, and that's how a want to remember her,' he explained.

Down in the street Arthur was surprised at how quiet it was. He had forgotten it was Sunday.

When he got to Bina's house the bairns were sitting around the table having their porridge.

Robina was sitting on her aunt's knee.

When they saw him, Annie jumped down and threw her arms round his knees. She burst into tears. 'Mammy's deid,' she sobbed.

Arthur bent down and lifted her up. 'A ken, lass, a ken.'

He looked at Bina and seeing her blotched face and swollen eyes felt ashamed again.

How selfish of him to think that only he had been affected by Mary's death. Here were the bairns and Mary's heart-broken wee sister equally grief-stricken.

'A'm sorry, Bina, am right sorry,' he said.

Bina nodded but said nothing as the tears again ran down her cheeks.

Arthur turned to Jamsie who still sat at the table his eyes staring down as his plate. He was biting his lip – trying to be a wee man- trying no tae greet like the lassies.

Arthur put Annie down gently and went to kneel beside him.

'It's aright, son, let yer greet oot,' he said, 'she was worth greetin for, yer Mammy.'

Jamsie threw his arms around his father's neck and burst into tears.

Soon they were all sobbing, even wee Robina who, mercifully, didn't know what they were weeping for.

After a while, Arthur, took out his hankie and blew his nose.

Bina got a towel and washed the bairns' faces then splashed cold water on her own.

'Faither,' Annie said, 'who will look after us now?'

'Dinnae worry lass, you've still got me, I'll look after you all, a promised yer Mammy,' he said.

But Arthur was worried. It wasn't going to be easy. He would have to work and the bairns were too young for school.

Bina's voice broke into his thoughts.

'Arthur,' she was saying, 'would ye be agreeable to Mary being laid to rest beside my faither and mither and yer bairn? It wis George's suggestion and it seems fitting.'

'That was right good o him, Bina, a would be very grateful,' he said.

And so it was that Mary was laid to rest in the Canongate Kirkyard beside her father, and her long dead mother who had filled her dreams in the days before she died, and the precious little son she had known so fleetingly in life.

Chapter 7

Edinburgh

December 1882

The work day had ended and Arthur trudged wearily up the road towards his home.

It was nearly six months since Mary had died and his sense of loss was just as sore.

Arthur felt it as an actual physical pain, an ache that made him feel bone weary. He woke in the morning as tired as when he had gone to bed.

At first his workmates had been sympathetic and tried to cheer him up by suggesting they go for a drink after work, or go to the Hibs match on a Saturday afternoon. However, when all their attempts met with a curt rebuff they lost patience and left him to himself.

Only the bairns brought him any comfort.

After Mary's burial Maggie Clark had pleaded with him to approach his mother and his family to help care for the bairns. But since he was estranged from his mother and his father had abandoned his family and now lived in England he had refused, his temper rising, the stubborn Delaney pride much in evidence.

'I wouldn't go crawling to them for help,' he said. 'You know they didn't approve of the marriage. Protestant Mary they called her behind her back. No matter how hard she tried they never accepted her. Why they hadn't even come to the funeral.'

Maggie pointed out that he hadn't even told them that Mary had died.

'That was no excuse,' he stormed, 'they knew, everybody knows everyone's business in this bloody toon.'

'Maybe they felt you should have told them yourself,' Maggie persisted, knowing the pride that ran right through that family.

The Delaneys had always acted as if they were a cut above most folk in the auld toon. Maybe it was the artistic temperament. Arthur's father was an artist who had taken up the new fashion of photography. James's brother, John, Arthur's uncle, was a famous actor down in England. He had even toured America with his productions on stage.

Arthur's granny, Helen, had married well the second time around. She was a widow of thirty when she had married Philip Boylan, a widower, twenty-five years her senior. He was a Master Tailor with a good business in the town. He had also invested in property which he rented out. This had made him a very wealthy man.

Not that Arthur had ever seen any of the money.

When old Philip died his large estate was inherited by Luke, his son with Helen, not by his stepsons the Delaney boys.

Eventually, Maggie had given up trying to reason with Arthur and had agreed to look after the bairns herself, with the help of Jeanie Flynn's daughter, Kate.

The lassie had been born with a club foot and found it hard to get work. She was happy to earn a few pennies a week helping to mind the bairns.

As he walked home Arthur's mind went back over the last few months.

They were lonely months.

He went out to work each morning and returned at night to a meal, prepared by Maggie, left warm for him on the cooking range. Afterwards he and the bairns would sit by the fire talking and Arthur would make up stories for them. Once they were tucked up in bed he would sit on, staring into the glowing embers, recalling happier times with Mary.

Maggie offered to come in again at night and sit with the bairns to let Arthur out with his mates to the pub.

'You've never been over the door in six months,' she said, alarmed at how low he was, 'it will do ye good, give ye a bit o company.'

But Arthur always refused. 'It's poor company a would be, Maggie, a have nae heart for it,' he said.

The only change in the family's routine came at the weekend when Arthur took over the care of his family. On a Saturday afternoon, or a Sunday, when the weather was fine, Arthur would make up some dripping pieces and fill a bottle with water and he and the bairns would set off for a walk.

They roamed everywhere that fine warm summer and autumn. Arthur came to know his bairns well and showed the same loving affection to them as their mother had.

Sometimes they would catch a horse-tram out to Liberton Dams. The bairns would take off their shoes and play at jumping the stepping-stones across the burn.

They squealed with laughter when one of them mistimed a jump and landed with a splash in the water.

On really hot days they would go to the sands at Portobello and paddle in the sea. Arthur, though, always worried when a breeze sprang up in case Annie caught a cold. They loved to walk out on the long pier over the sea and watch the day trippers coming ashore from the pleasure steamer, The Skylark.

The highlight for Jamsie though was always the train trip home from Portobello Station. The steam-train passed through the farmlands around Duddingston before puffing and hissing to a stop amid clouds of smoke in the Waverley Station. Arthur had to carry wee Robina up the steep Scotsman Steps and on to the North Bridge because, by then, she was usually fast asleep.

Once or twice each month they visited the Botanic Gardens at Inverleith, which Annie loved because it was also a favourite place with the gentry. The fine ladies of the New Town would stroll on the paths wearing their lovely gowns and carrying pretty parasols while Annie watched them with delight.

But their favourite place remained Arthur's Seat.

The bairns came to know it as well as their father did. They fed the ducks and swans on St Margaret's Loch with old bread. They walked around the Radical Road to Duddingston Loch while Annie and Jamsie chanted – "Round and round the radical road the radical rascal ran". They gazed down over the grassland and watched for the train coming along the Innocent Railway heading for St Leonards loaded with coal from East Lothian.

Jamsie, especially, came to love the hill in it's many moods and colours and dreamed of when he would be big enough to climb up Samson's Ribs, a dramatic rock formation. Meanwhile, he was only allowed to climb up as far as the ruin of St Anthony's Chapel above St Margaret's loch.

The bairns seemed to have accepted their mother's death and rarely spoke of her to Arthur. At first he had been surprised at this, and even hurt that they could have forgotten her so easily, she who had loved them so much. Robina, mercifully was too young to understand but he was surprised that Jamsie and Annie hadn't shown more reaction. But as time passed and his own grief hadn't lessened he was quite relieved that they didn't mention Mary. He doubted if his self-control would have held. At any mention of her by Maggie, or Bina, Mary's sister, Arthur felt his chest tighten and his eyes begin to fill.

Arthur was not to know that Jamsie and Annie missed their mother sorely and often sobbed out their sadness on Maggie's ample bosom. But the two bairns, wise beyond their years, were aware of how any mention of their mother upset their father. They had an unspoken pact never to mention her in his presence unless he did.

Things had continued this way all through that lovely summer and autumn. But now it was November. The nights were dark, the days dull and cold. Already there had been some snow. It was impossible now to take the bairns out for walks. Last Saturday they had gone instead to the fine Museum on Chamber's Street. The bairns had been entranced. Wee Robina eyes had widened when she saw the stuffed animals – the huge elephant and the giraffe - towering over her.

Arthur had felt his spirits lift as they had walked through the great lower hall, lit by many windows. His artistic eye had appreciated the impressive cast iron work and the clean soaring lines of the place. He had marvelled at the fine art objects on display from all around the world. He was himself a skilled craftsman and he would have loved to have created in crystal some of the exotic designs he saw here. He had even sketched a few on a scrap of paper intending to show them to the chief designer at John Ford's glassworks were he was employed as a glass-engraver.

Arthur remembered how he had felt when he had heard the great clock in the hall chime five and had seen the attendants walking through the museum ringing hand-bells to announce closing time. As they had left the museum sleet was falling and the children had shivered and gasped for breath as it stung their faces. Arthur's heart had sunk as they left the warm, brightly lit building to return to the empty, cheerless flat and another long lonely night.

Lost in these thoughts Arthur had reached Morrison's Close.

Though the gas lights were lit out in the street there were none in the Close. It took a few moments for his eyes to adjust to the darkness so he almost bumped into Jeanie Flynn who was standing at the stair doorway.

'Arthur,' she said, 'thank God you're here. Wee Robina's gone missing!'

'What!' Arthur shouted. 'Where's Maggie?'

'She's upstairs in the hoose, wi the other two bairns.....' Her words tailed off as Arthur pushed past her and bounded up the stairs.

Hearing him coming Maggie came out on to the landing between their two doors.

Arthur grabbed her arm. 'What happened, where's the bairn?'

'A'm sorry, Arthur,' Maggie said. 'Robina had been girnin a afternoon to get oot tae play wi Jamsie and Annie. A telt her she was too wee. A left her here in the kitchen til a went through tae make up their beds and when a came back she had slipped the latch and gone oot. Ye ken a canny manage doon the stairs easily my legs being so bad. A shouted up for Kate Flynn but by the time she limped doon the stairs herself the wee one was no where to be seen. Jamsie and Annie were playing in the back green and they didnae see her either. A the neebours are oot looking for her now....'

Arthur felt the blood rush to his head. 'Ye auld fool,' he said 'first ye kill ma wife and now ye lose my bairn!'

Maggie staggered back as if he had struck her and her hand went up to her mouth.

Then silently she turned and went into her own flat closing the door behind her.

Jeanie Flynn had come quietly up the stairs behind him and now stood open-mouthed, clutching her shawl around her.

Arthur turned to her. 'Will ye go in and mind Jamsie and Annie until a search for the bairn?'

Jeanie nodded, scared to speak, and edged cautiously round him and into the flat.

Arthur raced off down the stair and ran down the High Street. He searched every close, calling Robina's name. He climbed stairs and folk hearing the commotion came out onto their landings. But no one had seen a wee curly headed lassie. He went down into the Canongate. Surely she would not have wandered that far, he thought, but he searched again without success. At last, his heart pounding with anxiety he turned for home. Perhaps a neighbour would have found her by now.

When Arthur returned to his home he found Jeanie sitting in the chair by the fire with Annie sobbing on her knee. Jamsie stood close by the chair his face white and tear-stained. There was no sign of Robina but the neighbours were still searching. Arthur rested his elbows on the mantelpiece and covered his face with his hands. A nameless fear had him in its grip.

Just then a knock was heard on the door.

Arthur leapt to answer it, his nerves strung to breaking point.

As he opened the door a lady stood there and looking down Arthur saw she had Robina by the hand.

Arthur bent down and scooped her into his arms. 'Where have ye been ma wee pet, ye mustnae wander off like that, ye've given yer faither an awfy fright.' He hugged her tight, relief flooding through him.

The lady had followed him into the room and she approached Jeanie who was still sitting in the chair. 'Are you this child's mother,' she demanded?'

'Naw, naw,' Jeanie replied, rising and tipping Annie off her knee. 'A'm jist a neebor. A'm awa now,' she said to Arthur, and scurried from the room.

'Aye, ... thanks Jeanie,' Arthur called belatedly after her.

Turning to the lady he said, 'the bairn's mother's deid, a'm her faither.'

This caused the lady to pause, but getting her second wind she continued, 'Well you should think black burning shame on yourself letting a young child like that wander about in the dark. Do you know where I found her? Down in the Cowgate! She could have been run over by a dray or fallen into the Foul Burn. Anything could have happened to her! She was too young to tell me where she lived and I had to keep asking people until someone recognised her as your daughter and told me where to find you.'

As this tirade continued Arthur set Robina down and turned to face the woman.

He recognised her now as one of the Mission ladies who went about the Old Town handing out religious tracts. They hoped to convert the townsfolk to mend their drunken and debauched ways and repent. Arthur had always felt they might do more good handing out bread, rather than tracts, to folk whose poverty and despair drove them to drink and even prostitution. But now he felt an overwhelming gratitude, to this one, because she had brought Robina back safely to him.

He kept his usually quick temper and pride in check and took the tongue-lashing she doled out without demur.

'A thank ye for bringing the lass home,' he said, and went on to explain the circumstances he was in.

The lady listened and then made a suggestion. 'Why don't you put them in a Children's Home,' she said.

Arthur took a step back.

'Naw, naw', he said. 'They're no orphans they've got me. I promised their mother a would look after them.

'Well, you don't seem to be making a very good job of it,' the lady retorted. 'Letting a little one like that wander off, and look at the state of these children. Just look at this place. Her hand swept the room. If you put them in a Home they would be properly looked after and kept clean. You could still see them often. Surely that would be a better way of "looking after them", having them properly cared for?'

Arthur felt his temper rising but he didn't want to offend the lady after her returning Robina to him.

He went to the door and opened it saying, 'Thank you for your help, but no, the bairns stay here with me.'

The lady shrugged. 'Please yourself,' she said. She turned on the threshold and looking towards the children, all huddled together now on the hearthrug, said, 'If you change your mind take them to Miss Stirling's Home at MacKenzie Place. Tell them Miss Guthrie sent you.'

Before she descended the stair she pressed a tract into Arthur's hand. Arthur didn't answer. He closed the door and turned back into the room. He looked down at the little pamphlet in his hand – it read – "Suffer the little children to come unto me".

Arthur walked over to where the bairns sat together, in front of the fire, and for the first time in months he really looked at them.

Maggie had done her best but she was an old woman and had her own house to run as well. It wasn't right, he had expected too much of her.

Now he saw his bairns looked unkempt and he had been too wrapped up in his own grief to notice. Jamsie was grubby from top to toe. His hair was dull and matted. Annie was dressed in a thin dress that was now too short for her. Robina's dress was torn and filthy from her expedition to the Cowgate. Her curls looked like they had never seen a brush in weeks. No wonder the Mission lady had accused him of not looking after them.

Arthur filled pots with water and set them on the fire to heat. He lifted down the tin bath from its hook on the wall and set it down in front of the fire. He tore an old towel into strips and fetched a bar of soap. Once the water was warm enough he poured it over the soap in the bath filling it with soapy suds.

First, Robina was lifted in and rubbed all over with the soapy towelling and her hair washed. She squealed happily in the warm water, catching bubbles in her chubby little hands and blowing them at her father. Next it was Annie's turn. Arthur was gripped with anxiety when he saw how thin she was. Her shoulder blades stuck out and you could almost count her ribs. He washed her gently and wrapped a warm towel around her as she was lifted out. Finally, Jamsie was ducked protesting into the tub complaining that his father was hurting him rubbing so hard with the soapy cloth.

Once the bairns were dried and sitting again in front of the fire Arthur set to work with the brush on their hair.

Starting with Jamsie he soon realised that his hair was so matted it would have to be cut. Fetching a bowl from the press he placed it on top of Jamsie's head and cut round it neatly. Once he was shorn a pile of red gold hair was swept up and thrown on the fire and he was allowed to stomp off, still scowling, to bed.

Annie had long, fine hair which had dried quickly. Arthur brushed it thoroughly and then tied it back from her face with a ribbon. Though he had often watched Mary plaiting Annie's hair he felt that such a skill was beyond him.

Robina was the worst. Her thick black curls clustered tightly round her head and over the months they had become more and more tangled. Brushing was painful for her. Although Arthur was as gentle as he could be the wee one screamed and cried at the tugging. Arthur felt sure the neighbours would think he was murdering the bairn.

At last, clean and shining, the bairns all lay asleep in their shared bed. Arthur, exhausted by his efforts, and by the stress of the day sat in the chair by the kitchen fire lost in thought.

He looked up at the mantelpiece and fire surround. A legacy of the days when their flat had been part of a noble family's town house it was elaborately carved in oak. A swag and urn design ran along the mantelpiece and down each side of the surround a cascade of intertwining fruit and flowers tumbled. It was the bonniest thing in the room and it had been Mary's pride and joy. She had kept it waxed and polished and many a time Arthur had watched her lovingly trace the design with her fingers as she sat by the fire.

He reached up to touch where her hand had touched and saw that the wood was dull and his fingers came away covered in soot. The brass fender that used to gleam in the firelight was tarnished, as were the brass ornaments that Mary had kept bright and polished on the mantelshelf. Arthur's eyes travelled around the room and realised how untidy it now was, lacking a woman's touch. No wonder the Mission lady had looked so disgusted.

Perhaps she was right. No matter how hard he tried he couldn't be both father and mother to the bairns. He had to work and he had no one to look after them except old Maggie.

Maggie! Arthur suddenly remembered what he had said to her.

How could he have accused her of killing Mary!

Yet, Arthur knew, somewhere deep in his mind, he had always felt that Maggie was to blame. Blood poisoning the doctor had said. Well how had her blood got poisoned? It could only have happened during her labour. It had to be Maggie's fault.

But even as he reasoned this out Arthur felt ashamed and filled with remorse. Even if it had been something Maggie did that caused Mary's death she hadn't done it deliberately. She was only trying to help. She had been like a mother to Mary and he didn't know what he would have done without her since Mary's death. He would go in first thing in the morning and tell Maggie how sorry he was and hope she would understand and forgive him. But even if she did he could never expect her to take on the care of the bairns again.

What was he to do? Should he swallow his pride and go and see his own mother? But what would be the use. Even if his mother agreed to help what could she do? Ever since his father had walked out on them when Arthur was just a laddie his mother had had to work. Ann Delaney was not the easiest woman in the world to get along with, but for the first time, Arthur suddenly realised what a hard life his mother had had. She lived in the Cowgate with his sister Nellie and worked as a machinist in a tailor's shop. She was in no position to give up her livelihood and Arthur knew he could never earn enough to keep two houses going.

Though Mary's sister Bina continued to visit she was just a lass and had to work herself.

He thought about his father's family. Could any of them help?

His granny, Helen, who had married Philip Boylan as her second husband, was still alive and comfortably well off. But since his father had left Edinburgh, Ann, his mother, had little contact with her in-laws claiming they thought his father, James, had married beneath him. Granny Helen had always been kind to him and to his bairns, but she was an old woman now, even older than

Maggie Clark. She would hardly be fit to cope with three lively bairns.

Arthur's great-aunt, Sarah, who had married John Skiffington, had lived just a few doors down from Morrison's Close at 105 High Street, above their shop. She had always taken an interest in Arthur but she had died four years ago, the year he married Mary.

His great-aunt Jane, Sarah's sister, now lived in the house which she had inherited along with the Skiffington's business. Jane's husband, John Murray, was also dead so the business was run by Jane's large family. Jane herself was ailing with a heart complaint which sometimes confined her to bed for weeks at a time. There was no one there who could look after the bairns for him.

Arthur's closest relation was his father's brother, Thomas Delaney. He was a quiet, gentle man but he was the only one to brave his mother Ann's tongue and keep in contact with his brother's bairns all through their childhood. It was to his Uncle Thomas that Arthur turned for comfort and advice as he grew up with an absent father. Even in his adulthood the two had remained close. But Thomas and his wife, Margaret Maguire, had a large family of their own and Margaret's sister, Mary-Ann, lived with them to help look after their bairns while Margaret worked in Thomas's shoe-maker's shop. He couldn't expect any help from that side of the family. Nor would he have asked and embarrassed his uncle who would have done anything in his power to help his nephew.

His father had another brother, John, who had gone off to London to make his fortune on the stage. Arthur had often heard tales of the amateur productions that his uncle John had appeared in in St Pat's Church Hall in

St Mary's Street. One of the priests at St Patrick's Church, Canon Hannan, was dedicated to keeping the young men of the parish away from the temptations of the Old Town. He had formed a football team, named Hibernian, which went on to have great success in the Scottish League and had also formed an amateur dramatic group for those less sportingly inclined. Uncle John had been a leading light in these dramatic productions, mainly playing comic parts. As a result he had caught the acting bug, given up his trade as a printer, and turned professional. He had been a great success, touring around all the big Music Halls and Theatres in Britain and even going abroad, to America, on a whistle stop tour in his most famous role. He hadn't been back in Edinburgh for many years.

Arthur's mind had wandered and the fire had burned lower and lower. Eventually, Arthur stirred himself. He was getting nowhere and he was tired out. He would go off to bed and maybe in the morning he would think of something. He put a large lump of coal on the fire to keep it burning until morning.

As he prepared for bed Arthur tried to push to the back of his mind the one solution that he hadn't faced. It was the one that his workmate, Mike Grady, had suggested just that morning, during their tea-break, at the Glassworks.

'Why don't you marry again, Arthur? Get a mother for the bairns.'

The words were hardly out of his mouth before Arthur was on him. Taken by surprise, Mike fell backwards off the box he had been sitting on. The two men rolled over and over in the dust of the yard, pummelling each other. Workmates ran to separate them before the gaffer heard the commotion.

Mike, standing up and touching his bleeding lip, said, 'What the hell was that for?'

Arthur, still struggling to break free from the restraining hands of the two men who held him, shouted, 'Never say that again, no one will ever take Mary's place, no one you hear!'

They had made up their quarrel before the days work was over as they had made up after all the fights they had had over the years. They had met as laddies when both were enrolled in an Industrial School and lived in digs the school arranged down Easter Road near to the crystal works. Mike was more like a brother to him than his own brother, James, had ever been.

Arthur flushed, remembering the incident. He would have to start controlling his temper or he would have no friends left, Arthur realised, as he climbed into bed.

He fell at once into a fitful sleep and dreamed again the dream that had plagued him since childhood. He was crossing a wooden bridge across a river which foamed far below. There was a raging storm blowing and Arthur held the hand ropes on either side as the bridge swayed from side to side in the wind. There was an ominous creaking sound and ahead of him planks began to break from the bridge and plunge down into the water far below. Yawning gaps appeared at his feet. Unable to stand any longer he fell to his knees and began to crawl across, praying that none of the gaps became too wide to cross. And then the final horror. The bridge had collapsed ahead. He knelt on the edge of an abyss, the dark water below, there was nowhere else to go.

As always he woke bathed in a cold sweat.

Arthur sat up in bed shivering, staring into the darkness, and then he heard it, the rasping noise of Annie's breathing. She was having an attack of croup!

He leapt from his bed and ran to where Annie lay.

She was struggling to sit up but didn't even have the breath to call for him.

Oh God, oh God, thought Arthur.

Then trying to remain calm, and not distress his daughter further, he scooped her up in his arms and wrapped a blanket around her. Jamsie and Robina still lay fast asleep. He forced himself to say, 'It's aright ma wee lamb,' as he carried her through to the fire. He propped her up in the chair and ran out to the sink on the stair landing carrying a large pot to fill with water.

Luckily the fire had not gone out and he was able to rake it up and add more coal. He filled every pot in the house and set them on the range. It seemed like an eternity before the water started to boil and release the steam needed to ease Annie's breathing.

When Mary was alive she would cradle Annie in her arms and soothe her during such attacks while he filled the pots but now he had to leave Annie gasping in the chair while he ran out to the sink on the stair landing for water.

Arthur had never felt so alone in his life with no one to turn to. He could hardly go across the landing to old Maggie now for help. He would just have to manage.

Once the steam billowed out he was able to sit in the chair with Annie on his knee and comfort her and soothe the damp hair back from her forehead. Annie was crying, tears running silently down her cheeks. When at last she had the breath to talk the words came gasping out, 'A want ma Mammy, a want ma Mammy.'

'So do I, lass,' Arthur said, crying himself now, 'so do I.'

Eventually, Annie's breathing eased and she fell asleep in her father's arms but Arthur was afraid of a relapse.

He rose carefully and propped her up again in the chair while he put more coal on the fire and went for more water for the pots. He couldn't afford to let the water off the boil, the steam was the only thing that helped. Arthur was only six years old when his young sister had died in the local hospital as a result of croup. He well knew that any attack could prove fatal.

It was the longest night of his life.

Early next morning, before the bairns woke, Arthur went next door to Maggie Clark's house. When she opened the door Arthur saw from her blotched and swollen face that Maggie had been crying all night.

When she saw Arthur standing there her face hardened and she said, 'If you've come to ask me to mind the bairns you can forget it.'

'Naw a havenae, Maggie,' Arthur replied. 'A've come tae say a'm sorry. A dinnae ken what came over me. A dinnae ken what a would hae done withoot ye a these months. It was a ma fault, a expected too much.'

'How could ye say a had caused the lassie's death, and in front o Jeanie Flynn tae? A wid never have harmed Mary, ye ken she wis like a daughter tae me,' Maggie sobbed.

'A ken, Maggie, a ken, a must have been oot o ma mind. A've no been thinking straight a these months. A dinnae expect ye tae forgive me, but a really am right sorry.'

'What are ye going dae about the bairns?' Maggie asked.

'A dinnae ken, Maggie, but a will think o something. Dinnae you worry a couldnae hae got this far withoot ye. Ye've done mair than enough for us. Mair than ma ain flesh and blood,' Arthur said bitterly.

'Go and see yer Mither,' Maggie urged.

'Aye, I'll think aboot it, Maggie,' Arthur replied as he turned back into his own doorway.

When the bairns woke Annie was much recovered. He sat them all at the table and gave them their porridge. While they ate he sat by the fire thinking about what to do next.

He lifted down the tea-caddy in which Mary had kept the money saved from her house-keeping and counted out the coins. It came to three pounds, ten shillings, just over three weeks wages.

After the bairns had eaten and Arthur had tidied up he took the bairns with him down to John Ford's Glassworks in Holyrood Road. He saw his gaffer, John Campbell, and explained the situation saying he wouldn't be in for a few days. John was sympathetic but he warned Arthur that he couldn't guarantee to keep his job open for long.

'Ye ken times are bad, Arthur,' John said. 'If word gets oot that there's a job going there will be a queue at the door. If them up in the office get wind of it they will likely fill your job. Ye ken they were no happy about the time ye took off when yer bairn and then Mary died.'

'Aye, a ken that John, a ken they will show nae mercy. Business is business they will say. But what can a do – ye see ma situation,' Arthur said.

CHAPTER 8

Two weeks had gone by since the night that Robina had been lost and Annie had had her attack of croup, and Arthur was no nearer a solution. Indeed matters were worse.

Mike Grady had just left. He had brought Arthur his lying-time money and the news that the company had filled his job. Mike and his workmates had had a 'whip-round' on pay day and had added to the wages.

Arthur was touched and grateful but he knew it was not enough. Once he had paid the rent there would only be enough to keep him and bairns for another week. And where was next week's rent to come from?

Arthur felt bone-weary. He knew he kept putting off decisions but he somehow didn't have the energy to face facts. He watched the children playing on the floor at his feet. They couldn't go on like this. He would have to go to his mother for help.

He left it until late in the day when he knew his mother and sister Nellie would be home from work. He knocked on the door and his mother answered it.

'Well, well,' she said, 'would ye look at what the wind's blawn in, what brings ye here?'

'A have no where else to go, no one tae turn tae,' Arthur replied.

He had known that his mother would not welcome him with open arms and that he would have to swallow his pride, keep his temper, and take all she chose to dole out to him. As he took the tongue-lashing he felt again like the wee laddie he had been, suffering the effect of all the pent-up emotion, humiliation and bitterness that his mother felt as a deserted wife.

Nellie, his sister, tried to intervene and stem the flow of abuse.

Her mother rounded on her.

'Hold yer tongue,' she said, 'keep out of it, this is between myself and the fine bhoy here.'

She rounded again on Arthur. 'Ye chose the path ye took. Ye chose to marry a Protestant and not a dacent Catholic lass. Ye broke all ties with us. Ye left Nellie and me here on our ain, never a word from you. Ye hardly ever brought the bairns tae see me. My ain grand-bairns and a'm a stranger tae them.'

'Ye hadn't even the dacency to tell us when your wife died. We had tae hear it from others. Fine fools that made us look! And now you come crawling round here expecting me and Nellie to help look after yer bairns,' she stormed.

'A ken, a ken, but a'm at ma wits end. A've lost ma job and a'm no going tae be able tae pay the rent,' Arthur said.

The bairns had been cowering behind Arthur while the tirade continued and now it all became too much for wee Annie and she burst into tears.

At this Nellie could contain herself no longer and braving her mother's wrath she rushed forward and picked Annie up to comfort her.

Arthur waited for the explosion to follow but instead, for the first time, his mother's face softened as she looked at her namesake in Nellie's arms. She took Annie from her daughter and carried her to the chair beside the fire. Sitting her on her knee she rocked the bairn in her arms.

'There, there,' she soothed, 'dinnae mind yer granny's tongue. It's no yer fault ye've a fushionless faither. There, there, a didnae mean tae upset ye.'

Nellie had now lifted up Robina and her eyes met Arthur's over their mother's head. There was only a year between brother and sister and up until his marriage to Mary they had been close. He read in Nellie's eyes the message that the storm had passed and all would be well.

Nellie was the peace-maker in the family. Gentle, like her father, anything for a quiet life. Arthur knew he was like his mother. Quick temper, hasty tongue but easy-going in-between.

His father, James, the artist and dreamer, had never come to terms with his wife's volatile nature. Eventually, when he could take no more, he just up and left. He moved into a high-class boarding house just further up the street. Annie never got over the humiliation of it all. She was never the same again.

In a way it was better for her when her husband moved to England and continued his photography profession in Wigan. From time to time money arrived from him, especially while his children were small, but now, they rarely heard from him.

His mother and Nellie had to work to keep a roof over their heads and food on the table. Arthur suddenly saw clearly just how hard life had been for his mother and despite her quick temper she had never deserved her lot.

The storm over they sat around the fire talking, each with a bairn on their knee. As Arthur had known, his mother was not prepared to give up her job, nor would allow Nellie to do so. They had had a hard struggle and she had no intention of giving up her independence now. However, she suggested that Arthur and the bairns move in with them meantime, which would at least give them a roof over their heads.

Nellie worked in Luke Boylan's pawn-shop and said she would see if Luke could suggest some work for Arthur, that he could do when Annie and Nellie were home to mind the bairns. Luke Boylan was their Granny Helen's son from her second marriage and thus their father James's half-brother. He was a well-respected and prosperous business man in the town with many contacts in the business community.

It was agreed that Arthur and the bairns would return to Morrison's Close that night and pack up their possessions. Meanwhile his mother and Nellie would try and make some space for them in their small house so they could move in next morning.

Years later Arthur could never pass Morrison's Close without seeing, in his mind's eye, his final departure from his home that morning.

He saw himself with Robina in his arms, Annie by the hand and Jamsie trotting alongside, leave the gloom of the Close and come out into the bustle of the High Street. He saw himself turn at the entrance and look back into the Close. He remembered again how it had felt, as if he was leaving all his happiness behind. As if he was abandoning Mary's gentle ghost there in his deserted home and going out into an uncertain future.

And so it had proved to be.

Arthur and the bairns lived with his mother and Nellie for just two weeks.

Luke Boylan found Arthur work as a house-painter working in a friend's grand house in the New Town. To his surprise, Arthur found he enjoyed the work. It involved painting the carved plasterwork ceiling and gilding the ornate cornice of the elaborate public rooms of the house. The work had to be meticulous but Arthur had been used to that in his trade as a crystal engraver and the concentration required kept his mind off his troubles for a few hours. Luke's friend had not yet moved in so Arthur was able to work hours to fit in with his mother or Nellie being home to mind the bairns.

In truth he was glad to get out of the house in the Cowgate.

His mother and Nellie tried hard but they had lived together for a long time. They had their own way of life. Having Arthur and the bairns living with them in just two rooms put a great strain on them all. Arthur was also worried about the effect on the bairns. They were unnaturally subdued and seemed to be going on tip toe all the time. They found it hard to cope with their grandmother's mood swings. Arthur and his mother were not getting along any better, they were too alike, and in spite of Nellie's best peace-making efforts Arthur knew things could not continue as they were much longer.

After two weeks the house that Arthur was painting was finished and he was again without work. When he had returned that night and told his mother, she was tired after a day's work and in a black mood. She made some comment about hoping that he wasn't expecting her and Nellie to keep him and his bairns.

Arthur, his pride hurt, had lost his temper and a blazing row had ensued. In the midst of this Arthur suddenly caught a glimpse of the bairns. They were all huddled together on one bed, their arms around each other, and they were cowering.

My God, Arthur thought, what am a doing to them?

Abandoning the argument he dropped to his knees beside them and gathered them into his arms rocking them gently to soothe them.

The rest of the evening passed in a tense silence. His mother looked shamefaced but her pride would not allow her to bend.

The following morning, after his mother and Nellie had gone off to work, Arthur was alone in the house with the bairns. He heard a knock at the door and when he answered it he saw to his surprise Miss Guthrie standing there.

She was handing out tracts and didn't recognise him at first, but then she caught sight of Robina.

'What are you doing here?' she enquired.

Arthur explained his situation.

'You mean, you all live here,' she said incredulously, 'looking round the room. Have you got a job?'

Arthur said he found it difficult to get work to suit when he had the bairns to look after.

'Well, that settles it,' she proclaimed, 'you must put the children into Miss Stirling's Home. She has many children there whose mothers are dead and whose fathers are in the same situation as you are. What is your alternative?'

Arthur had to admit he had none. No home of his own. No job.

Miss Guthrie saw his indecision. 'Leave it with me,' she said, 'I will arrange everything. Bring the children to MacKenzie Place this afternoon.'

Arthur was so tired and depressed it was almost a relief to let someone else take charge

What could he do, he thought? He had promised Mary he would look after the bairns and maybe this was the only way he could keep that promise. He would still see the bairns everyday and when they were a bit older, and able to go to school, he would bring them home again.

Arthur closed the door on Miss Guthrie and turned back into the room.

Three pairs of eyes were watching him closely.

'What's a Children's Home, faither?' Annie asked.

Arthur took Robina on his knee and sat down in the chair, by the fire, the other bairns at his feet.

'It's a special hoose run by a very kind lady called Miss Stirling. She looks after bairns like you whose Mammy is deid so that the faithers can go tae work.' Arthur explained.

'A didnae ken that other bairns hadnae a Mammy either,' Annie said. 'A thought it was just us.'

'Naw, naw, ma wee pet. There are lots o' bairns like you in the Home and you'll a be able tae play the gether – ye would enjoy that, wouldn't ye?' he pleaded.

'But what aboot you, faither,' Jamsie asked. 'Where would you be?'

'A would stay here wi yer Granny. But a would be able to get a job. Then after work a could come and see ye all,' Arthur replied.

'A'm no goin,' Jamsie declared.

'Ye hae tae son. A cannae look after ye and work tae. Without work a wouldnae hae any money tae feed us or anything. It will no be for long. Once you and the lassies are big enough tae go tae school we will get a hoose and we can a be thegether again.'

To stop himself weakening Arthur put Robina down and started to get their things together.

His mother and Nellie were both skilled needle-women. Once the bairns had moved in and they had seen their meagre wardrobe of clothes they set to work. As a result all the bairns were now warmly dressed. Annie and Nellie had also made them little nightshirts. Robina and Annie's had flowers embroidered on the collars and Jamsie had a steam engine on his. They had also made the girls a rag doll each with bright dresses and long braided hair. Jamsie had been given a brightly coloured felt ball stuffed with rags.

It was as he was packing all their possessions into the trunk he had brought from Morrison's Close that Arthur began to waver and his eyes filled with tears. But he knew there was nothing else to do. He had struggled for six months to look after the bairns and now he had exhausted all the possibilities.

He sat the bairns at the table for the last time and filled their bowls with the soup his mother had left hot on the hob. He broke some bread into Robina's bowl and spooned the mushy mixture in to her mouth which opened and shut like a little bird's beak.

The two other bairns were quiet and Arthur wondered what they were thinking.

After they had finished eating Arthur strapped the trunk containing their belongings to his back and lifted Robina into his arms and they set off. Turning up the High Street Arthur kept to the opposite pavement from Morrison's Close and averted his eyes as he passed it.

They walked over the North Bridge and along Princes Street until they came to Hanover Street. When they reached Queen Street Arthur stopped and set Robina down to rest his arms. It was one of those bright, clear winter days rarely seen in Auld Reekie. The sky was blue and you could see for miles. Looking down the street Arthur saw the sea sparkling in the distance. The trees in the Queen Street Gardens lifted their bare branches to the sky.

He adjusted the trunk more comfortably on his back, picked Robina up again, and with Jamsie and Annie trotting by his side started downhill towards the village of Stockbridge.

He found the address he had been given in MacKenzie Place and rang the bell. It was answered by a maid, a child of about ten.

She took them into a small office off the main hallway. A lady sat at a desk.

'My name is Miss McNee,' she said. 'I'm afraid our Foundress, Miss Stirling, is not here at the moment but Miss Guthrie has explained your situation and I am sure Miss Stirling would wish us to consider admitting your children. It will be necessary for us to have your children examined by Dr Notley to check the state of their health,' she continued.

She rang a bell on her desk, the door opened and the same little maid entered.

'Tilly, please take the children to the doctor's room,' she instructed.

The children followed Tilly out and Miss McNee turned her attention to Arthur.

'Now, if I could just take down a few details,' she said, drawing a leather-bound Register towards her.

'Why is it you wish the children admitted?'

'Because their mother is dead and a have no one tae look after them,' Arthur replied.

'And your full name is?' Miss McNee enquired.

'Arthur P. Delaney,' he answered.

'Delaney,' she repeated, 'that's an Irish name isn't it? Are you a Papist?'

'It is an Irish name, but a was born here as was my father before me,' Arthur replied.

'It's just that Miss Stirling does not permit any Popish priest or nuns to enter any of her Homes,' Miss McNee explained. 'Would that be a problem?'

Arthur was exhausted. What difference did it make, he thought? He had prayed to God to spare Mary's life but his prayers had been ignored.

'It would not be a problem,' he said.

'Good,' she replied. 'Now where do you live?'

'At present I am living with my mother in the Cowgate,' he answered.

There was a knock on the door and when Miss McNee called, 'Enter,' a tall, stooped man ushered in the three children. He approached the desk and Miss McNee said to Arthur, 'This is Doctor Notley.'

Dr Notley turned to Arthur and said, 'The children have been well cared for and are generally in good health. The child called Annie is a little chesty but that is not uncommon and need not concern us.' Then addressing Miss McNee he said, 'There would be no problem in admitting them.'

'Thank you doctor,' Miss McNee said as the man turned to leave the room.

'Now which child is Annie?' she asked.

When Annie stepped forward she said, 'And how old are you child?'

Annie looked at her father.

'She's four,' he said.

'And the other children?'

'Jamsie is five and Robina is nearly two,' he answered.

'Well I think we can find places for the children,' Miss McNee said.

'There is, of course, a small charge,' she continued. 'We do not exist just for people's convenience - so that they can dump their children here and escape their responsibilities.'

Arthur rose from his seat.

'It was Miss Guthrie suggested I bring them here', he said. 'I was doing my best tae look after them. A did not ask for your charity!'

Miss McNee saw that she had gone too far. 'Quite so,' she said. 'I did not intend to offend you. I do understand your difficult circumstances.'

'The charge will be five shillings altogether.'

Arthur was taken aback. He had not expected it to be so much.

He had only been earning seven and six a week for the painting job. Even if he got a full time job he would be unlikely to earn more than fifteen shillings. But what could he do. He had come this far and he had nowhere else to turn. He would find the money somehow.

'A do not have that much on me,' he said.

'Never mind, you can bring it with you when next you visit the children,' Miss McNee assured him. 'Now,' she rose, 'if you will just follow me I will show you around the Home.'

The Children's Home was in a large house. They climbed the stairs to the attic floor and Miss McNee opened the door of a low-ceilinged room. Rows of mattresses lined the room. A pillow lay at the top of each and a neatly folded blanket at the bottom. The next door on the landing was opened to reveal a bathroom. It contained a large bath tub, a wash-hand basin and a water closet. The bairns had never seen a proper bath before and stared wide-eyed.

Arthur was impressed in spite of himself. Everything was clean and shining. The brown linoleum was polished and the wood of the staircase stained and waxed.

So far they had seen no evidence of any children but now they returned to the ground floor.

Miss McNee opened the door and they entered a very large, bay-windowed, room. The winter sun streamed in. It was full of children. Some sat at a table spread with picture books while a lady helper read to them. Some were writing on slates. The pencil screeching along made Arthur's blood run cold. A tiny girl pushed a doll in a carriage around the room and another pulled along a truck full of wooden blocks. In the bay-window stood a large rocking horse with a flowing mane and tail.

Annie could not contain herself. She ran forward. 'Can a hae a shot on it?' she pleaded.

'Of course,' Miss McNee replied. She lifted Annie up and then turned and placed Robina in front of her sister. The two girls rocked back and forwards joyfully.

Arthur turned to Jamsie. 'Would ye no like a shot', he said.

Miss McNee intervened. 'I'm sorry,' she said. 'this is the girls' Home. The boys have a separate house.'

'Ye mean they'll no be a thegether,' Arthur exclaimed.

'I'm afraid not,' Miss McNee replied.

'But...they have never been separated,' Arthur said, his heart sinking.

'Don't worry,' she assured him. 'They will still see each other. Both boys and girls eat all their meals here.'

Arthur looked at Jamsie's crestfallen face. What was he to do?

But he knew he had no option.

'Perhaps you would like to say goodbye to the girls now?' Miss McNee suggested.

Arthur went forward to the rocking horse. 'A have tae go now, ma wee lambs, but a'll be back tae see ye soon,' he said, and kissing them both he turned quickly before they could see the tears well up in his eyes.

He took Jamsie by the hand but they both turned at the door and looked back at the girls. Annie was waving and she lifted Robina's hand and made her wave too.

'If you will just follow me I will direct you to the boy's Home,' Miss McNee said.

From the directions it was obvious that the boy's Home was some distance away.

Arthur decided to take a horse-drawn tram as he felt it was a bit far for Jamsie to walk.

Arthur rang the bell at the house on Bayton Terrace and they were admitted.

Arthur handed over the note that Miss McNee had given him. This house was much smaller and nosier but it was organised on the same lines as the girls' Home. As they were shown around Jamsie gripped his father tightly by the hand.

When it was time to leave, Arthur knelt down beside his son. 'Dinnae leave me, faither,' Jamsie pleaded. 'The lassie's are wee. They can stay. But a'm bigger. Take me hame wi ye.'

'A cannae son, ye ken that. Try and be a wee man, for ma sake. A telt ye it will no be for long. Dinnae make it any harder than it already is,' his father pleaded.

Jamsie had always been old for his years and he realised it was hopeless. He blinked back the tears as his father's arms went round him and then one of the lady helpers came and led him away.

Arthur turned to the lady who had shown them round. 'A'll be back down tomorrow to see how he has settled,' he said.

'I'm sorry,' she replied. 'I'm afraid that won't be possible. With so many children to care for we must have a routine. Visiting time for parents is between two and four o'clock every Saturday. It would be much too disruptive to have people coming and going all the time.'

'But...a thought a could see them every night,' he said.

His heart sank. What had he done!

'I'm very sorry,' she persisted, 'but those are the rules. You saw how upset your son was. You must see it would be most unwise to put him through that every day.'

Arthur, upset as he was, could see she was right.

He agreed to return the next Saturday and bring the money with him.

Walking up the road Arthur could hardly see were he was going. Tears blinded him.

He was attracting the stares of passers-by so he took out a handkerchief and blew his nose, trying to compose himself.

He walked on trying to convince himself he had done the right thing.

He would get a job and save every penny. He would get a house for them to come home to when they were a bit bigger. The Homes looked comfortable. The bairns would be cared for meanwhile.

It wouldn't be forever.

EMMA'S STORY

PART ONE

Hillfoot Farm.
Aylesford,
Halifax
Nova Scotia.

30 May 1886

Miss Auld,
62 Northumberland Street,
Edinburgh.

My dear Miss Auld,

Thank you so much for your most welcome letter giving us all the news from home. I am very honoured that our kind friends and supporters have asked for information about me and how I came to begin my life's work. I will endeavour to answer their request as best I can.

I was born in 1838 in Edinburgh. My ancestors the Stirlings of Cadder were landowners who could trace their origins back to the 12th century. My paternal great-grandfather had been a linen manufacturer in Glasgow. He exported some of this linen to the United States and imported tobacco from Virginia on the return voyage.. He later expanded the business by importing raw cotton from the United States and set up cotton-spinning mills in Manchester. Some of the family then diversified into banking in the great metropolis of London. My father, John Stirling, had his country estate at Eldershaw when he married my mother, Elizabeth Willing of Philadelphia. My mother was the grand-daughter of Thomas Mayne Willing. He lived to the great age of 89 and was both mayor of Philadelphia and President of the first chartered bank in America. He was a man of high principle being one of only two delegates to the Continental Congress who had refused to sign the Declaration of Independence as it would have meant him breaking the oath of loyalty he had sworn to King George III. So as you may imagine I find myself quite at home on this side of the Atlantic!

I was the youngest of eleven children. Shortly after my birth our family moved from Edinburgh and set up home in St. Andrews. My home was in a large old fashioned house close to the ruins of the Cathedral in St. Andrews. It was a picturesque old place, standing in its own courtyard and garden, which were surrounded by high walls. These were our only defence against the inroads of our somewhat troublesome neighbours, "the Fishers", whose dilapidated dwellings formed, at that time, the east end of North Street, except where the line was filled up by our stretch of high walls. From our upper windows I had ample opportunity to observe the doings, and compassionating the misery of swarms of the fisher children, the dilapidation of whose clothing was only rivalled by that of their dwellings. Our chief meeting place, however, was the open sunny space between our gate and the Cathedral, which was the favourite playground of our troublesome neighbours. Our gate itself was a curiosity, for over it were the Douglas arms - the bleeding heart - and, if it could have spoken, might have told many a tale of all who had come and gone beneath its arch since the days of its original possessor, the celebrated Bishop Gawaine Douglas before the Reformation days.

While the fisher children took their noisy pleasure in the open space aforesaid, our favourite playground was within the precincts of the ruined Cathedral, where my brother and I played happily many a summer's day beside an old and highly respected friend, who united in his own person the functions of custodian to the Cathedral and factotum to my father. So it came to pass that in our baby days our favourite stories were told us by David about the Protestant Martyrs and John Knox complete with certain gruesome details.

These stories came to life most vividly when we visited the nearby ruined Castle, with the window still remaining where Cardinal Beatoun looked out at the spectacle of the Protestant Martyr George Wishart burning in front of the castle gate, and at which window he in turn speedily met with the retribution due. My brother and I would with much trembling look down into "the Bottle Dungeon" in which so many victims of ecclesiastical tyranny were immured until death put an end to their sufferings. Who can wonder that I grew up a staunch Protestant?

We children had been brought up strictly in the Protestant faith and impressed from our earliest years with a perfect horror not only of the Romish Church but of that portion of the Episcopal Church now known as Ritualistic, then commonly called High Church or Puseyite. We attended the Scotch Episcopal Church, where my father held the office of vestryman, and it seemed to me, as a child, that his whole efforts in connection with the Church were concentrated in resisting all the various forms and ceremonies - "innovations" they were called - which have since brought so much misery, and, as it now appears, real danger in the way of false doctrine into the Episcopal Churches in both England and Scotland. His instructions and advice to me on these points, and as to the sufficiency of THE BIBLE ONLY as a rule of life, were most solemn and made a deep impression on my mind. My mother also held these views quite as strongly, we, therefore, were never allowed to make any Roman Catholic acquaintance or to mix much with those who were known to be High Church. No doubt our parents were considered very narrow-minded. I have often since been glad it was so.

However, in spite of the good example of our parents as children we could be described as more dutiful than devout. Everything changed when I was about twelve years old and one of my brothers, a young soldier, came home from abroad, deeply impressed with the importance of eternal things. He lost no time in speaking to me about my soul and the need of salvation. But I sturdily resisted all such appeals and attempts at evangelising with all the little strength and obstinacy of twelve years old. My remembered obstinacy caused me much distress later when that brother was killed in the Crimean War.

I was quite a lonely child as, sadly, so many of my brothers and sisters died in their youth but I was close to my brother, playmate of my childhood. Imagine then my distress and that of my dear parents when that brother also was killed in the same war.

A short time after this my dear elder sister, Mary, thirteen years older than I was, who had long been in delicate health, was called by the Lord in a remarkable way, and having found peace in believing in Him, naturally tried to lead me to Him too, but it seemed without success. The effort did not last long for she was summoned to leave earth for heaven just a fortnight after her conversion, and died after a few days illness, rejoicing in her newly found Saviour. During her illness I had read to her constantly from her little Testament, which was very precious to her, but it was not until the day after her death that I took refuge in the Testament, too, and in the 17th Chapter of St. John found the Lord and Saviour Jesus Christ. It is a long time ago now, but He has never failed me since, and I believe soon began to use the child He called then as a means of helping other children.

I felt that He wanted me to do something for Him, and the people most within my reach were the fisher-children in the adjoining street. These now became the object of my life. I even overcame my hatred of plain sewing, and one of my greatest pleasures was to make what I could, in the way of clothes, for them. Later, when I was older, I was permitted to become a visitor at the Fisher's school close by and for fourteen years thereafter I took the role of Honorary Secretary. This only ceased when I was disabled as the result of an accident which laid me on the sofa for nearly six years, and from the effects of which I have never entirely recovered.

My beloved father died the year after my sister Mary in 1853. However, I give thanks that I did have enough strength to care for my dear mother and after she went blind I spent many hours reading to her and nursing her in her growing infirmity. Great was my sorrow then when she too was called to the Lord, dying in 1874. With her death my childhood home was too large for me alone and was sold up. I went to live in the neighbourhood of Edinburgh, the town of my birth. I was somewhat of an invalid, being still lame from my accident and I was a good deal alone in the world. My surviving sisters were much older than me. Ann had married a stockbroker and Jane an advocate and both lived in Edinburgh's Georgian New Town and were much about in society. My sole surviving brother managed the family's business affairs and had thirteen children of his own to attend to. I felt my weakness keenly and often wondered if I would ever again be of any use. I often asked God to give me something to do for Him. I could not help it. It is so sad to feel of no use.

After residing in Edinburgh for some months a friend told me she had been shocked by the fearful stories she had heard of the ill-usage of young children in the Old Town. The result was that, using an inheritance from my mother, I opened a Day Nursery early in 1877, where mothers who worked during the day could bring their babies and little children below seven years of age, and by paying a small sum, leave them to be well taken care of till night.

The offer I made in return for 2d. a day was a warm house, three meals a day and a piece for those who had teeth to eat with. For the bottle babies I provided the best milk I could get and an unlimited supply of crusts and drinks of milk for the teething children. Some friends used to shake their heads gently and murmur, "Irregularity". But the proof of the pudding was literally in the eating and the starving mites grew fat and even rosy. I employed a number of motherless girls who, with good looking after, made very efficient nurses. We had a good many cradles and swing cots and I had a wonderful chair in which I could nurse five little ones at a time.

I spent the greater part of my days at the Day Nursery only going home to sleep. The work was hard, but most interesting from a missionary point of view, as in living the life and sharing the burden of the poor, it gave one the opportunity of speaking words for Jesus. Because of the strictness of my upbringing I was ignorant, at that time, of the devices of the Romish priests, of whom, no doubt, I had a wholesome horror as aforesaid. However, my love and compassion for poor little children were so overpowering that these feelings quite overcame any fear or prejudice I might otherwise have had in dealing with Roman Catholics of the poorer classes. My whole object was to alleviate the misery of these poor little ones for the sake of Him who so loved the little children. I received ALL ALIKE, contenting myself with the stipulation that no popish practices or idolatrous prayers should be permitted in my houses and that no priests or sisters should, on any pretence whatever, be allowed to visit the Day Nursery. If I shut the door to keep the priests out, while I let the children in, it was only because I instinctively dreaded the fascination of the Old Enemy ROME!

I think I loved the old Nursery better than any of the Homes for I spent so many of the early days of the work there and learnt so many hard lessons concerning the children of the poor. One of my greatest pleasures in looking back to the old nursery days is the recollection of the pleasant and affectionate intercourse with you dear Miss Auld, who was so true and kind a friend to me and all our children all through those years of (it must be confessed!) the anxiety and drudgery of Day Nursery work.

I remember how you came in all weathers to look after us and see we had all we needed in the way of housekeeping; how you cheered us up by taking the best view of everything, coaxed the bairns with sweeties – I always said it made me jealous, but I did not think it – how you controlled rebellious and provoking girls – kept up the spirits of the nurses - conducted mothers' meetings once a week, and scolded me roundly for my imprudence in various directions and not taking care of my health! I wish you were here with me now, that's all I can say.

Well I must close now, my dear old friend, my duties call me to the schoolroom. I will get this short account off to the post but I will write again soon and let all our supporters back in the old country know a little more of how my work continued to prosper.

Your affectionate friend

Emma Stirling

Hillfoot Farm
Aylesford
Halifax
Nova Scotia

30 June 1886

Miss Auld,
62 Northumberland Street,
Edinburgh.

My dear Miss Auld,

Thank you for your most welcome letter. How I wish I could have been there and seen so many of my most supportive friends gathered together in your lovely garden for afternoon tea. I am so pleased that they found my humble jottings on my life and early work of interest. Your encouraging words have inspired me and so here I sit at my desk in our Parlour to pen a few more words describing the progress of the work I began so tentatively all those years ago.

A few months after I began the Day Nursery work I felt constrained to open a home in the autumn of 1877, as I found so many children who had no home to go to at night, unless the common lodging- house could be called so, and so many others brought by fathers, the mother having died and left the poor things to the care of the even more-to-be-pitied man, who now had to be father and mother and all. Need I say it likewise grew?

At this time in 1878, I consented to have a board of Directors. When I accepted their co-operation, I kept in my own hands three items; - provision and amount of food, entire control of the servants and admission of cases. This I thought fair and reasonable, as I had undertaken to be responsible for the expenses of the Institution.

Many and harrowing were the cases for which my help was asked from all quarters. Sometimes help was needed only for a limited period, sometimes until in a year or two I could put the child in the way of doing for themselves. More frequently the little ones were left a burden on my hands altogether, until at last I had, for a long time before I left Scotland, 300 children to feed every day, to say nothing of clothing and education. All my Home children went to the public schools so the school fees were a heavy item.

By 1880 the work had attracted a good deal of public attention and a good deal of criticism. When the British Association met in Edinburgh it was the subject under discussion and it provoked most decided, and it seemed to me, most unjust opposition. I took the opportunity to plead the case of the innocent little children, whose only crime was their poverty. At the close of my appeal a gentleman made a most touching and eloquent speech in defence of the cause. That speech, I am certain, turned the tide of public opinion in Edinburgh, and the speaker was J.H.A. MacDonald, then Sheriff of

Perthshire, later Lord Advocate and now Lord Kingsburgh, the Lord Justice Clerk of Scotland.

The Homes once started grew rapidly til by 1883 I had Homes for girls and little ones at 11, MacKenzie Place, Stockbridge in Edinburgh and at 1, Craigholm Crescent, Burntisland in Fife. There was also a boys Home in Burntisland at 1 Craigholm Crescent and a small home for eight boys at Bayton Terrace, Granton in Edinburgh. I may mention that my servants in the Homes, except the housekeepers, were all taken from the elder girls who had behaved well enough to deserve such promotion. I lived in my own private homes at Merleton, Wardie when I was in Edinburgh and at 16 Craigholm Crescent when in Burntisland. I often took into my own home little ones and delicate children who needed special attention. I was careful only to admit children who were either victims of cruelty or really homeless. Though it is true to say that at that time of general depression and want of work, consequent on the commercial crisis many became destitute whose parents had been respectable and well to do people.

In December, 1884 I added the Shelter from Cruelty, 150 High Street, to the list of houses. The reason for this was that I was finding it necessary to receive so many children requiring special protection from cruelty at my own home at Merleton, and as this was extremely inconvenient for myself and my household, I thought it better to incur the expense of another house somewhere near the

Police Office. Besides, it was extremely desirable to have a kind of test house through which doubtful children could pass on their way to the Homes.

I know some friends objected to having so many houses on the score of expense and increased difficulty in supervision, but, after all, the Home is the first necessity of a homeless child, and I am convinced, that a real home, and therefore individual attention, can only be secured where there is a manageable number of children; beyond that it ceases to be a home and becomes merely an institution, which I have always been most careful to avoid for our children.

At this time there was an idea of some other friends beginning a new society for the same end, i.e. of Prevention of Cruelty to Children, but finding how fully the Edinburgh and Leith Children's Aid and Refuge (which was the name now given to my work) occupied this ground, these friends thought it better to join us and all work together.

In May, 1885, we were greatly cheered and encouraged when the Earl of Aberdeen, who was at that time Lord High Commissioner, did us the honour to visit the Shelter on his way from the annual General Assembly of The Church of Scotland, accompanied by his lady wife and his mother. He expressed his satisfaction with the arrangements and especially commended the manners and appearance of the children whom I had brought from the Homes for his inspection.

The upkeep of all these Homes was a severe burden on my finances. You will say, "Did you get no financial help?" I answer, "Very little in proportion". The Town Council of Edinburgh and other public bodies gave annual grants, the public contributed latterly about £500 a year and I charged parents who placed children with me 2/6 each child per week. However, it was understood I was responsible for the expenses of the various branches of the institution, which before I left Edinburgh had amounted to a total of £8,000. This seems a large sum but when you consider this paid all the expenses for eleven years working out at about £720 a year it is a very moderate computation for so large an enterprise, involving over 3,000 children.

As early as 1882 I had begun enquiries relative to the emigration of children to Canada, and the protection to be obtained for them. The Canadian Government was keen to encourage as many children as possible to take up employment as farm labourers and domestic servants and was prepared to give me very liberal grants if I undertook such a child migration scheme.

My journey to Canada in the summer of 1885 therefore met with great success and I obtained promises of help, of various kinds, from various people.

The matter having become financially serious, so far as I was concerned, I told the directors I must avail myself of the opening, with such children as could not be provided for otherwise. I told the directors eighteen months before that this was the only way I could see of continuing the work. I further said that if they (the directors) wished to withdraw from the undertaking, which had so outgrown its original proportions, I could only be obliged to them for what they had done. If they, on the other hand, decided to go on with me, I should be glad of their help. They decided to go on. I may mention that complete lists of the children were submitted to the Directors before starting.

On my return to Scotland in 1885 I took a short lease on a farm at Leadburn Park in the Scottish borderland as an outlet for our older boys, and as a means of employing them profitably, and training them for farm work in Nova Scotia.

In March, 1886, I accepted the invitation of the London Society for the Prevention of Cruelty to Children to attend a meeting held at their Shelter in Harpur Street. The Rev. Benjamin Waugh greeted me most warmly and introduced me to the meeting as a "veteran in the work", having been fighting the children's battle against cruelty since 1877, while, as he was pleased to say, stronger people had only awakened to the necessity in 1884. We Scotch representatives urged on the meeting the necessity for legislation in Scotland. We were advised to seek the help of any parliamentary or official friends on whose support we could rely. I brought the case before the Hon. J.H.A. Macdonald, who was the Lord Advocate at the time. He set up a meeting with other Scotch MPs and I was invited to attend by special invitation to represent Edinburgh, which I believe was an unusual honour for a woman!

As a result of our meeting, the law regarding cruelty to children was eventually altered. Praise the Lord! I am thankful to have thus been the means of laying the foundation and developing in Edinburgh the work which since, by joining the Glasgow Society, has become the Scottish National Society for Prevention of Cruelty to Children.

After I returned from London I immediately began my preparations to return to Canada. It was May of 1886 when I sailed again for Nova Scotia and by then I had closed my two private houses at Merleton and Burntisland. However, I still had eight houses full of children, besides many boarded in the country.

This system of boarding out I had been obliged to have recourse to in 1884 when house accommodation failed. I was very careful in the selection of those with whom they were placed, and the children were arranged in groups of four or six, so that the friend who acted as Treasurer and paid their board monthly, could see how exactly they were attended to, and look after them in every way.

If you ever see any of those friends in the country, especially Mrs Paterson, of Buckrigg Farm near Beattock, who so efficiently carried on this part of the work, the results of which were, to my mind, extremely satisfactory, please give her and them my sincere gratitude. I will never forget their kindness. Many were the lamentations alike of nurses and children when boarding out proved too expensive to be continued, and our children had to be moved to other quarters, on my winding up my personal connection with the work previous to leaving Scotland. But, under the circumstances, with 300 children to provide for, I was forced to see what I could do in the new country, unless, indeed, I accepted the alternative of giving up the children, which I could not do.

As I could not make up my mind to resign them to the hands of strangers for the selection of their future homes, I preferred going with them and buying a farm where I could make a home for the little ones, and headquarters for those who had already been placed; for it would obviously be worse than useless to send boys and girls across the sea, without a home within reach of them, with their own people there to look after their interests, and to hear constantly how they are getting on.

I must stop now, dear friend, lest I weary you and our generous supporters with too long winded an account but I hope they will find something of interest within. Should they wish to know of our subsequent journey to Nova Scotia and how we have fared I will happily write again.

Meanwhile my thanks to you for forwarding the generous donations you collected from our friends in Biggar. Please also convey my thanks to Mrs Murray, of 13, Hatton Place, for the boys' shirts, petticoats and stockings and let her know her most welcome parcel arrived safely.

Keep well, dear old friend. I wish you were a better sailor and were able to visit us here in our new home but though the miles separate us we will never forget your kindness to us.

Your affectionate friend

Emma Stirling

Hillfoot Farm,
Aylesford,
Halifax
Nova Scotia.

25 July 1886.

Miss Auld,
62 Northumberland Street,
Edinburgh

My dear Miss Auld,

At your request, and that of our generous supporters in the old country, I am persuaded to continue to relate how my work progressed after I determined to leave Scotland with our children to begin a new life in New Scotland.

Having decided to go and transfer my efforts to the new farm, where I could feed the little ones at a cheaper rate than in Scotland I gave the Directors notice of our departure.

In May, 1886, I sailed with twenty-five children and sufficient helpers to take care of them, leaving the rest to follow when I was ready to receive them. We set out, not knowing exactly where we should find a home, but trusting in the same God who has led us and fed us all these years, and He has not disappointed us.

Kind friends in Edinburgh invited us to breakfast with them the morning we started for Liverpool and wished us God speed. It seemed very hard to leave so many kind friends that morning. It seemed as if they were sorry to see us go; but still for "our children" what cannot one do? Wae's me, there seemed to be little bread in Scotland, especially for "our children"; and so, when we heard the last "good-bye" and "God bless you" on the railway platform, and had seen the last friendly face at the carriage window, we could only be thankful that so many would think of and pray for us and our little ones, while we were far away doing what we could.

But as you know dear Miss Auld we had not left all our friends in Edinburgh for, to our great joy and delight, you appeared on the platform at Liverpool.

The children were so surprised and thought your appearance in that "far awa place" (as they called it) almost supernatural! But there you really were, full of kindness and help, and with an immense stock of sweeties. You helped us settle the children in bed in our lodgings and were still there when the next morning saw us early up and away to the Alexandra Dock, until soon it was finally time to board the big ship Caspian. You said good-bye; we said good bye too, the children gave a cheer for you; some of us felt a little as if we could cry; ropes, chains etc., seem to make a little more noise, and we are off! I will never forget the sight of you on the dockside, waving and waving, until you disappeared from our view. I confess my resolve almost left me to have to leave such a dear friend behind as we embarked on our great adventure.

On board our children attracted a great deal of attention, with their Scotch tongues, neat cloaks, and bright fishermen's caps, which I devised as a means of keeping them in sight; for when I saw the red knitted cap, we knew that the little head inside must belong to one of "our children". Remember so many were under eight years old, four below four years. I took the very little ones with us, for I knew those to follow would have enough to do without such a heavy handful. The youngest of the party, a fat good-natured baby of two years seemed to enjoy the whole thing as well as any one.

There was plenty to do to look after the children on board. The matron and girls were kept busy doing everything. I'm afraid I lapsed into uselessness and felt ashamed of doing nothing. I cannot help it for I am a shocking sailor but as there is no other way to Nova Scotia, I had to make the best of it. Our children too were extremely ill to begin with, and then, with the fickleness of youth, become lively and active, and used to the ship as if they were old sailors. Mercifully, the rest of our party were excellent sailors and by- and- by I too was able to be dragged up on deck, and we had some great times.

The passengers were very kind to the children, and liked to hear them sing their Scotch songs and school rhymes, as well as the hymns of which they are so fond.

Some days into the passage we began to see ice, and then our progress became slow, owing to the fog being more dense than usual. Eventually we reached St John's, Newfoundland. We did not go ashore but enjoyed the warm day on deck, when the sun had broken through the fog, and shone brilliantly on the rocky cliffs of St. John's harbour, and some of the vessels of the squadron lying there. It was a pretty sight, and land is pleasant after being ten days at sea.

After we left St. John's we saw many more icebergs. I counted seventeen from the deck of the ship in one day! We saw several whales, and whenever they were visible the excitement was overpowering.

The ships company and passengers were extremely kind to our children. Many were the words of counsel and encouragement, as well as gifts of fruit and goodies which found their way to our quarters. But for all the interest and pleasure of the voyage, I was truly thankful when we all got safely off the ship. Our children had had such a merry time dancing about on deck, with skipping ropes and games that I had felt a little nervous that one or two might have skipped overboard! We landed in Halifax, Nova Scotia, on the 5th June 1886 and went into temporary quarters until I could arrange our future plans.

Here I must call a halt as the Supper gong has just gone and I must be about my duties. My sincere thanks go to you Miss Auld and to all in the old country who sent parcels of clothing and monetary donations.

Yours in gratitude

Emma Stirling

Hillfoot Farm
Aylesford
Halifax
Nova Scotia

25 August 1886

Miss Auld,
62 Northumberland Street,
Edinburgh

My dear Miss Auld,

It was so good to hear from you at last. I was becoming very concerned that some time had elapsed since last I wrote to you and no reply had been received. You always urged me to take better care of my health and now I must urge you to take your own good advice. Influenza can be such a debilitating illness and I thank the good Lord that you have made a complete recovery. You and the ladies from the Church Guild are so kind to say they enjoyed my description of our voyage with the children to Nova Scotia and want to know WHAT HAPPENED NEXT!

After settling the party in Halifax, I went in search of our future home, and in a few days saw what I thought extremely suitable for the purpose. I had been guided by the advice of Dr Lawson, Secretary of Agriculture for Nova Scotia, as to the points to attend to in choosing a farm; and the value of his assistance has become more and more apparent as time has gone on. When it came to the "short leet" I had the benefit of practical help from Mr Herbert Skier and Mr Leander Eaton, both well known as excellent practical farmers in the province.

Now I must try and describe Hillfoot Farm as I found it when we arrived in June. It lies in the Annapolis Valley, about one hundred miles from Halifax, in what is known as the Garden of Nova Scotia, sheltered by the North rugged steeps or uncultivated moorland - a green swelling range of hills with here and there a wood. Spruce and hemlock trees are abundant, but there is also a variety of beech, maple, ash, and oak. There are also plenty of "willows by the water courses"; some of them had been planted by the French when Nova Scotia was called Acadia. In many places the hillside was broken up by the plough, and an excellent crop of potatoes and oats were growing on it. Lower down in the valley more Indian corn and squash were to be seen and quantities of hay.

All over the valley, whether on hill or in the valley, apples grow as natural fruit; of course the orchards consist of trees grafted with fine kinds, and the effect was beautiful in the early summer when the blossom was on the trees.

Later, of course, we were to see the trees bending with the weight of their splendid fruits, of all colours, red, crimson, golden russet, bright green, pink and yellow. From August till the end of October, it is the principal industry to gather and pack for sale the wealth of the orchards.

I still think our farm is one of the prettiest in this pretty neighbourhood, lying as it does on the sunny side of the mountain; the house is shaded by some large willow trees. The orchards lie behind it, and on the tableland at the foot of the mountain there is an excellent area which we have now filled with more fruit trees which have brought the orchards into one. It is well sheltered by the rising ground to the west.

In front of the house lay a fine meadow of fifty acres, fairly well cleared, but with the stones left in heaps of various sizes, which I knew we would find a use for sometime in the future. The rest of the tillage land and pasture extended to 210 acres, well sheltered by the "Woodlot" or natural forest, and dotted here and there with clumps of spruce and deciduous trees and any quantity of apple trees. There was also large quantities of wild raspberries, blackberries and blueberries so I knew we would be at no loss for jam.

There were lovely views in every direction. Two miles of was the village of Aylesford, with its pretty houses, railway station, post office and three churches.

Hillfoot was a small, old-fashioned farmhouse when I first saw it. It measured 30x40 ft., with a small L shaped wing for kitchen and woodshed, and one and a half stories high, the lower flat divided into a wonderful number of tiny rooms, with two staircases so narrow and steep it was to me a marvel how any person of ordinary proportion ever succeeded in getting up and down.

I however, did manage to get to the top and found myself in what is known in Nova Scotia as an "unfinished chamber", that is, an attic merely partitioned with rough boards, with no plaster, but with windows, and in warm weather quite fit to sleep in. The roof slopes down to nearly the floor.

It was obvious that much needed to be done before the accommodation could be made in any degree sufficient for our large family. I therefore, as soon as possible, rented two cottages in the neighbourhood, so that we had no lack of bedrooms, and used to meet at the farm in time for breakfast. The house there being speedily in the hands of workmen, we lived chiefly outside!

The first thing I did was to knock down all the partitions in the house. There is only one room left now as it was then, always known as the parlour. When the rest of the space was cleared, it gave us a good sized hall and staircase in the middle, the parlour to the west, and to the east a larger room, divided from the hall by folding doors, which, when finished, was in those days the living room of the family. However, while all these alterations took place the parlour was the only room we had. In it the grown ups had their meals.

The children, fortunately, were content with the greater freedom of the porch. When the table was cleared of food it was speedily replaced by sewing, clothes to be ironed, letters to be written, apples to be pared, and a host of odd jobs too numerous to mention - all had to be done in that wonderful room. No wonder I still have a liking for it - for the memories of that first struggling season.

At the beginning I did all the driving of the express wagon necessary, having no one else to do it. The first day I was in Aylesford after the children came, I drove fourteen hours - from 5.30am until 8.30pm., with very short intervals for breakfast, dinner and tea- in order to get our goods from the railway station and the necessaries of life that we could not do without.

It was obvious that we needed to add an extra storey to the house, and I was told the easiest way to do this was to raise the roof bodily and build chambers in between. I must say I felt a little nervous when I looked up and saw that the roof, under which we were to sleep raised on blocks about nine feet above its original position, like an umbrella. However, I was told there was no danger, and in the belief of this we slept like tops! I have since been thankful the nights were calm.

All this time, our children were leaving us and going to new homes, where they received a warm welcome, and gave great satisfaction.

In September the second party arrived - thirty-six. I went to meet them in Halifax, and when we reached Aylesford the whole neighbourhood assembled at the railway station to bid us welcome, and brought their "teams", or wagons, to help us carry the party and their baggage home; and as they kindly thought I should be less comfortable at our unfinished house, from the influx of so many of our children, they had arranged that I should visit each of the neighbours in turn until my rooms were supposed to be fit to be occupied; and I must say their evident sympathy with, and pleasure in, the welfare of our children was very comforting and reassuring.

We are now well settled and after just four months Hillfoot Farm already feels like home. I do hope you and my other dear friends enjoy hearing of how we have begun our work in New Scotland. I will write and keep you informed of our continued progress. Meanwhile, please do look after your own health my old friend. You can rest assured that all goes well with our children here so do not be concerned.

Your affectionate friend,

Emma Stirling.

CECILIA'S STORY

PART ONE

CHAPTER 1

Edinburgh

1st September 1886

Cecilia Delaney bustled around the kitchen of her new home at 147 Cowgate. She had been married to Arthur for four weeks.

The kitchen range was freshly black-leaded and the copper cooking pots on it gleamed in the firelight. The kitchen table was scrubbed white and set with the new crockery that had been a wedding present from her bridesmaid, Catherine McGrain.

Cecilia's mother, Mary-Ann Clifford, had trained her daughter well in the art of house-keeping and Cecilia was taking pride in having her own house spick and span.

She was waiting for Arthur coming home from work so she sat in the rocking-chair beside the range, leaning forward from time to time to stir the stew in the pot. How strange it felt to be a married woman with her own place, she mused.

Cecilia had seen Arthur about in the town and had learned from his neighbours of the tragedy that had befallen him in losing his wife and baby son, then having to put his other bairns into a Children's Home, but she didn't actually know him. That had all changed one night in St Patrick's Chapel. Cecilia had a great devotion to the Blessed Virgin and she would always go in to say a decade of the Rosary, in front of Our Lady's statue, anytime she passed the chapel.

On this particular evening she had been making her way home to the Cowgate. Her way had taken her down South Gray's Close and so she had taken the chance to slip into the side door of St Patrick's for a visit to Our Lady.

The inside of the church had been dark except for the pools of light around the candle-lit altar and statues so Cecilia had thought the chapel empty. But as her eyes had become accustomed to the gloom she had seen a man kneeling in the front pew, his head bowed.

Not wishing to disturb his prayer Cecilia had knelt down quietly in front of the statue of The Virgin, in the side aisle. Her rosary beads had slid through her fingers as one "Hail Mary" followed another. So engrossed had she been, in prayer, that it had been a while before she had become aware of a muffled noise.

Looking down towards the man she had realised he was weeping!

Unsure what to do Cecilia had looked up at the statue of Our Lady and had seen that the face was full of pity.

She had risen from her knees and had moved silently down the aisle towards the man. As she had drawn near she could see that his shoulders were shaking. She had touched him gently on the arm, and, startled, he had looked up. Cecilia had recognised Arthur Delaney, but she had also smelt the raw whisky on his breath.

Oh no, she had thought, not another crying drunk!

As she had turned to leave Arthur had caught her by the sleeve.

"Dinnae go," he had said, "dinnae leave me."

Cecilia couldn't have explained why she stayed. Why she had slipped into the pew and knelt beside him. Was it the look of desperation in his eyes or the look of pity she had seen on the face of the statue? So she had stayed and she prayed. Prayed that he would be released from this torment he was in.

Gradually, Arthur had become calmer.

"'A'm sorry," he had said, "a hiv nae right tae ask ye tae stay but a'm at ma wits end. A tried the drink, it disnae help – a thought if maybe a came in here a wid be helped. Daft o' me. Why would God listen tae someone like me when a havenae been tae Mass for years?"

Cecilia's faith was very simple but it was very strong. "God always listens to those who seek his help, to those who are full of sorrow, a doubt ye would be any different," she had said.

And then the whole story had come pouring out like a dam had burst. He had told of his loss of Mary, of betraying his wee son by denying him his name, and finally of his sense of breaking his promise to his wife by putting his bairns into a Home.

After he had finished, Cecilia had said, "Dae ye no think ye are being a bit hard on yourself? A dinnae see what else ye could hae done."

Arthur had turned his face towards her in astonishment. "Dae ye think God could forgive me," he had pleaded.

"A'm sure He has forgiven ye any faults already since ye are sae sorry, it seems tae me yer problem is ye cannae forgive yerself," Cecilia had replied.

They had left the church together and, as it was now late and very dark in the close, Arthur had asked if he could walk her back to her home.

Cecilia had agreed, and as he had left her at the foot of the stair, Arthur had said, "Thank ye for yer kindness, a didnae deserve it, but a'm right grateful."

He had turned and walked away and she had stood looking after him, for a moment, before climbing her stair.

The next day was Sunday and Cecilia sat beside her mother in their usual pew. As they rose to leave at the end of Mass she had been surprised to see Arthur sitting in a pew at the back.

If Cecilia was surprised Fr Hannan was astonished!

As they left the church together the priest had said, "It's been a while since I've seen ye here, Mr Delaney, but ye are very welcome for all that."

Once outside, Cecilia had been touched to see how Arthur had tidied himself up from the night before. He had really made an effort. He was clean-shaven. He had on a clean shirt, he had brushed his hat and his boots were highly polished. He had fallen into step beside her as she followed her mother and a neighbour down South Gray's Close and again thanked her for her kindness.

And that is how it began.

Every Sunday after that he was at Mass and walked her down the close. After a few months he had asked her if she would walk out with him. Cecilia had agreed and on their first walk he took her to Arthur's Seat. They had strolled round the Radical Road with Arthur pointing out views and landmarks. He seemed to love the place. Cecilia, who had never been up the hill, was entranced.

When Cecilia had told her mother, Mary-Ann Clifford, that Arthur had asked her to marry him her mother had advised her to think long and hard on it.

"A'm right fond o Arthur," her mother had said, "he has a good heart and life has no been kind tae him, but he has three bairns, Cissy. Are ye willing tae take on a ready made family?"

Cecilia hadn't yet met Arthur's bairns because, though he had taken her to MacKenzie Place to see the lassies and to Wardie to see young James on several occasions, none of the bairns had been there. The last time they had gone the matron at MacKenzie Place had said that Annie and Robina were boarded out at Moffat for the summer months. She thought they might be back in September. The matron at Wardie had said that James was down in the Borders working on a farm that Miss Stirling had bought to teach the boys farming tasks, and would be back at the end of the season.

Arthur had made clear that he wanted to bring his bairns home.

When he had proposed, he had said, "A'm asking a lot, because it wouldnae jist be me ye are taking on but ma bairns as well."

Cecilia had thought long and hard but she had also prayed about it and what kept coming back to her was the look on the face of the statue of the Virgin that night in the chapel.

So Cecilia had said yes and they had been married on 30th July 1886 by Fr Culhane in St Patrick's Church where it had all begun.

As she had walked down the aisle on her brother Ned's arm, with her friend, Catherine McGrain, following behind as her bridesmaid, and had seen Arthur standing there, his Best Man, Patrick McKenna, by his side, Cecilia's heart had told her she had made the right decision.

They had taken their vows, repeating after Fr Culhane, "For better, for worse, for richer for poorer, in sickness and in health, til death do us part."

So deep in thought was Cecilia that when the door burst open and Arthur ran into the room she nearly fell off the chair with fright.

'Cecilia,' he shouted, 'she's taken ma bairns away tae Canada!'

Cecilia leapt from the chair and grabbed Arthur by the arms.

His face was drained of colour and he was shaking. She could see he was in deep shock. She led him to the chair she had just vacated, beside the warm range, and pressed him into it.

As she busied herself making tea Arthur told her what had happened.

He had been making his way home down the High Street when he heard someone calling his name. He had turned and seen Kate Hanlon running after him. Kate and her family had lived beside Arthur in Morrison's Close. She worked beside his sister, Nellie, so Arthur knew her well. When she caught up with him, Kate explained that her brother, Paddy, worked as a carter and that early that morning he had been sent by his boss to an address in MacKenzie Place, in Stockbridge. He was to pick up boxes and trunks and take them to the Caledonian Station.

When he arrived his load was already piled up on the pavement.

While he was loading it on the cart a large wagon drew up behind him. The door to the house opened and a group of bairns filed out along with some elderly women. The women carried wee bairns and toddlers in their arms. As Paddy watched the bairns and the women were helped up onto the wagon.

A laddie with bright red hair caught his attention and Paddy recognized young James Delaney. Paddy was wondering if he was mistaken but just then the laddie saw Paddy and waved to him. Paddy waved back but he wondered where they were all headed.

A maid was standing on the pavement, wiping her eyes on the corner of her apron, so Paddy had approached her and asked where the bairns were going. She said they were going 'awa across the sea tae a new life in Canada'. Paddy couldn't believe his ears!

He had looked back at the cart and saw that James was still waving at him, but though he looked round at the rest of the bairns he couldn't make out if the other Delaney bairns were there. Apart from James they were all wearing red knitted fishermen's caps and it was hard to recognize any of them.

The lady in charge of the group had noticed James waving at him and had said to Paddy, 'You, my man, why are you standing there staring, get that baggage off to the railway station.'

Was James trying to tell him something? Paddy didn't see what he could do so he leapt into the cart, flicked the reins, and the horses moved off at a steady gallop.

When he reached the Caledonian Station he was directed towards a platform where a train was waiting. Its baggage van doors stood open. He was kept busy unloading the trunks and helping the porters load them in the van so he didn't see the bairns board the train. When every trunk was safely stowed in the van Paddy ran down the length of the train looking for the bright red hair of James Delaney.

The guard was walking along slamming shut the doors of the carriages, then he blew the whistle and the train was off. It hooted and clouds of smoke filled the air.

At last, as a carriage was speeding past, Paddy caught a glimpse of bright red hair. He was sure it was young James, his face pressed against the window, looking his last on his home.

When the guard walked back towards him Paddy had asked him where the train was going and was told that its final destination was Liverpool.

Paddy had said that he had heard the bairns were bound for Canada and the guard had said that was likely because Liverpool Docks were where a lot of the ships left from for the Americas.

He had looked at Paddy, 'Tae Canada?' he had said, 'Why would anybody take wee bairns like that tae Canada? It's a frozen wilderness, or so a'v heard,' and he shook his head in puzzlement.

Paddy had felt ill at ease all day at his work and as soon as his sister got home he had told her all about it.

'Surely,' he had said, 'Arthur Delaney wouldnae have agreed tae his bairns being sent tae a frozen wilderness?'

Kate had set off at once to let Arthur know and by chance had seen him walking down the High Street ahead of her.

When Arthur had finished telling Cecilia the news he got up from the chair. 'My God, a'v got to dae something,' he said, 'ma bairns, ma poor bairns.'

Cecilia pushed him back into the chair and put the mug of tea in his trembling hands.

'Ye can do nothing the night, look,' pointing at the window, 'it's dark already, everywhere will be closed. Leave it til morning,' she said.

Reluctantly, Arthur agreed, and after having their meal they sat talking at the table. It was decided that first thing in the morning Arthur would go to the Homes and demand an explanation from the matrons.

'A these weeks, Cecilia, they have been telling me a pack o lies, telling me the bairns would be back soon,' Arthur raged.

Cecilia, as usual, thought of the church.

'We could go and see Fr Hannan,' she said. 'Am sure he would advise us what to dae.'

CHAPTER 2

Edinburgh

2nd September 1886

They rose after a restless night. Arthur had suffered the nightmare that had plagued him since childhood. He was on a bridge which was breaking up beneath him. He had wakened Cecilia up with his groaning and throwing his arms about. She had held him and tried to assure him it was just a dream, all would be well, but neither of them were reassured.

Cecilia made breakfast of porridge and forced Arthur to sit and eat it. It was still dark and the wind was howling and throwing squally showers against the window panes.

It was weather to match Arthur's mood. He felt as if the very heavens were weeping. All his guilt came flooding back.

'A should never hiv put them in that place,' he cried.

'Arthur, we've been over this time and time again. What else could you do in the circumstances you were in?' Cecilia argued.

As soon as it was light Arthur set off for MacKenzie Place.

When confronted by a furious Arthur, the matron had admitted that a group of children had gone off to Canada but she refused to give him any information about whether any of his children had gone. She had referred him to the Secretary of The Edinburgh & Leith Children's Aid & Refuge Society.

Arthur had set off for Pitt Street where the Secretary had his office.

When he got there Arthur had demanded to speak to the Secretary. Eventually he was shown into an office where a man sitting behind a desk introduced himself as Mr MacDonald.

He had remained seated and asked, 'What can I do for you, Delaney?'

Arthur had demanded to know where his bairns were but the Secretary denied knowing anything about them. He told Arthur he would have to make enquiries and advised him to return the next day.

Arthur had to go straight to work as he was already late so it was evening before Cecilia heard all this.

They spent another restless night. Cecilia was worried that Arthur had gone from a state of shock to one of red hot anger. The worry about the bairns, wondering how they would cope with a hazardous sea journey, despair at the thought that he might never see them again made him angrier than Cecilia had ever seen him. Since meeting Cecilia, Arthur was a changed man. Contentment had brought out the easy-going side of his nature. He was happier than he had been in years.

ARTHUR'S STORY

PART TWO

CHAPTER 1

Edinburgh

3rd September 1886

Before he left the house, Cecilia had begged him to keep his temper in check. Getting lifted for a breach of the peace would not help the situation, she argued.

When Arthur arrived at the office he was shown in to see Mr MacDonald. The Secretary reported that he had checked the books and that Robina had been sent to Canada three months before but as far as he knew James and Annie were still in Homes in the country but he refused to tell him where they were.

Arthur nearly collapsed when the Secretary said that wee Robina was already in Canada! How could a wee one like that manage in such a wild country? His youngest! She was just a wee bairn and she was miles away from home, from him.

Forgetting Cecilia's advice, Arthur banged his fist on the desk and lent over it, his other hand raised to grip MacDonald's necktie.

The Secretary looked frightened and lent back to escape Arthur's hand.

'Ye are not much of a Secretary then mister, for a know for a fact that my laddie, James, was in a group that left from the Caledonian Station two days ago so don't be telling me a pack o lies!' Arthur shouted.

'A want ma bairns back. Ye had no right tae send them away. Where is Annie?' he raged.

Arthur's shouts had alerted other people in the building and they ran into the office. Feeling more confident now that help had arrived Mr MacDonald rose and ordered Arthur from the office or he would call the police.

Remembering Cecilia's advice, at last, Arthur shrugged off the restraining hands and left.

When he left the office Arthur was in too much of a state to go in to work so he returned to their house in the Cowgate.

When he related what had happened to Cecilia she had taken her shawl from the hook, wrapped it around her and said they must go and see Fr Hannan.

They walked along the Cowgate and climbed the steep cobbled path of South Gray's Close. They passed the side entrance to St Patrick's Church where they had been married just a few weeks before. The priest's house was a fine stone building set a bit back from the Close with a small garden in front. The strong winds of the last few days had already stripped some of the leaves from the trees and they lay in golden heaps on the path.

They climbed the short flight of steps to the imposing, black painted front door and pulled on the gleaming brass bell-pull. After a few moments the door was opened by old Bridget Daly, the priest's housekeeper, who showed them into the small room on the left of the hallway and went off to fetch Fr Hannan. Soon, Arthur and Cecilia heard footsteps descending the wooden staircase, the door opened and Fr Hannan entered the room.

Seeing the distress on their faces the priest invited them to sit by the fire while he took up position behind the desk.

Arthur related all that had happened and he could see that the priest was very concerned. Arthur remembered that Fr Hannan had actually baptized the bairns they were talking about. He knew these bairns, had welcomed them into Holy Mother Church.

The priest listened carefully then said that it seemed to him as if they would need to take legal advice on the matter.

Arthur turned his hat nervously in his hands explaining that they didn't have much money. Would this cost a lot, he asked?

Fr Hannan said not to worry about that side of things meantime, he would try and raise an appeal for funds.

He wrote a short note and handed it to Arthur.

'Take that to William Considine at that address,' he said, indicating the envelope. 'He is one of our few Catholic solicitors. I have explained that you will give him the details but he has my authority to take what proceedings seem necessary and report back to me. Let him have all the information he needs. After that leave it to him and me.'

Cecilia and Arthur thanked the priest for his support and after receiving his blessing they left the house.

Cecilia returned to their house but Arthur wanted to waste no time and set off for Mr Considine's office.

When he returned he said that Mr Considine had been reassuring saying he would contact the Edinburgh & Leith Children's Aid and Refuge Society at once and demand his children be returned to Arthur.

'He said it was quite indefensible in law, no one had the right to deprive a father of his children when he wanted them,' Arthur said. 'I have to leave everything in his hands.'

After mass, the next Sunday, Arthur and Cecilia stayed behind to speak to Fr Hannan. Arthur explained what Mr Considine intended and he asked Fr Hannan what would happen about the solicitor's fee. The priest had assured him not to worry. He had it all in hand. He intended to ask some of the business people in the congregation to subscribe to a legal fund to fight the case. He was sure, once they heard the circumstances, they would be willing to help.

EMMA'S STORY

PART TWO

Hillfoot Farm
Aylesford
Nova Scotia

2 November 1886.

Miss Auld,
62 Northumberland Street,
Edinburgh.

My dear Miss Auld,

I do not want to alarm you but great trouble has made a visitation upon us.

I must come home to Edinburgh, urgently. I can say nothing further, at present, but I must throw myself on your mercy.

I plan to sail on the S.S. Carthaginian, from Halifax on the 8th November and hope to arrive in Liverpool around the 18th weather permitting. I would thereafter travel to Edinburgh by train and arrive as near to the 20th as possible.

My dear old friend could I beg for temporary lodgings for myself and two of our children? Please do not mention my return to anyone, not even the Directors, and please keep secret that I will be bringing the two children with me. So very much depends on this. I know I can trust to your utmost discretion.

I will explain all when we arrive.

Your most grateful friend,

Emma Stirling

P.S. Could you telegraph me on receiving this letter as all haste is needed.

ARTHUR'S STORY

PART THREE

Chapter 1

Edinburgh

3rd December 1886

The weeks had dragged on. Each Sunday after Mass, Arthur would ask Fr Hannan how things were going and he was assured that they were progressing.

Arthur was restless. He could settle to nothing and was inconsolable. He knew Cecilia was desperately concerned for him but she felt helpless. He realised it was not the way she had imagined starting married life.

Eventually, a letter came from Mr Considine. Arthur opened it and his face lit up. He swept a surprised Cecilia from her feet and birled her round and round.

'They're back, Cecilia, ma bairns are back!' he shouted.

When Cecilia at last got her feet back on the ground she took the letter from him and read it.

Dear Mr Delaney,

I saw Miss Stirling's agent today. I gather that the children have been brought back, but Miss Stirling refuses point blank to part with them unless compelled by law to do so. It is plain there will be heavy fighting before the children can be recovered. Before taking any steps, I would like to have a meeting with the very Rev. Canon Hannan.

William Considine.

When he had calmed down she handed the letter back to him.

'It looks like things are no going tae be sae easy, Arthur,' she said.

When Arthur re-read the letter his mood changed. He had been so elated at the fact that the bairns were back home that the significance of the rest of the letter hadn't really registered.

'A have to dae something, Cecilia. If the bairns are here a have tae go and find them,' he said.

CHAPTER 2

Edinburgh

4th December 1886

Early next morning Arthur set off for the Home in MacKenzie Place. He demanded to see the matron and insisted she return his bairns. He was taking them with him.

The matron assured him the children were not there.

Arthur refused to believe her. He pushed past her and went into the large kitchen were he knew the children breakfasted. With a protesting matron behind him he threw open the door. Startled children looked up from the long table around which they sat. His eyes swept the room but he could see that none of his bairns were among them. He turned and raced up the stairs to the attic floor where the children usually slept. The room was deserted. He searched every room on all the floors, startling their occupants, but there was no sign of his bairns.

By now the matron had called their handyman, a big burly lad, and he took hold of Arthur by the arm. Arthur shook him off and ran from the house.

He set off for the Home in Granton. He ran down Granton Road and hammered on the door of the house in Bayton Terrace where James had lived.

A maid answered and he pushed past her into the house. The matron came out into the hall demanding to know what was going on. He demanded to know if James Delaney was here. She denied it but Arthur ran through the house opening doors anyway. This was a much smaller house than the one in Stockbridge so it did not take him long to realise that James was not there. In fact there were no boys in the house. Only then did Arthur remember that the boys took all their meals at MacKenzie Place.

He ran from the Home and down the hill to Miss Stirling's private residence in Boswall Road. It was a large stone house, called Merleton, which stood in its own grounds.

He rang the front door bell but there was no reply.

A broad carriageway leading to stables behind ran alongside the house.

Arthur ran up it and round to the back of the house.

The place was deserted.

He looked up at the back of the house and realised that every window had its wooden shutters closed tight.

He hammered on the back door and shouted the bairns' names.

No response.

He was like a man possessed.

He turned to go when a small door in the scullery offshoot opened and an old bent man stood there peering out.

Arthur rushed back and demanded to see Miss Stirling.

The old man looked frightened at being confronted by a very angry man.

'The mistress isnae here, she's in Canada,' he quavered. 'The hoose is shut up, a'm just the caretaker.'

Seeing he had frightened the old man Arthur felt some remorse.

'A heard she had come back,' he explained.

'Well if she has she is no here and a kent nothing aboot it,' the man protested.

Arthur knew that the man was telling the truth. The house was shut up. It was obvious there was no one there but the old man.

Arthur turned and left.

'A'm sorry to hiv troubled ye,' he called over his shoulder.

Arthur trudged wearily home to the Old Town. He was remembering the day he had put James into the Home in Bayton Terrace. He had walked this very road, tears blinding him. The bairn had begged him to take him home with him but Arthur had refused pleading wi the laddie to understand. How could a wee laddie have understood! He had promised to bring him hame when he was bigger but he had let his son down. He had been taken to the other side o the world.

But now he was back and Arthur vowed never to let his bairns go again. Now he had Cecilia and a home for the bairns. Surely the law would make that old witch give him his bairns back.

There was a biting wind coming of the sea and as he walked on it started to snow. Great white flakes landed on his jacket. He had rushed out without a coat and by the time he walked through the door of his house he was wet through.

Cecilia was waiting for news and his uncle Thomas had come by.

'Where hiv ye been!' Cecilia exclaimed. 'A was that worried aboot ye!'

Then when she touched him she realised that he was wet through.

'Let me get that jacket off ye, and come and sit by the fire, you'll catch yer death o cauld,' she said.

Arthur sat by the fire and told them what had happened.

'Well,' old Thomas said, 'once ye dry off we will go and see that manny, MacDonald. Hear what he has tae say.'

Cecilia insisted Arthur wear his coat and saw them off. He was glad his uncle was with him. Thomas had been like a father to him ever since his own father, James, had deserted his family and gone to England.

They were back within an hour.

Mr MacDonald had at first denied knowing anything about the bairns being back and when Arthur had persisted and accused him of lying he had admitted that his instructions were to give Arthur no information. When Arthur had said he would go to law to have his bairns returned MacDonald had simply scoffed at the idea and ordered Arthur and Thomas out.

After Thomas had left, Cecilia and Arthur sat on by the fire talking and Arthur vowed that he would not give up. He would pester MacDonald until he told him where the bairns were hidden.

CHAPTER 3

Edinburgh

14th December 1886

Arthur was as good as his word. He was back at MacDonald's office so many times that eventually the Secretary agreed he would try to persuade Miss Stirling to return the children. He admitted it would be wrong to keep them but he refused to tell Arthur where the children were claiming Miss Stirling had refused to tell him.

But the weeks went by and still no information about the bairns was forthcoming.

Arthur had been refused admittance to MacDonald's office several times so he took to waiting outside, on the street, until MacDonald emerged and demanding the return of his bairns. Eventually, Mr MacDonald said that if Arthur didn't stop following him he would call a policeman and have him arrested for breach of the peace.

When Cecilia heard this she was really worried and made Arthur promise not to approach MacDonald again.

Seeing her concern, and realising the wisdom of her words, Arthur promised.

'We will go and see Fr Hannan again,' Cecilia said.

They went again to the priest's house and told him what Arthur had been doing.

Fr Hannan agreed with Cecilia that Arthur could get into trouble if he persisted in badgering Mr MacDonald. He advised Arthur to leave it in Mr Considine's hands and do nothing further meanwhile. Arthur asked him how the subscription was going and the priest explained he had collected some monies and was hopeful of getting more.

They returned to their house and Cecilia tried to calm Arthur down.

'We have to leave it to Mr Considine and the law, Arthur, please take Fr Hannan's advice and don't do anything further yourself,' she pleaded.

The meeting with the priest had taken place just a few days before Christmas. It was a bleak Christmas that year and the following week neither Arthur nor Cecilia felt able to celebrate Hogmanay, even though it was their first in their own home.

Arthur's grandmother, Helen Boylan, had invited them to her house on George IV Bridge for Hogmanay, but they had refused explaining they would be poor company. Arthur knew that she understood and he also knew she was desperately worried about him.

So as the old year passed Arthur and Cecilia sat alone by their fireside. They heard the bells peal out the old and ring in the new. Neither of them spoke of it but each knew what was on the other's mind. What would the New Year of 1887 bring?

CECILIA'S STORY

PART TWO

CHAPTER 1

Edinburgh

8th February 1887

Cecilia answered a knock on the door of their flat and saw big Phil Clarke standing there. Phil was her mother's cousin's son and Cecilia was surprised, but delighted, to see him. She ushered him through to the kitchen where Arthur was sitting, reading the paper.

'Look who's here!' Cecilia announced.

Arthur rose from his seat, a look of delight on his face.

'Phil man, it's right good tae see ye. I've jist been reading of your exploits in the paper!'

Big Phil Clarke was one of the players in the Hibernian Football Team that had been started by Canon Hannan in St. Patrick's parish. He was a very popular inside left. A tireless runner and a prolific goal scorer.

'Come and sit doon, Phil,' Cecilia urged. 'And tell us all yer news'.

The man sat in the chair beside Arthur. He held up one of his huge hands.

'This is the hand that shook that of Michael Davitt,' he announced with pride.

Neither Cecilia or Arthur needed to ask who Michael Davitt was. The founder of the Irish Land League which fought to give farmers the right to own the soil of Ireland. The man prominent in the movement to give Ireland Home Rule he was as well known to the residents of Edinburgh's 'Little Ireland' as he was at home.

'How did ye come to meet him?' Cecilia gasped.

Phil explained that Michael Davitt was on a visit to Edinburgh and Michael Whelahan, the founding Captain of the Hibernian Football team, and John McFadden had taken Davitt to Hibernian Park to see the team training. Afterwards he was introduced to the whole team.

'A don't mind admitting,' said Phil, 'that I had a tear in me eye and, sure, do ye know what he did then?'

Arthur and Cecilia shook their heads.

'He presented Mick Whelahan with a lump of shamrock studded turf from blessed Ireland and Mick placed it reverently on the centre spot of the 'Holy Ground',' Phil announced, with a catch in his throat. 'It took me a' ma strength to stop from dropping to me knees and kissing the turf so it did.'

Cecilia said nothing but she was amazed that this giant of a man could be so emotional about such a thing but glancing across at Arthur she could see that he too was moved.

The three sat in silence for a moment or two then Phil seemed to give himself a shake.

'Anyway,' he said. 'It's about Hibernian that I'm here.' He turned towards Arthur.

'How would ye like to travel to the cup final in Glasgow wi' the team?'

Arthur's face lit up and Cecilia thought that it was a long time since she had seen him look so happy. She guessed what was behind Phil's offer. The fact that Arthur had suffered the loss of his bairns was common knowledge among their relations. This was Phil's way of trying to cheer Arthur up and she gave thanks for the man's kind heart.

'Dae ye really mean it?' Arthur asked.

'Sure I have yer ticket in me pocket at this moment. If ye agree ye can travel with us in the special train laid on for the official Hibernian party from Waverly Station,' said Phil.

Now it was the turn of Arthur to have tears in his eyes as he shook the big man's hand and accepted the precious ticket.

Cecilia showed Phil to the door as Arthur sat down in his chair his eyes never leaving the ticket.

'That was right kind of ye, Phil,' Cecilia said.

'Ach it's little enough after all he's been through,' Phil said, pulling on his cap as he set off down the stair.

Chapter 2

12th February 1887

Arthur had to work on Saturday morning but his gaffer had let him go in early so that he could get away sharp for the game. Cecilia was watching from the window and she saw him come running into the street. Moments later their door was thrown open and Arthur rushed in. Cecilia had left his Sunday clothes and a clean shirt laid out on the bed and after a quick wash he went through to change. He wouldn't stop to eat the soup that she had made so Cecilia quickly made him a piece of bread with cheese and handed it to him as he rushed back out the door.

'Give them a cheer from me,' she called after him.

'Aye, a will that,' he replied, as he disappeared down the stair.

Cecilia returned to the window and watched as he ran up the street. He was wearing a new green tie and had a green handkerchief showing in his top pocket. Phil had told him this was a new idea. All the officials and players intended wearing the club colours of the Emerald Isle. As Cecilia watched she saw other supporters making their way towards the train station and most were wearing something green.

The special train carrying the officials and players was leaving from the Waverly Station at 1.00 pm and

Arthur was terrified he would miss it. Cecilia had never seen him so excited, but he was not alone. The whole of the Old Town was in a fervour. So much was at stake for the Irish community. Hibernian were not just a football team they were a symbol of Irish pride among a people who had never felt accepted in the host country. But now an Irish organization was in the final of the Scottish Cup and defeat was unthinkable!

Cecilia turned from the window. She felt restless and couldn't settle to her housework. Eventually, she took her shawl from the hook and walked down to visit her sister, Mary McGrain. It was a cold, brisk day but dry and bright and Cecilia walked through near deserted Old Town streets. Only the children were out on the streets. The lassies were at their skipping games and some had chalked peevers on the pavements and were hopping about on them. The laddies, of course, were playing football, emulating the match their heroes were playing in far off Glasgow. They had made footballs with rolled up balls of newspapers trussed up with string and their coats were being used as goalposts. Cecilia stopped to watch one group, in Chessels Court, and was amused to see that there was only one set of goals. Presumably, no laddie wanted to be in any team but the Hibernian so they took turns in shooting in goals! As she passed various pubs she could hear an excited buzz of conversation from those men who had been unable to make the journey to Glasgow.

When she reached her sister's house she found that Mary was in alone. Her husband, Patrick McGrain, had also gone to Glasgow. He hadn't been able to get a train ticket but the railways had laid on freight wagons and that's how Patrick intended to travel.

'He was like a daft laddie, wi' excitement, when he left the hoose,' Mary said.

The two women sat and chatted over a cup of tea but both were aware that their minds were not really on the gossip.

Eventually, Mary said, 'Dae ye feel up to walking up to Paddy McGrail's shop in the Canongate? A heard that they were going to telegraph the score from the match to him.'

Cecilia was five months pregnant but she said she felt fine so both women grabbed their shawls and made their way to 266 Canongate. They couldn't get near the shop for the crowds that thronged the pavement outside. Cecilia saw one of Arthur's workmates standing near the door.

'Dae ye ken the score, Mick?' she shouted.

'It's 1-1,' he shouted back. 'Dumbarton's Aitken scored a goal in the 60th minute and then big Phil Clarke made a brilliant pass to James Montgomery and he scored for Hibernian.'

Cecilia and Mary looked at each other, their eyes wide, caught up in the excitement.

Just then a telegraph boy on his bike, ringing his bell furiously, sped down the Canongate and the crowd seeing him parted to allow him in to Paddy's shop.

'What does it say?' the crowd outside shouted.

The tension was unbearable. And then such a roar went up from inside the shop that no words were needed.

Mick, nearest the door, shouted through the noise to Cecilia.

'The Hibernian have scored another goal! It's 2-1,' he yelled.

A man standing beside Cecilia shouted back at him. 'Did it say who scored?'

'It wis 'Darlin' Willie Groves,' he roared.

Even Cecilia, who took very little interest in football, had heard of the great Willie Groves.

The crowd were dancing jigs in celebration. 'The lads have done it – they have won the Scottish cup for ould Ireland,' a man shouted.

The man beside Cecilia urged caution. 'Sure, lets not be too hasty,' he said. 'The games no finished yet.' That quietened the crowd down and the tension rose even higher.

'Mick, can ye see the time on the clock?' an old man shouted.

Mick craned his neck to see through the doorway. 'Ten minutes to go,' he called back.

The crowd fell silent and Cecilia found herself praying for a victory for Hibernian. She didn't know what Canon Hannan would say when she went to Confession and said she had prayed for such a thing, but she had a feeling he wouldn't be too hard on her!

A short time later, though it seemed an eternity to the waiting crowd, the same telegraph boy again cycled down the road. This time he was lifted off his feet and passed over the heads of the crowd into the shop!

After a short pause an enormous roar went up from those inside and travelled out onto the street. Nothing needed to be said. They had done it – the team from poor 'Little Ireland' - had won the Scottish Cup!

As the noise spread out into the street windows were thrown up in the houses. Women lent out on their window sills, smiling and waving to the crowds below. One woman draped an Irish flag from her window.

Mick shouted up to her, 'Missus will ye throw me down yer flag?'

The woman complied and Mick caught it and waved it above his head.

'Follow me, men of Ireland,' he yelled.

He was lifted shoulder high, bearing the flag aloft, and the crowd formed a procession behind.

Cecilia and Mary looked at each other and giggled. What were they thinking of? A couple of respectable married women, one pregnant, following the mob!

Up the Canongate they went, down St. Mary's Street, into the Cowgate, the crowd growing by the minute, everyone knew where they were headed. They poured through the gates of St. Patrick's Church and there they came to a halt. There was a pause as the end of the procession caught up and then the voices rose in one accord. 'God Save Ireland' they sang.

It was dark by the time a tired, but happy, Cecilia made it home to their house. She warmed some stew on the hob and after she had eaten sat with her feet up on a stool beside the range.

She must have dozed off because she came to with a start at an explosion of noise outside her window. She looked out and saw a mass of folk moving along the street and she thought she could hear the sound of a flute band in the distance.

The team must be on their way back!

She grabbed her shawl and hurried downstairs. She walked up to the Tron and found a spot on the corner where she could see right down the North Bridge. The noise rose to a crescendo and now she could definitely hear a flute band.

As Cecilia watched, not one, but two flute bands marched into view. As they came nearer she saw that the leading band was that of their own St. Patrick's Catholic

Young Men's Society and the other, judging by the banner they carried, must be the Leith Harp.

And now she could see the horse-drawn brake carrying the triumphant Hibernian home.

It turned at the end of the North Bridge into the High Street and Cecilia caught a glimpse of the banners that adorned it. One read – *Welcome Hibernian Winners of the Scottish Cup 1886-1887* - and the other – *God Save Ireland – Hurrah for the Green Jerseys*.

As it turned at the Tron, the Young Ireland Flute band, which had been entertaining the crowds with patriotic Irish songs, marched up behind it. The crowd was going wild, shouting and cheering and throwing their hats in the air!

Cecilia could see the looks of amazement on the faces of some of her neighbours, who were not Irish, at this outpouring of exuberant joy. But then how could they ever understand just what this meant to the Irish. To a people regarded not just as second class citizens but hardly as citizens at all.

Cecilia saw that a huge procession was snaking behind the brake and she heard her name being called. Arthur detached himself from it and joined her on the pavement.

'Is this no just the most amazing thing,' he shouted, above the noise. 'A have so much to tell ye.'

'It's great, Arthur,' Cecilia said. 'But get back into the procession. You don't want to miss a minute of this,' and she gave him a gentle push.

Soon Arthur was swallowed up in the crowd.

Cecilia followed the procession down, keeping to the pavement, as the crowds streamed past her. Ahead the brake carrying the team turned into St. Mary's Street.

The street was flooded with an eerie glow. Every window in every tenement was lit by a green limelight.

The doors to St. Mary's Halls were flung wide open and in the gaslight Cecilia could see Michael Flannigan, President of the Catholic Young Men's Society, standing in the flickering light to welcome the Hibernian team home. She knew that over a thousand people had been invited to a special Reception and Arthur, as Phil's guest, was to be one of them!

Cecilia watched until the doors closed behind the invited guests. The crowd outside was still huge and they had no intention of leaving. They burst into a spirited rendition of 'God Save Ireland' and she knew that the singing and cheering would go on into the wee small hours but now she was feeling tired and made her way slowly down into the Cowgate through the rejoicing people. Arthur would tell her all about it when he came home.

Once back in their flat, Cecilia put more coals on the fire. It was a cold February night. She hadn't noticed it out in the street but now she could feel the chill. She warmed her nightdress on the fireguard while she washed her hands and face and then took off her clothes and snuggled into her nightie. She climbed into the high bed in the kitchen and propped herself up on the pillows drawing the feather quilt around her. She would be warmer in bed while she waited for Arthur to return.

She must have drifted off to sleep because she woke with a start as a nearby church clock struck midnight. Arthur was still not back but now she was awake. She rose and put the filled kettle on the hob to boil then climbed back into bed. Before the kettle had boiled she heard Arthur's key in the lock and he came in on tiptoe, trying not to wake her. His face lit up when he saw she was awake and Cecilia realised it would be some time before either of them got any sleep!

Arthur made the tea and handed it to her in bed then drew up a chair beside her.

'Tell me all about it,' Cecilia said, 'right from the beginning'.

A delighted Arthur, his eyes still glittering with excitement, was happy to oblige.

Cecilia heard all about the journey through on the train, with the team, their arrival in Glasgow, where they were met by important members of the town's Irish Community and taken to catch their onward train to Hampden.

He described the atmosphere so vividly that Cecilia felt she had been there herself. There was a huge crowd of supporters at the Park. They had sold 15,000 tickets. The biggest amount ever sold for a Scottish Cup Final, Arthur explained. The official party, with Arthur among them, had been shown to their seats in the stand.

'We had a grand view over the ground,' Arthur recounted. 'Already the ground seemed to be packed to bursting point, and then a huge commotion broke out! A suddenly saw even more men pouring in at the back. We heard later that crowds of Irish navvies from Edinburgh and Irish miners from the coalfields of Lanarkshire had walked all the way to Hampden. They hadn't any tickets but they rushed the gates and the polis were powerless to stop them!'

Arthur started to laugh. 'In the end they reckoned that 20,000 fans watched the match!'

Once everyone was in place the Hibernian crowd had burst into a rendition of 'God Save Ireland.'

'We were in the stand above the players dressing rooms,' Arthur explained, 'And when our lads heard the crowd singing they joined in from down below. Then we were all on our feet cheering!

'We were playing a team called Dumbarton who ran out wearing blue and white jerseys but when the Hibernian ran out in their green jerseys there was such a roar from the Irish that the opposition looked ready to run back into the dressing rooms,' Arthur chuckled.

'It was a tough game, Cecilia. The play ranged back and forth, the tension was unbearable, and then after 60 minutes Dumbarton scored! You ought to have heard the groan of despair that went round the ground,' Arthur said.

'But the fans rallied and roared the Hibernian on and our Phil responded with a brilliant pass to James Montgomery and James put the ball in the back of the net! The place was in an uproar – we had equalised! But 'Darlin' Willie Groves wasnae prepared tae settle for a draw! He began one of the dribbling runs that he is famous for. A tell ye the Dumbarton defence didn't know what had hit them and then he calmly shot the goal into their net – we were winning 2-1!

'The crowds on the terraces were in an uproar, the noise was unbelievable, but there was still about ten minutes to go. The longest ten minutes of my life! And then the final whistle blew and the boys were carried shoulder-high from the Park.

'It was amazing, Cecilia. The team from poor 'Little Ireland', had won the Scottish Cup!'

Arthur described how after the players had got cleaned up and changed they were escorted from the ground with the rest of the Hibernian party and they were all taken to the east end of Glasgow.

'They have a St. Mary's Hall, tae,' Arthur said, 'And all the prominent Irishmen in the city were waiting to meet us. There were town councillors, priests and the leader in Scotland of the National League. He is known as 'Honest' John Ferguson and he was full of praise for the achievement of the Edinburgh Hibernian. We all sat down at long tables and were served a great meal. Then there were more speeches and many songs sung before we made our tired but happy way back to the train.

'An well ye saw for yerself what it was like when we arrived back in the toon,' Arthur said.

'Aye,' Cecilia said. 'A had never seen anything like it in ma life and a doubt a will again. But tell me what happened when ye got into St. Mary's Hall?'

'The team and the officials were escorted up on to the platform. A hardly recognised oor Hall. There was green bunting strung up everywhere. A sat down on one of the benches on the floor of the Hall with all the jostling, cheering crowd. Then Michael Flannigan came to the front of the stage and made a speech. A can almost remember it word for word,' Arthur recalled.

'He congratulated the team on their victory and said that they had brought great credit to our Society, St. Patrick's Church and Edinburgh. In fact he said they were a credit to every Irish Catholic in Scotland. Hibernian had shown with a mixture of skill, fitness, courage and fighting spirit just how good the Edinburgh Irishmen were. He also praised the Hibernian Secretary, John McFadden, for building such a strong band of players and planning the strategy that won us the Scottish Cup, a feat that at one time seemed totally impossible. Then he raised both his hands above his head and shouted out – 'God Save Ireland' and the crowd leapt to it's feet.

'They were still shouting and applauding when John McFadden himself rose to deliver his reply and it was several minutes before he could make himself heard,' Arthur said.

'He began by saying he would accept no praise for the day's great deed. He would leave all praise to the players who showed that the green jerseys are made of no mean stuff. He then went on to thank our Captain, James McGhee, for his support both on and off the pitch, and all the unsung work done by Canon Hannan, Michael Whelahan and Robert McGeachan. There was another burst of applause in response and then he held up his hand for quiet – 'Last, but not least, I must thank you gentlemen, our brothers of St. Patrick's Catholic Young Men's Society, after all Hibernian are your team!'

'A thought they would never stop cheering,' Arthur said.

Arthur explained that more speeches were made and the celebrating continued. Michael Flannigan had urged all present to be on their best behaviour as the rejoicing continued all over 'Little Ireland'.

Arthur said, 'A knew Canon Hannan was anxious in case things got out of hand and might result in police action, and disgrace for St. Patrick's, but a met him on my way home and he had just come from the polis office up the High Street. He had been told that not even one arrest had been made in connection with the celebration!'

Cecilia's eyelids were drooping so Arthur took her cup and tucked the quilt around her.

'A'm sorry, lass, ye must be tired oot, and in your condition, too. A dinnae ken what a wis thinking of keeping you awake this late,' he said.

Cecilia reassured him that she had wanted to hear every detail and as she finally drifted off to sleep she gave thanks for the fact that in all the excitement Arthur had never mentioned his bairns once. He had had at least one day of pure happiness.

CHAPTER 3

Edinburgh

April 1887

It had been a bitterly cold winter and the pavements were icy as Cecilia returned from visiting her mother-in-law, Ann Delaney. Ann had been bed-ridden for weeks suffering from bronchitis and Cecilia had been really worried about her. She had gone to see her every day, taking her soup, and making bread poultices to put on her wheezing chest. In truth, Cecilia had been glad of something to keep her busy as Arthur had heard nothing further about his bairns.

She knew that Arthur had taken to hanging about outside the various Homes, whenever he wasn't working, in the hope of seeing his bairns. As he had promised her and Fr Hannan he made no attempt to enter the houses but he watched and he waited hoping against hope.

When Cecilia pushed open the door of her house she saw that the postman had been. She bent and picked up the letter that lay on the mat and her heart quickened as she recognised Mr Considine's handwriting.

When Arthur returned from work she handed him the letter. He ripped it open and as he read it she saw the disappointment on his face.

'He asks me to go and see him in his office. There is nothing about the bairns in it,' Arthur said.

Arthur went to see the solicitor next day. Mr Considine explained that he had everything prepared to present a Petition to the Court on Arthur's behalf but it would cost £25 in legal fees to do so. Arthur could not believe the amount – it was a fortune! Mr Considine advised him to check with Fr Hannan if this amount could be raised and Arthur promised to do so.

After the meeting Arthur went straight to the priest's house and told him how much would be required. To his horror Fr Hannan explained that raising such an amount would be impossible. He had approached as many of his congregation as possible for donations but had been unable to raise as much as he had hoped. He had enough to meet Mr Considine's expenses so far but he could promise no further help.

When Arthur returned and reported this meeting to Cecilia he was devastated. He could never raise such a sum he would have to go back to searching for the bairns himself.

CHAPTER 4

Edinburgh

April 1887

Cecilia climbed slowly up the cobbled roadway of South Gray's Close on her way to morning mass. It was April yet a bitter wind was blowing needles of sleet into her face. She wrapped her shawl more tightly around her as if trying to warm the bairn that now kicked vigorously within her. Cecilia was almost six months pregnant and her increased bulk and the effort of walking into the full force of an Edinburgh wind took her breath away.

She stepped into the doorway of St Patrick's and just being out of the wind brought instant relief. She entered the church and making her way towards the sanctuary genuflected before the gilded tabernacle. She sat for a few moments, getting her breath back, before sinking to her knees.

It was dark in the church. The blue, green, red and yellow of the stain glass windows curving above the sanctuary, which glowed jewel-like when the sun shone through them, were now subdued in the poor light of a winter's morning. Only the candles on the altar, and those banked in front of the statues of the Virgin and St Patrick, allowed light to pierce the gloom.

The church was filling up, mainly with women all with their black shawls covering their heads. A few old men entered removing their caps and dipping their fingers in the holy water stoups.

A bell rang and they all stood as Fr Culhane entered followed by an old bent altar server. The priest stood in front of the altar with his back to the congregation and the old Latin liturgy, familiar to Cecilia since she was a child, unfolded as it had done since time immemorial.

Fr Culhane made the Sign of the Cross and intoned-

'In nomine Patris, et Filii, et Spiritus Sancti.'
(In the name of the Father and of the Son and of the Holy Spirit)

The old altar server responded – *'Amen'*.

Still standing at the foot of the altar steps the priest continued with the prayers of the mass. *'Confiteor Deo omnipotenti'* –*(I confess to Almighty God, ...)* The prayer of contrition for sins continued evoking the name of the Virgin and the saints, and the people present....*mea culpa, mea culpa, mea maxima culpa'* – *(through my fault, through my fault, through my most grievous fault).* At each phrase the priest struck his breast. The great *Confiteor* ended with the priest asking the saints and all present to pray to the Lord for him.

When the priest had finished the server responded, on behalf of the people, by repeating, in Latin, the *Confiteor*.

Though the congregation did not say the Latin responses each one of them present could have. They knew them off by heart. The language was as familiar to them as the Irish or Scots they spoke every day.

The congregation knelt, or bowed, or stood, in the great ritualistic dance of the liturgy as the mass continued.

The sacred moment of the Consecration came, Fr Culhane raised the Host high above his head. The people bowed in reverence then raised their heads in adoration each silently saying the prayer –'My Lord and my God'.

Afterwards the priest moved down the steps, chalice in hand. The people filed forward and knelt at the altar rails. As Fr Culhane approached, Cecilia put out her tongue to receive the Blessed Sacrament.

Afterwards she knelt and prayed fervently for her husband, Arthur, and his lost bairns, and for this bairn of his that she carried deep inside her.

As the mass ended the priest began the final blessing. Raising his voice he declared – '*Benedicat vos omnipotens Deus,...*' then finally turning to face the congregation he continued, '*Pater et Filius, et Spiritus Sanctus*' – while blessing them with the sign of the cross.

The people responded – '*Amen*'.

Once Fr Culhane had entered the sacristy people began to drift away, but leaving her wicker basket on the pew Cecilia made her way to the statue of the Virgin. She lowered herself carefully on to the kneeling stool feeling very clumsy now at this stage of pregnancy. She took her Rosary from her pocket and the beads slipped through her fingers as one decade followed another. Time passed, as it always did when Cecilia prayed the Rosary, without her really noticing it, but when at last she struggled to stand she realised how chilled she was.

Though the church gave shelter from the wind it was unheated and on this unseasonable April day it was bitterly cold.

She returned to the pew and collected her basket.

In the porch she pushed open the outside door and a gust of wind seized it and banged it against the exterior wall. Cecilia jumped in fright and then struggled to close it behind her.

Fr Culhane appeared in the porch.

'Leave it child, I'll do that,' he said.

It always amused Cecilia that the priest called her child since he was scarcely older than her, but when she teased him about it he had said that he saw all his flock as his children. Since he could never marry or have children himself Cecilia thought it must be some consolation to him to think that way.

So she just smiled and said, 'Thank ye, Father,' as he pulled the door closed.

Cecilia was glad to see that the sleet had stopped, though the wind was still gusting strongly. As she passed the priest's house she saw that the trees in the garden were being bent over with the force of the wind. Though the sleet had stopped it still lay white on the cobbles of the close so Cecilia walked very carefully, afraid of slipping while in her condition.

She came out through the archway and down the few steps into the High Street. Here the pavements were paved and so not as hazardous as the slippery cobbles she had left behind in the close.

In spite of the bad weather the street was busy, as usual, bustling with people. Housewives carried their baskets from shop to shop, brewery drays rumbled up the cobbled roadway, and a horse-drawn coal cart stood to her right outside Tweeddale Court, the horse stamping its hooves and its breath steaming in the cold air. The horse waited patiently, unattended, as the coalmen answered the calls from the women leaning out of the windows above and heaved a sack of coal on their backs to deliver to the customer. It was hard, dirty work, many of the tenements were six or seven stories high.

A coalman called out Cecilia's name as he approached a doorway. At first she didn't recognise him, so black was his face with the coal dust, but then she realised it was Tammy Bain and raised her hand in greeting. He was a distant relation of Arthur's family, though Cecilia had never quite managed to untangle the relationship.

Tammy lived out of town in the village of Gilmerton. The men of the village were always referred to as "the corduroy men" as most of them were involved in the coal-mining industry and wore work trousers made out of that hard-wearing material.

Cecilia made her way across the road and walked up the pavement towards the vegetable barrow that stood in the roadway outside Arthur's Aunt Sarah's old shop. It felt strange to look through the window and see others at work in the shop. All the time that Cecilia was growing up the name Skiffington had been painted above the door. Even after Aunt Sarah died and her sister Jane Murray ran the shop the name stayed the same. But now Auntie Jane, too, was dead and the business had been sold off.

Auntie Sarah's will had stated that on the death of her sister her inheritance was to pass to Jane's bairns. None of the bairns had wanted to continue the business and so it was sold. The Murray bairns had all received a very good inheritance and were doing well for themselves in different businesses in the town.

When Cecilia's turn came after queuing at the barrow she filled her basket with potatoes, turnips, carrots, leeks and cabbage.

'Are ye sure that's no too much for ye tae carry, Cecilia?' Mary Daly, the barrow-woman said, 'In your condition an all.'

Cecilia laughed, 'Ah, Mary, ye'll not be making a fortune if ye discourage yer customers like that!'

Mary smiled but she turned to her son, young Joseph, and said, 'Here you, take Mrs Delaney's basket hame for her.'

When Cecilia protested and said she could manage, Mary said, 'Aye maybe, but that's too precious a bairn o' Arthur's for ye tae be taking any chances.'

She took the basket from Cecilia's hands and gave it to her son, 'Take that doon to the Coogate and leave it at the door.' She turned to Cecilia. 'It's 147 isn't it?' Cecilia nodded.

Cecilia thanked Mary and paid over the coppers she owed.

'Mind how ye go,' Mary called after her.

In truth Cecilia was glad to be relieved of the basket as she had a stitch in her side which was causing her some discomfort.

She decided to return home by St Mary's Street as, unlike South Gray's Close, it was paved, not cobbled, and therefore safer to walk on.

As she walked she thought about Mary Daly's comment about Arthur's "precious bairn". Cecilia thought, I suppose most folk in the old town who knew them, knew about Arthur's lost bairns and would realise how important this bairn she was carrying was.

Cecilia herself had wondered when she realised there was a bairn on the way. Arthur was still spending any spare time he had waiting outside the various Homes in the hope of catching sight of his bairns. Miss Stirling was still refusing to disclose where she was keeping them, and his attempt to get them back through the law had foundered for the lack of money.

However, when she told Arthur she was pregnant, his face lit up and he lifted her off her feet and swung her around in his arms. One look at his face and all doubts vanished. That this was a most wanted bairn, a "precious bairn" as Mary Daly had said, was obvious.

Cecilia stopped off at the butcher's shop on the corner of St Mary's Street and bought a piece of flank mutton for the soup she was planning to make. Luckily, Arthur was working as a house-painter, so at least he was indoors, but it was such a bitterly cold day that she wanted to have hot soup ready when he got home.

Arthur was a bit later home than Cecilia expected. The wind was throwing handfuls of sleet against the window panes. Surely he wouldn't have gone down to Stockbridge, to the Home, on such a night as this, she worried.

Just then the door opened and Arthur came in on a blast of cold air.

'Look at ye, ye are soaked,' she cried, as he struggled out of his wet jacket. He shook the sleet from his hair and it sizzled as it landed and melted on the hot range.

'Ye surely didn't go down to Stockbridge in weather like this,' she exclaimed.

Arthur looked surprised, then glanced up at the clock on the mantelpiece.

'Is that the time?' he said.

'Naw, a wasn't doon at the village, a wis just coming doon the close and a thought a would stop by the Chapel on ma way past and say a wee prayer,' he said.

Cecilia felt her heart lift. It was ten years since Arthur's first son, James, had been born. Arthur was a very different man from the laddie he had been then, who hardly saw the inside of the chapel from one year to the next. Now he seemed to get the same comfort from his faith that Cecilia herself had always had.

EMMA'S STORY

PART THREE

Hillfoot Farm,
Aylesford,
Nova Scotia

24 May 1887

Miss Auld
62 Northumberland Street,
Edinburgh

My dear, dear Friend,

What would have I done without you over the past few months in Edinburgh. Without your caring support such a satisfactory outcome would not have been possible.

We have arrived safely in Nova Scotia. We were such a large party of fifty-six children and, of course, the adult helpers, that we seemed to fill most of the ship! The children were very sick at first but soon found their sea-legs and began to enjoy the voyage.

I, as usual, was very sick and took much longer to recover. I was very fortunate to have with me Mr Peggie, a farmer, who had worked for me for many years at home. My farmer at Hillfoot had indicated his desire to move to British Columbia to farm with a cousin so I was able to offer his position to Mr Peggie. It was my great good fortune that he agreed to accept. While on board he supervised the helpers and kept the children under control, while I was indisposed, which was a great relief to me.

Now to more of my news. As I explained, when I was with you, I had left all in order as far as I could for completing the new wing before I was so rudely recalled to Edinburgh.

This wing was to contain the kitchen, laundry, nursery, storerooms, bathrooms, downstairs and upstairs, as well as six good large bedrooms and above that the boys' attics.

As I told you this part of the building was framed, roofed and finished outside before I left but inside much had to be done.

In the time I was away the inconvenience of this was considerable for those left behind to cope. However, with good fires, and happily a milder winter, no one seemed to suffer from it.

On my return I was delighted to find that all the work is now complete and the buildings are looking quite splendid.

It was so very good to see you, my dear Miss Auld, and spend time in your company, in spite of the unfortunate circumstances. I will remain forever grateful for your support and that of my other friends in Scotland. Hopefully, all that unpleasantness is behind us, I am sure we will not be troubled from that quarter again.

I may well have bemoaned Edinburgh's cold and blustery climate when I lived there but, believe me, compared to Nova Scotia, the most vile Edinburgh winter day would seem positively balmy! I would certainly not wish ever to spend a winter here. I hope next winter to spend some of the time in the South of France and the rest in Edinburgh, if I could impose again on your hospitality.

As I explained, when I was with you, before I departed from Nova Scotia last November I had gradually emptied Hillfoot Farm of children. Only a few remained to be placed. I have a plan, which must be adhered to, before placing children and though I was not here myself I feel sure that those I left behind were as scrupulous as I would have been myself as to the respectability of the employers they were placed with.

Only the babes and toddlers, too young for any kind of work, were left. As soon as they are able we train the girls in housework and the boys work on our own farm but I prefer not to place them with farmers until they are around eight or nine years old and can be of use. As a result of this policy we have acquired a reputation for providing children who give satisfaction.

Given the constant demand for our children, and the fact that I now had space available, I was able to bring another fifty-four with me when I returned from Edinburgh to Halifax with the Delaney children. The largest group so far. So in spite of my travails in Edinburgh it all worked out very well.

How I enjoyed the time spent with you in your lovely cosy home. Edinburgh's New Town is such a handsome and so very civilised place.

I cannot begin to tell you how much I miss it but most of all how much I miss you, my dear.

I have never had such a caring friend and I give thanks for you every day.

However, I must not complain. Though Aylesford seems very crude by comparison with the 'Athens of the North' it is none the less very pretty.

Our return coincides with blossom time here and the trees are laden with flowers of every hue from white and cream to pink. There will be a good crop of apples, pears, plums and cherries in the autumn. Or the 'Fall' as they call it here.

I look forward to hearing from you soon. I rely on you, dear friend, for all the news from Scotland.

Your ever grateful friend

Emma Stirling

EMMA'S STORY

PART FOUR

Hillfoot Farm
Aylesford
Nova Scotia

15 October 1887

Miss Auld
62 Northumberland Street
Edinburgh.

My dear friend,

I am writing to ask if I can impose on your kindness, once again.

I am returning home earlier than expected as there have been new developments in the matter which brought me to Edinburgh last year and which I had hoped were finished with.

I have been advised, by my man of law, that I should return to Scotland as soon as possible and dispose of my personal assets and responsibilities towards the Homes still remaining.

Could I again beg your hospitality?

After this visit is over I intend to have severed all my links with Scotland and will transfer my efforts to forwarding the interests of our children in Nova Scotia.

My farm manager, Mr James Peggie, is returning with me to visit his wife in the Scottish borders. He can be spared from Hillfoot Farm because with the approach of winter nothing can be done on the land. Very often we have snowdrifts several feet high!

He will return in March next year to escort Mrs Hill, matron of one of the Girls' Homes, who will be bringing out a party of boys and girls. Once again we have been able to send so many of our children away, to different parts of Canada, that we now have space at Hillfoot.

If you are able to accommodate me, dear friend, I will stay until April next year by which time I hope to have disposed of all my properties and assets in Scotland.

It will be a very trying time for me, both as regards the history of the work, in leaving the Homes in Scotland, where I had worked so long, and been the means of rescuing so many children, to be carried on by others.

It will be trying too as regarding my own personal feeling. I am aware that I will be leaving all - my own home, and its comforts, country, friends and kindred.

I will be going away for at least three years, to fight a hand-to-hand battle with poverty and hard work, heavily weighted with a number of young and helpless children.

Surely no one can doubt the love for them that induced me to do this!

Could you telegraph me as soon as possible and let me know if this would be convenient for you?

Your ever grateful friend,

Emma Stirling.

CECILIA'S STORY

PART THREE

CHAPTER 1

Edinburgh

January 1888

Cecilia sat beside the range, her hands busy at her knitting, her foot rocking the wooden cradle in which her baby son, Arthur, lay. Her mind went back to the day he was born. It was the 12th of August 1887.

Arthur had left for work when her pains began, but fortunately her own mother, Mary-Ann Clifford, had come by to see how she was. As the hours passed and the pains grew stronger Cecilia had huddled in the chair doubled over with the strength of each contraction.

Her mother had taken her by the arm. 'Get up Cissy,' she had said, using her family name, 'ye need tae walk aboot – it will make it easier for you in the long run.' Cecilia was reluctant but her mother had hauled her to her feet and walked her up and down the room.

'A should send word tae, Arthur', Cecilia had said, between gasps.

'Ye will do no such thing,' Mary-Ann had said. 'This is no place for a man – he wid jist get in the way, but we will send for Mary now, a will need her tae gie me a hand.'

She had opened the door and walked across the landing to Cecilia's neighbour, Sally Doyle, and rapped on the door. When Sally answered, Mary-Anne sent her to Mary's house up the street to bring Cecilia's sister, Mary McGrain.

'Tell her Cissy's time has come,' she had said, as Sally set off.

In no time, though it seemed like an eternity to Cecilia, her sister had come through the door.

'Keep her walking,' her mother had ordered, 'while a get things ready. She's a lucky lassie – a don't think she is going to be long.'

Cecilia remembered feeling far from lucky!

Mary-Ann had set pots of water boiling on the range then stripped the bed in the recess of its coverings. She had laid old newspapers on the flock mattress to protect it, then spread a clean white sheet from Cecilia's cupboard over them.

'Right ma bonnie lassie, let's get ye into yer nightgoon now,' she had said.

Cecilia remembered standing helpless as her mother and sister undressed her and slipped an old cotton nightgown over her head. They had then lifted her bodily up onto the high bed.

Sweat had run down Cecilia's face. She remembered the room had felt hot. Steam had poured from the pots on the range. The pains had been coming closer and closer together.

Suddenly, the door had opened and Arthur had come in. He had taken in the scene at a glance, his face had filled with anxiety and he had started towards the bed.

But Mary-Ann was too quick for him, 'No ye don't, ma manny,' she had said, turning him round. 'Dinnae worry, she's doin jist fine. Get ye through to Sally Doyle's hoose – a dinnae want ye under ma feet.'

Cecilia had seen Arthur look over his shoulder at her before the door had been closed firmly behind him.

It had been just as well because, the next moment, Cecilia remembered, she had let out an almighty shriek! Her mother had been at her side in an instant, 'Push Cissy, push, yer doing grand,' she had urged. Cecilia had done as she had been told and, at last, there he was.

'A fine big laddie,' her sister had announced from the foot of the bed.

Mary-Ann had cut the cord then wrapped the bairn in a clean white towel and laid him against Cecilia's breast. She remembered looking down at his damp hair and had felt such a rush of love for this bairn that she had been sure would be with her all her days.

'Let's get ye cleaned up, Cissy,' her mother had said, 'and then we can let that man o' yours back in before he starts kicking the door doon!'

Half an hour later Cecilia, washed and in a fresh nightgown with her still damp hair clustering in dark curls around her face, was propped up on pillows with her new wee son in her arms.

Mary was sent across the landing to the Doyle's house to announce the news of a safe delivery to an anxious Arthur.

He rushed through the open door and ran to the bed.

'Are ye alright, lass,' he had asked, with a tremble in his voice.

'A'm fine, Arthur, jist fine,' she had replied.

She had lifted the sleeping bairn and had held him up to his father.

'We have a son, Arthur,' she had said.

Arthur had taken the bundle in his arms and had stood looking down at the bairn, and then the tears had started to run down his face and soon he was sobbing.

Arthur had been followed into the room by Sally Doyle and her man Seamus. Seeing Arthur in tears, Seamus had shuffled his feet and looked down at his shoes. He was embarrassed. You would never see a grown man weeping in the old town - unless he was drunk - it just wasn't done!

But the four women understood only too well the reason for the tears as he held his wee son in his arms.

'Ye'll be calling him, Arthur, a suppose?' Mary-Ann had enquired.

This query brought a fresh burst of tears, but this time only Cecilia knew the reason. Arthur was remembering his dead son, who had gone to his grave without his father's name.

At last, pulling himself together, Arthur had returned the bairn to his mother and had blown his nose hard.

'He's a fine laddie, Cecilia,' he had said. 'A'm right proud o' ye.'

Seamus had then moved forward and had shaken Arthur by the hand.

His wife was bending over Cecilia in the bed to admire the bairn. 'Ah, he's right bonnie, sure he is, is he not Seamus?'

Her husband had nodded his agreement. 'He's a broth of a boy, right enough,' he had said.

Sally had reached into her apron pocket and extracted a silver sixpence. She had placed it carefully in the folds of the bairn's shawl, as was the custom. 'Here's some lucky silver for ye, laddie, may ye never be without,' Sally had said. 'Come on now, Seamus, let us away by and let the lassie and her bairn get some rest.'

Mary-Ann and Arthur had thanked Sally for her help and the pair returned to their own home.

'Will a heat up that stew?' Mary-Ann asked her son-in-law. 'Ye must be famished by now.'

'Naw, naw, a'm fine,' Arthur had responded. 'Sally insisted on feeding me. A think she did it tae make me sit doon and no wear her rug oot wi ma pacing,' and he laughed.

He had bent down and picked up his son again and began pacing around the room his eyes never leaving the bairn's face.

The three women had looked at each other and smiled.

'Ah well,' Mary-Ann had laughed, 'a suppose it's a right if ye wear oot yer ain rug!'

Seven days later they had taken the bairn to be baptised in St Patrick's Church. Sally and Seamus's son, wee Liam, who had been the first person they had seen on leaving the house to go to the chapel, had received the traditional "Christening Piece" of a silver sixpence, a slice of bread and cheese, and a piece of cake wrapped in greaseproof paper.

The bairn had been baptised by Fr Culhane, and his god-parents had been Cecilia's bridesmaid, Catherine, and her brother-in-law, Patrick McGrain. They had named him Arthur.

As if reading his mother's thoughts wee Arthur woke up and started crying. Cecilia put her knitting down, picked up her son and put him to her breast were he settled contentedly.

The door opened suddenly causing Cecilia to start as Arthur rushed into the room.

'A've seen her, Cecilia,' he shouted.

'Seen who?' she asked.

'Auld Stirling,' he said.

'Ye've seen Miss Stirling?' Cecilia repeated in amazement. 'Where did ye see her?'

'A saw her carriage driving up the High Street. Ye ken she's got that fancy carriage wi' the coat o' arms on the doors, ye could hardly mistake it,' he said.

'A followed it to the Children's Shelter in Assembly Close and watched till a saw her get doon from the carriage and walk into the close. A waited a few minutes until a was sure she was inside, then a rang the doorbell and told the maid a wanted tae see Miss Stirling. Of course, she didna know who a was and after a few minutes she came back and showed me into a room.'

'She had a man in there and a wee lassie. When she saw me, she said in that hoity-toity voice of hers – this is Detective Constable McPherson, Delaney - so you had better behave yourself. As if a was a wee laddie!'

'What did ye say?' Cecilia asked. 'Ye didn't lose yer temper did ye, Arthur?' she asked anxiously.

'Naw, a kept ma temper, a wisnae gaun tae gie her a chance to have me lifted, but a demanded to know were ma bairns were and she refused to tell me. She said that I would have to go to law to get them back as she intended to keep them.'

'She kept looking towards the Constable, as if she expected him to intervene, but he was refusing to meet her eye. A looked at him maesel and a thought he looked sorry for me. A think she saw it tae, because she said if I did not leave she would send to the Police Office and have me removed.'

'So what did you say then?' Cecilia asked anxiously.

'A said she needn't trouble because a wis gaun there maesel, this very instant, to lay charges of child-stealing against her.

'As a turned and left, a heard her berating the Constable for not arresting me and a heard him respond, in a soft Highland voice.

' "And what would I be after charging him with, my lady?" before the door closed behind me.

'A went straight to the Police Office in Parliament Square and asked to speak to an officer. A senior police-man came and took down the details. He was very sympathetic when he heard about the bairns being taken away, but he said it was too complicated a case. A would have to bring proof before he could get a warrant for her arrest. He advised me to get a lawyer,' Arthur said bitterly.

'It cannae be right that ye cannae get justice unless ye can afford to pay,' he exclaimed.

'Arthur, why don't you do as Mr Considine suggested and try and get yourself on the Poor Roll', Cecilia said.

After Fr Hannan had said he could do nothing more for him, could raise no more funds for a court case, Arthur had been filled with despair.

He had gone back to the solicitor, William Considine, to inform him that he would not be able to pursue the case for the return of the bairns because of lack of funds. The solicitor, seeing his distress, had suggested Arthur try to get himself admitted to the Poor Roll. He could then get free legal assistance to pursue the case. Mr Considine had explained that there were lawyers prepared to represent clients too poor to pay their own legal costs. Arthur's pride had been hurt and he had protested he was not a pauper - he was in work.

The solicitor had asked how much he earned and on hearing the amount had explained that, on such a low income, he might still qualify for legal help.

Arthur had been reluctant to declare himself a pauper. The age-old stigma of the workhouse still lingered, so instead, he had gone back to haunting the Homes were he felt his bairns might be hidden, but all in vain.

He suddenly became aware of the bairn at his wife's breast and his face softened. He reached down and stroked wee Arthur's downy head, 'A still have you ma bonnie wee man and no one will ever get to take you away,' he said.

Then, he straightened up and looked at Cecilia, 'You're right,' he said, 'a have to do everything a can to get the bairns back. A will go the morn and see about getting on the Poor Roll.'

Chapter 2

Arthur put in his application to be admitted to the Poor Roll the next day, but three months passed before he heard his application had been approved.

He lost no time in approaching a Poor Roll lawyer and he was fortunate in obtaining the services of Mr Ross Stewart. He and Arthur got on right from the start. Ross Stewart was a man who believed strongly in justice for all. Though he would have made more money in private practice he was fired with zeal for the underdog.

It seemed to Arthur and Cecilia that the processes of the Law were grindingly slow but, at last, Ross Stewart had presented Arthur's Petition to the Court of Session in Edinburgh on 15 November 1888.

He sent Arthur a copy of the Petition.

It read -

COURT OF SESSION
EDINBURGH

15 November 1888

Custody case for the return of children of the petitioner, ARTHUR DELANEY.

MINUTE for the Petitioner, lodged 15th November 1888.

ROSS STEWART, for the minuter, stated that the petitioner, in the month of December 1886, on the day after his hearing that his children had been brought back to this country, called upon Mr MacDonald, Pitt Street, Edinburgh, the then secretary of the Edinburgh and Leith Children's Aid and Refuge, and inquired where his children were.

He was summarily dismissed, with an absolute refusal of the information he desired. The next day the petitioner called at one of the homes of the said Institution in MacKenzie Place, Edinburgh, but no one there could tell him where his children were. The petitioner went twice to Miss Stirling's residence at Wardie, but failed to obtain an interview with her. He accordingly called again upon Mr MacDonald who told him that if he would 'just wait patiently', he would arrange with Miss Stirling that the children would be given to him, but he gave the petitioner no information as to where the children were.

In or about the month of January 1887, Mr MacDonald informed the petitioner that Miss Stirling was out of the country and would return in three or four months, and that he would advise her to give the petitioner back his children. She did not return within that period, but, to the best of the petitioner's knowledge, remained away till the beginning of the present year.

During the whole period from January 1887 till January 1888 the petitioner has very frequently called upon Mr MacDonald to hear if there was any news of Miss Stirling's return. On many of these occasions he was accompanied by his uncle, Thomas Delaney.

In the end of January 1888, the petitioner, immediately on hearing that Miss Stirling had returned, called upon her and demanded his children. She, however, refused to deliver them to him.

The petitioner was at that time so poor, that he was unable to procure the services of his former law-agent, but as soon as possible obtained admission to the Poor's Roll, and instituted the present proceedings.

The petitioner denies emphatically that he ever intimated to the respondents, or authorised any one to intimate on his behalf, that he had abandoned his claim to the custody of his children, or that he had given up his intention of taking proceedings for their recovery.

Signed – D. ROSS STEWART.

By then Cecilia and Arthur had two sons, Bernard having been born to them in 1888. But Arthur was as determined as ever to get his bairns back from Canada.

Cecilia was fully behind Arthur in his endeavours. If anything, now that she had bairns of her own, she realised the heartache that was with Arthur every day of his life.

On 23rd November 1888 the judge approved Arthur's Petition stating there was a case to answer. The Directors of the Edinburgh and Leith Children's Aid and Refuge Society were ordered to appear before the Court to explain why they had not returned Arthur's children to him.

The trial date was set for 1st February 1889.

EMMA'S STORY

PART FIVE

Hillfoot Farm,
Aylesford,
Nova Scotia.

30 November 1888

Miss Hope Johnston
Marchbankwood,
Scotland.

Dear Miss Hope-Johnstone

My sincere apologies for the delay in writing to thank you for your great kindness and hospitality to me during the last fortnight of my visit to Scotland.

Marchbankwood is such a lovely place, truly a paradise on earth! It was so very kind of you to invite me and our friend, Miss Auld, to spend that time with you.

My stay with you enabled me to regain sufficient strength to enable me to undertake the voyage, worn out as I was by the work, care, and anxiety consequent on such an undertaking.

I believe, but for this timely rest and tender nursing, I would not have been able either for the voyage or for the work which lay before me on my landing; and I shall be grateful all my life.

My tardiness in writing is, because, almost as soon as I arrived at Hillfoot, another party of children were sent by the directors. They were accompanied by Mrs Vass and by my farmer's wife, Mrs James Peggie.

Our party was supplemented by several children from Miss Croall's Home for Destitute Children in Stirling.

Once they had arrived, we lost no time in using the fine weather to complete the house accommodation required for a permanent colony.

So you see we have been very busy indeed. Nonetheless it is a poor excuse for my delay in writing to thank you and I hope you will forgive me.

As you were kind enough to say that you would be interested in hearing of our progress here I will write again with more news.

Your sincere friend

Emma Stirling.

CECILIA'S STORY

PART FOUR

CHAPTER 1

1st February 1889

Cecilia sat in the public gallery of the Court of Session as Arthur's custody case for the return of his bairns was about to be called. She looked down into the well of the Court and could see Arthur, his mother, Anne Delaney, and his uncle, Thomas Delaney, sitting below.

The Court Usher called out 'All rise' as the judge entered and took his place on the bench overlooking the Court.

After they were seated the usher announced-

'Custody case for the return of the children of Arthur Delaney.

'The lawyer for the Petitioner, Arthur Delaney, is Mr. Ross Stewart.

'The lawyer for the Respondents, the Directors of Edinburgh and Leith Children's Aid and Refuge Society is Mr C. J. Guthrie.'

Cecilia watched as a be-wigged Mr Guthrie rose to his feet.

'I call Mr John McDonald,' he intoned.

A short, stout man entered, climbed into the witness box and took the oath.

Mr Guthrie – 'Could you please give your Statement to this Court.'

Mr MacDonald –'I am an accountant and am Secretary of the Edinburgh and Leith Children's Aid and Refuge. I became Secretary in December 1885. Prior to that Mr Alexander Young was secretary. When I became secretary I found a minute-book containing minutes, commencing the time when the directors were appointed. The first minute was dated 1st May 1884. The shelter in connection with the refuge is at 150 High Street and the home in MacKenzie Place, Stockbridge. At one time there were a number of homes but latterly there have been only two.'

Mr Guthrie –'Who was in charge of the homes when you became secretary?'

Mr MacDonald – 'When I became secretary, Miss Stirling had charge of the homes. She had been the foundress of the homes, and spent a very large sum of her own fortune on them. When there was any deficiency of funds, she supplied it. She has spent about £8000 on the homes.'

Mr Guthrie – 'Is Miss Stirling still in that position with regard to the homes?'

Mr MacDonald – 'No, in October 1887, she sent a letter of resignation to the directors, and ceased any connection with them.'

Mr Guthrie – 'Did the directors have anything to do with sending children away from the homes to Nova Scotia?'

Mr MacDonald – 'No.

From the time my connection with the homes commenced in 1885 down to 1887, the homes and the children were under the charge of Miss Stirling. It was she who had to do with sending the children away: these matters were not brought before the directors at all.

Prior to October 1887, the sending of children away was never brought before the board, of course, the board were aware that children were sent away, but they did not consider the individual cases.'

Mr. Guthrie sat down and Cecilia watched as Ross Stewart rose to his feet.

Mr Stewart – 'Did the directors, at any time, send children away to Nova Scotia?'

Mr MacDonald – 'After Miss Stirling ceased the connection with the homes, the directors did consider the sending of children away. Dr Affleck and Dr Bell, who are mentioned in the Petition as directors, had resigned before the Petition was brought; and Dr Gilmour, whose name is also mentioned, was dead.'

Mr Stewart – 'When was Miss Stirling last in this country?'

Mr MacDonald – 'Miss Stirling left this country last in March 1888. So far as I know she has not been in this country since. Prior to March 1888 she had been in this country from October 1887. She came home then from Nova Scotia. She was in Nova Scotia from May 1887 to October of the same year. Prior to May 1887 she had been in this country from November 1886.'

Mr Stewart – 'Do you have details of the three children in your records?'

Mr MacDonald – 'Yes. I find in the books of the homes the names of three children, James Delaney, Annie Delaney and Robina Delaney. That was in a book previously kept by Miss Stirling and now kept by me.

'It goes back to 1877 but those entries were copied in afterwards.

'It contains entries of a large number of children who were admitted before 1884, when the directors were appointed. Amongst others who are entered as having been admitted, are the names of those three children.'

Mr Stewart – 'Are these the children of the Petitioner?'

Mr MacDonald – 'Yes, they are but I do not know anything of their admission beyond what I see in the books.'

Mr Stewart – 'Could you please read out the details from the book.'

Mr MacDonald – 'The entry in the book relating to James Delaney is No. 83. The writing at the bottom of the page under the heading "Remarks", is in the hand of Miss Stirling. At the end of that writing is another entry – "Sailed for N.S. 1st September 1886". That is in the handwriting of one of my clerks.

'No. 84 in the book relates to Annie Delaney. The entry under the heading "Remarks" is in Miss Stirling's hand.

'Entry No. 85 refers to Robina Delaney. Part of that entry is "Sailed for Nova Scotia 25th May 1886."'

Mr Stewart – 'Can you tell us when Annie Delaney went to Nova Scotia?'

Mr MacDonald – 'There is no entry for as to when Annie Delaney went to Nova Scotia and, as a matter of fact, I don't know.'

Mr Stewart – 'When did Miss Stirling acquire the property in Nova Scotia?'

Mr MacDonald – 'Miss Stirling acquired the property in Nova Scotia in 1886. The board of directors have no connection with that property, nor any interest in it whatever.

'The homes here are now entirely supported by public subscription. The directors give their services gratuitously.'

Mr Stewart – 'When did you first see the Petitioner, Arthur Delaney?'

Mr MacDonald – 'I first saw the Petitioner, I think, in September, 1886. He came to ask for his children – where they were and I told him they had gone with Miss Stirling to Nova Scotia.'

Mr Stewart – 'Did Mr Delaney call on you frequently regarding his children?'

Mr MacDonald – 'He called on me more than once.'

Mr Stewart – 'How many more times?'

Mr MacDonald – 'I can not say for sure.'

Mr. Guthrie indicated he wanted to ask a question and Ross Stewart sat down.

Mr Guthrie – 'Was the petitioner in arrears of board for his children?'

Mr MacDonald – 'During the time I have been secretary – since December 1885 the petitioner has never paid any money for the support of his children in the homes.

'From the books kept by Miss Stirling. I find he paid board in varying amounts in 1882, 1883, altogether £1.17s. I know that application was made to him for board without result.'

Mr Guthrie – 'When did you next hear of the matter?'

Mr MacDonald – 'The next I heard of this matter after the petitioner called on me, was a letter which I received from Mr Considine, S.S.C., in September 1886.

'I wrote on 22 September giving the address of James and Robina as Aylesford, Nova Scotia and stating that Annie was still in one of the homes in this country.'

Mr Guthrie – 'Did you make contact with Miss Stirling regarding this matter?'

Mr MacDonald – 'On 2nd October 1886 I telegraphed to Miss Stirling; "Directors are taking action against Delaney, (for non payment of board) but advise you bring the children home."'

Mr Guthrie – 'And did she bring the children home?'

Mr MacDonald – 'The children were brought home in November 1886, and Mr Gray, our legal-agent, intimated that fact to Mr Considine, Mr Delaney's law-agent.'

Mr Guthrie – 'When did you last see Miss Stirling?'

Mr MacDonald – 'I went to Liverpool to meet Miss Stirling and accompanied her and James and Robina Delaney to Edinburgh. The last I saw of them was at the Caledonian Station, when I saw them into a cab with Miss Stirling.'

Ross Stewart then rose to his questioning.

Mr Stewart – 'Do you know where the children were taken?'

Mr MacDonald – 'Since then I have known nothing at all of their whereabouts. That also applies to the whereabouts of Annie Delaney. Neither James nor Robina have been in any of the homes since then.'

Mr Stewart – 'Do you know what became of Annie Delaney?'

Mr MacDonald – 'I don't know what has become of Annie. Miss Stirling took her away from Dumfries were she was boarded. I paid Dumfries originally : she was in the habit of boarding children there. I don't know when she was taken away. If she went abroad I don't know when it was.'

Mr Stewart – 'Did you make any contact with Miss Stirling after seeing her off at the Caledonian Station?'

Mr MacDonald – 'I wrote to Miss Stirling on 27 November 1888, and I received a reply on 24 December 1888.'

Mr Stewart – 'So, in fact, you did know where the children were?'

Mr MacDonald – 'I did not know, for certain, that the children were with her.'

Mr Stewart – 'In the circumstances do you not think it was your duty to convey her address to Mr Considine?'

Mr MacDonald – 'Not if Miss Stirling did not want it.'

Mr Stewart – 'How many meetings have you had with the Petitioner, Arthur Delaney?'

Mr MacDonald – 'I have had four or five interviews with the Petitioner since September 1886. I mean interviews in my office.

'In addition to these he may have spoken to me on the street. He has done so more than once. He has also spoken to me here.

'I knew the children had been brought back to this country but I did not know where they were.

'The Petitioner's agent had been told the address of the children in Nova Scotia.'

Mr Stewart – 'Is it the case that you dismissed the demands from Mr Delaney for the return of his children in summarily manner?'

Mr MacDonald – 'It is not the case that I ever summarily dismissed the Petitioner with an absolute refusal of information as to where his children were. I would simply refer him to his law agent, Mr Considine.'

Mr Stewart – 'But Mr Considine did not know where the children were – did he?'

Mr MacDonald – 'I did not know, for certain, where the children were in December after they came home.'

Mr Stewart – 'Is it not the case that you told the petitioner that you would try to persuade Miss Stirling to return his children to him?'

Mr MacDonald – 'Before the children were brought home I told the Petitioner that I would try to persuade Miss Stirling to bring the children back to this country. I never told him I would arrange with Miss Stirling that the children be given to him.

'In January 1887 Miss Stirling was still in this country and had been since November 1886 and she remained in this country until May 1887.

'I knew Miss Stirling's whereabouts in the end of 1886 and beginning of 1887 because I was in constant communication with her.'

Mr Stewart – 'Did Mr Delaney call on you at that time?'

Mr MacDonald – 'The Petitioner called on me during the time Mr Considine had the case in hand but not after that, so far as I recollect.'

Mr Guthrie then intervened.

Mr Guthrie – 'Was it the case that the petitioner was in arrears of board for his children?'

Mr MacDonald – 'When I became Secretary I examined the books to see which of the parents were in arrears for ailment of their children. I found that the Petitioner was due, I think, £28. I wrote to him asking for payment. I have no copy of the letter I sent: it would be one of the printed forms we have for the purpose.'

Mr Guthrie – 'Were you acting on the instructions of the directors at all times in this matter?'

Mr MacDonald – 'I was not acting on the instructions of the directors.

'During Miss Stirling's absence from May to November 1886; Miss Stirling was still acting as Superintendent although she was away. She acted through a lady deputy. Miss Auld and Mrs Young acted as deputies for her when she was absent.'

Ross Stewart rose and resumed questioning.

Mr Stewart – 'At that time you could have delivered the child Annie to her father, could you not, since she was still in this country?'

Mr MacDonald – 'I declined to deliver Annie Delaney to the petitioner, because I could not deliver her without Miss Stirling's consent: Miss Stirling was responsible.'

Mr Stewart – 'Didn't you think that since Miss Stirling was responsible for the children she ought to bring them back?'

Mr MacDonald – 'Yes.'

Mr Stewart – 'Why did you not communicate the fact that you had met Miss Stirling and the children at Liverpool to Mr Considine, the law-agent?'

Mr MacDonald – 'We communicated the fact that they were here which was surely enough.'

Mr Stewart – 'Why did you not write to him stating in an open manner, Miss Stirling has returned, she was at

Liverpool, and I saw the children and they are in this country?'

Mr MacDonald – 'I did not write to that effect. I told the Directors. If I informed Mr Considine it would be through our law-agent. Our law-agent was told at that meeting.

'I could not ascertain where the children were to be taken to, because Miss Stirling would not tell me. She said she would not tell me because she alone was responsible for the children and she meant to keep them.'

Mr Stewart – 'Did you ever receive any intimation from Mr Considine that the Petitioner had instructed him to drop the case?'

Mr MacDonald – 'I don't remember receiving any intimation from Mr Considine that he had resolved to take no proceedings in the matter; I don't think I did.

'I told Miss Stirling that the Petitioner was asking about his children and wanting them.'

Mr Stewart – 'Did Miss Stirling tell you to give Delaney no information about where his children were?'

Mr MacDonald – 'Very likely.'

Mr Stewart – 'Is it true that Mr Delaney called frequently at your office demanding the return of his children?'

Mr MacDonald – 'He called five or six times since September 1886. I cannot tell when he came last. I don't think he called any more than six or eight times after December 1886. I always referred him to his law-agent.'

Mr Stewart – 'Is it not the case that Mr Delaney came so often to your office that you threatened him with the police?'

Mr MacDonald – 'It is not the case but I threatened him with the police for following me on the street and giving me impertinence. He would probably be asking about his children – speaking about the case.

'I have no doubt we asked Miss Stirling where the children were, but she would not tell us.'

Mr Stewart – 'Is it not the case that you told Mr Delaney to be patient and that he would get his children back?'

Mr MacDonald – 'I have no doubt I advised the Petitioner at one time to wait and his children would be given to him but that was before the children came home. I never said that to him after the children came home: he never got any answer from me after that, except to refer him to his law-agent.'

Ross Stewart then sat down and Mr. Guthrie then called Mr. Robert Collie Gray.

Mr Guthrie – 'Could you describe your role in this case?'

Mr Gray – 'I have been a director of the Edinburgh and Leith Children's Aid and Refuge since March 1886. Miss Stirling was Superintendent and took charge of the homes at that time. She acquired a property in Nova Scotia at the end of 1885 or beginning of 1886. Our directors had nothing to do with that place. During last year she ceased to have any connection with our homes and we have no control of her in any way.'

Mr Guthrie – 'When did you first hear about the Petitioner's children?'

Mr Gray – 'I first heard about the Petitioner's children about October 1886, when he applied to Mr MacDonald to have them sent back to him. A correspondence ensued between me and Mr Considine, and we had several meetings.

'The object of the communications was to make plain to Mr Considine, as petitioner's agent, that the directors did not desire to interfere between him and getting possession of his children if it was right that he should have them.

'At that time I understood that the children were in Nova Scotia.

'My statements given at that time were based on my information and understanding at that time.

'I understood that of the two who were taken away on August, 1886 Miss Stirling had taken one of them with her from Edinburgh and had picked up the other at Dumfries on her way as she had done in other cases.'

Mr Stewart for the Petitioner intervened.

Mr Stewart – 'But since this was not the true facts your correspondence and meetings with Mr Delaney's then agent were in fact based on error. Is that not so?'

Mr Gray – 'It was only inference on my part that that was how she did it. I did not know it. I cannot say of my own knowledge when the children were taken away by Miss Stirling for the first time to Nova Scotia. I have only the information of the secretary on the subject.

'The directors had no doubt the correct course was to bring the children back. I informed Mr Considine that in the directors' opinion the removal of the children was entirely the act of Miss Stirling, and that they had wired her advising her to bring them back.

'When the children were brought back the fact was communicated to the directors and the information was given to Mr Considine. I also informed him that Miss Stirling refused to give them up.

'The children were never in the custody of the directors after they were brought back, and the directors had no information as to their whereabouts.

'We tried to get their address, but Miss Stirling gave us to understand she thought it best not to tell, as it would then be impossible for us to tell any other person.'

Mr Stewart – 'Do you think your acceptance of that position was an honourable one to take as a law-agent?'

Mr Gray – 'I can only say that it was outwith my control.

'I was aware that the Petition was framed with a view to Delaney recovering his children. The Petition was not proceeded with. I cannot tell why.

'The failure to proceed with it was in no way due to the directors. I expected him to go on with it at the time.'

Mr Stewart – 'Yet is it not a fact that you urged Delaney, through his law-agent, to delay the proceedings?'

Mr Gray – 'I asked him to delay proceedings until the children had been brought back to the country, when it would be possible to get the children under the Petition.'

Mr Stewart – 'So you are of the opinion that it would be right and proper for Mr Delaney to regain his children?'

Mr Gray – 'We had no desire to put any obstacle in the way of Delaney getting back his children. We had no interest to do so.'

Mr Stewart – 'Don't you think it was your duty as directors and managers of this home to know where those children were?'

Mr Gray – 'Certainly: if the proceedings had gone on we would have had to ascertain that but they had only been threatened.'

Mr Stewart – 'Did you receive any intimation, in your position of law-agent, that this case had been abandoned?'

Mr Gray – 'I received no intimation from Mr Considine, or the petitioner, that the petitioner had abandoned his children but I assumed it, nothing having been done for more than a year.'

Mr Stewart – 'Was your threatened action against Mr Delaney on the question of his arrears intended to discourage him from seeking to proceed with this Petition?'

Mr Gray – 'I don't think a claim for ailment was ever seriously made on the petitioner: it was simply mentioned at a meeting that he was a large sum in arrears.'

Mr Stewart – 'In arrears to your Society?'

Mr Gray – 'Yes: I mean in arrear of the board which we understood he had agreed with Miss Stirling to pay.'

Mr Stewart – 'In whose name was that standing – the Directors' or Miss Stirling's?'

Mr Gray – 'It was in no one's name: there was an old book in which Miss Stirling kept note of payments of board, and in it there were entries of some payments by Delaney amounting to 27s.'

Mr Stewart – 'Mr MacDonald told this court that he had informed Miss Stirling that an action was being raised against Delaney in respect of the arrears. I ask you again – in whose name would such an action have been raised?'

Mr Gray – 'As I said such an action was never seriously considered.'

Mr Stewart – 'Then I am afraid that the court can only conclude that the threat was to deter Mr Delaney from taking legal action to have his children returned to him. That the arrears were in fact a purchase price to be paid for the children.'

At this the Judge intervened.

Judge – 'It was suggested by one of the Directors that a claim should be made against Delaney for arrears of ailment. Had that any connection with the claim of Delaney to have his children returned?'

Mr Gray – 'It arose at the same time and of course it was the demand of Delaney for his children that brought it to the mind of the director who suggested it your Honour.

'But I can only repeat that the Directors had no interest in hindering the petitioner from getting back his children.'

Mr Stewart – 'Had you no interest in doing what you could to get them back for him?'

Mr Gray – 'Not if the father did not wish them. He never asked for them, directly or indirectly, after the time I have mentioned so far as I know.'

Mr Stewart – 'Were you not informed that Mr Delaney was unable to proceed as a result of insufficient funds being available for further legal action?'

Mr Gray – 'I may have been. I cannot recollect.'

Mr Stewart – 'Had you no interest, as a director of an institution which had received three children from the petitioner, to get them back for him, or give him the information to enable him to find the children?'

Mr Gray – 'Since this Petition was brought I have had correspondence with Miss Stirling in Nova Scotia on many occasions. I have done my best to help the Petitioner to get his children.'

Ross Stewart requested that the correspondence be read out in Court.

Cecilia listened carefully as the Court Usher read out the letters.

The usher announced -

'LETTER ONE, dated 10 July 1888.

Dear Miss Stirling,

I understand a communication will have been made to you regarding a Petition at the instance of Arthur Delaney for the custody of his children, and as I think it right that you should know the terms of the answers which have been put in for the directors, I now send you a print of these answers.

The agent who formerly represented Delaney is not now acting for him, but the case has been taken up by one of the agents for the poor, who will thus not be entitled to any expense unless he gains his case.

The Court have to-day delayed doing anything in the case, pending the intimation to you of the petition.

Of course I do not now say anything at all as to the merits of the case, because you will no doubt be communicating with your agents, Messrs Stuart and Stuart, with whatever instructions you think proper, but I may add that practically nothing can now be done until the Court resumes in the middle of October next.

Robert C. Gray'

'LETTER TWO dated July 24, 1888

Hillfoot Farm, Aylesford, Nova Scotia.

Dear Mr Gray,

I saw from the 'Scotsman' a short time ago that Delaney's case was coming on, and am very glad to see the answers which the directors have put in, which seem to me perfectly reasonable and satisfactory.

As to my communication with my agents, I have none, as Messrs Stuart have nothing to do with it, and I don't see my way of troubling them further or indeed doing anything. October is a good way off.

You have only (so far as I know) told one story or fib in your answers. You say Miss Stirling took the children, on their return in 1886, to her own house, Merleton. I did not. They never set foot in Merleton, as it was closed at the time. All the rest of your statements are substantially correct.

If the court goes on delaying at this rate, they will have legislation before they know where they are, and the law on the right side. I am told on good authority it is coming quickly.

Emma M. Stirling'

'LETTER THREE dated November 10,1888

Dear Miss Stirling,

The Delaney case was before the court to-day, when the Judges ordered Delaney to put in a statement in writing as to what he had to say with regard to the third article of our answers, in which we say that he took no steps after the children were brought back in November 1886.

Several of the judges, however, seemed to entertain the view that, after getting you to bring back the children, then the directors should have got the children restored to one of the homes, or looked after them in some way or another, and one of their Lordships put the question whether, since this Petition was raised in June last, we had ever asked you to tell us distinctly where the children were, or to restore them to this country, if they had again been taken out of it.

This question was not pressed further to-day, pending the putting in of the statement ordered from Delaney, but as it will, no doubt, be again repeated when the case is in Court again, I have been instructed to ask you regarding it, and I hope you will be so kind as let me hear from you in direct course of post.

Of course, the Directors have no desire to anything but what they are advised is right and proper.

Robert C. Gray'

'LETTER FOUR dated November 28 1888.

Hillfoot Farm, Aylesford, Nova Scotia.

Dear Mr Gray,

As to the view of the Judges that the directors should have had the Delaney children restored to the Homes in November 1888, or have looked after them in some way or other, I frankly say that the directors did ALL that they could in that direction, and are entirely free from any blame.

They also did "have them looked after" most efficiently, as I gave them personal and repeated assurances to that effect.

As to where they now are, they were a considerable time ago located in excellent homes in Canada, and therefore having been away from my home, and beyond my control entirely, I can hold out no prospect of restoring them to the old country.

Emma M. Stirling'

Cecilia, sitting above, saw the colour drain from Arthur's face as this letter was read out and he gave an audible gasp.

The Court Usher continued.

'LETTER FIVE dated November 27, 1888.

Dear Miss Stirling,

A draft of this letter was read at a full meeting of the directors yesterday, and they instructed me to press upon you the expediency of meeting the orders of the Court, and by doing so put an end to the difficulties.

Robert C. Gray'

'LETTER SIX, dated December 24, 1888

Hillfoot Farm, Aylesford, Nova Scotia.

Dear Mr Gray,

I have taken a little time to consider before answering your letter of the 27th of November.

Also, in view of the very serious nature of its contents, I have taken legal advice on the subject.

The result is that I can only repeat the answer I honestly gave to Mr Gray's letter of the 10th of November, viz., that the Delaney children being now out of my hands, and beyond my control, I cannot do anything more in the matter.

Of course I feel very strongly (and think the directors should inform the Court) as to the very pitiable condition from which the children were originally taken. The father's shocking and most heartless conduct in deserting them for four years; his well known idle and intemperate habits, which to all appearance were unchanged up to April last; and finally, that when the children were in

Scotland in 1886 he made no attempt to recover them, or to pay the debt he had incurred for their support.

I say, in view of all these facts, I am credibly advised it is very improbably that the court here will order them to be given up by those in whose hands they are, as I am told the view taken by the Courts here is not the same as in such cases as it appears to be in the old country.

While I am sorry I cannot meet the views of the directors in this matter, this is all I have to say.

Emma M. Stirling'

'LETTER SEVEN dated January 19, 1889

Dear Miss Stirling,

Since Mr Macdonald received your letter of 24th December, the Court have settled that the evidence in the Delaney case is to be taken soon before Lord Adam.

With reference to what you now say as to the children being in Nova Scotia, but out of your hands, our counsel, Mr Guthrie, thinks it would be necessary for us to know the exact addresses of the children, as there is no doubt we will be questioned on this point.

I am sure you understand that the directors are not wishing to give you any trouble in this matter, but of course they have to answer to the Court, and it would only be right that they should not be put in the position of seeming to refuse information.

Would you kindly let me hear from you at your early convenience.

Robert C. Gray'

After the letters were read out to the Court Mr Gray stood down.

Mr. Guthrie called Mr. James Colston to the witness box.

Mr Guthrie – 'Could you indentify yourself and your role in this case?'

Mr Colston – 'I am a printer in Edinburgh, and a Justice of the Peace and a Deputy–Lieutenant of the County. I am one of the directors of the Edinburgh and Leith Children's Aid and Refuge. I became chairman of the board in 1884. Prior to that I was president of the committee of advice.

'Miss Stirling was the foundress and she was also the largest contributor to the funds. I think the directors felt a diffidence in interfering owing to that fact.'

Mr Guthrie – 'When did you first hear of this case?'

Mr Colston – 'I first heard about Delaney when Mr Considine threatened us with an action, towards the end of 1886.

'I had an interview with Mr Considine and Mr Gray, and I stated that I had not the slightest objection to giving the children back.

'In November of the same year I heard from the secretary that the children had been brought back and Mr Considine was informed of that fact.

'Miss Stirling refused to give the children up; she thought they were her property.'

Mr Stewart for the Petitioner intervened.

Mr Stewart – 'Do you consider that children should be regarded as "property"? Something that could be traded in the marketplace?'

Mr Colston – 'The directors did not concur in her view but Miss Stirling refused to give them up unless the law compelled her.

'She refused to tell us where they were.'

Mr Stewart – 'When you heard that Mr Delaney's children were in this country, why didn't you obtain from Miss Stirling information as to where they were?'

Mr Colston – 'One man may take a horse to water but he cannot make him drink.

'Mr Considine knew Miss Stirling's residence at Merleton, Wardie. He was told that the children were with Miss Stirling.'

Mr Stewart – 'Did you know that on leaving finally for Nova Scotia that Miss Stirling had closed up her house at Wardie?'

Mr Colston – 'I do recall that the secretary had informed us of that fact.'

Mr Stewart – 'So what would have been the point of Mr Considine making a submission to Merleton in Wardie if neither Miss Stirling or the children were there?

Mr Colston – 'The fact must have slipped my mind.

'We have been all along and are now quite willing that the children should be restored to their father; we have no desire to have any litigation on the subject.'

Mr Colston then stood down.

Ross Stewart then called William Considine S.S.C to the witness stand.

Mr Stewart – 'Could you give this court your name and state your involvement in this matter?'

Mr Considine – 'I am William Considine and I am a S.S.C. I was agent in 1886 for the petitioner, Arthur Delaney.

'My business book shows the different meetings between me and my client, and also the letters written by me on his behalf to Mr MacDonald and Mr Gray.

'At the meeting with Mr Colston and Mr Gray they told me they had telegraphed to Miss Stirling to bring the children back from America.

'I had a meeting after that with Mr Gray who said that Miss Stirling declined to give up the custody of the children. He could give me no information about them other than that they had returned; he did not know where they were.

'I wrote to my client that same day, 3 December 1886.'

The letter was read to the court.

'Dear Mr Delaney,

I saw Miss Stirling's agent today. I gather that the children have been brought back, but Miss Stirling refuses point blank to part with them, unless compelled by the law to do so. It is plain that there will be heavy fighting before the children can be recovered. Before taking any steps, I should like to have a meeting with the very Rev. Canon Hannan.

Mr Considine'

Mr. Considine continued.

'Canon Hannan had introduced Delaney to me. I had a meeting with Canon Hannan and a Petition was drawn up.

'I wrote to Mr Delaney on 6 January 1887 asking him to call and go over the Petition.

'I had a further meeting with Canon Hannan and went over the Petition with him.

'I wrote to Mr Delaney on 28th January, 1887 asking him to call on me. He called at my office after that date.

'There was nothing further done by me after 28th January 1887.'

Mr Stewart – 'Did you have any further contact with Mr Gray?'

Mr Considine – 'I had no further meetings with Mr Gray but I met him once or twice, accidently in George Street and had some conversation with him. He asked me why I was not going on with the Petition and I have no doubt I told him I was in want of funds.'

Mr Stewart – 'Can we be clear why did you not proceed with the Petition?'

Mr Considine – 'The sole reason why I did not press the Petition was because I had no funds.'

Mr Stewart – 'Did you, at any time, inform the Directors that you had abandoned the claim for the custody of the children?'

Mr Considine – 'I never intimated to the respondents in this case that I had abandoned the claim.'

Mr Stewart – 'Did Mr Delaney ever say to you that he wanted to abandon the claim?'

Mr Considine – 'Mr Delaney never authorised me to abandon the claim.'

Mr Stewart – 'Did the directors ever write to you about arrears of ailment?'

Mr Considine – 'The directors never wrote to me about arrears of ailment.'

Mr Stewart – 'Did the directors at any time write to you with information as to where the children were in December 1886.'

Mr Considine – 'No.'

Mr Considine stood down.

The judge ordered that the case be resumed on the 8th February 1889 and the Court then adjourned.

Cecilia rushed downstairs as soon as the judge had left the bench. Arthur came through the swing doors from the Courtroom. His face was ashen and he was trembling.

'Did you hear that, Cecilia, auld Stirling says she doesn't know where my bairns are,' he said. His eyes were glistening with unshed tears.

'Now dinnae fash yerself,' his mother, Anne, said as she came to stand beside them. 'Sure, she's just saying that to put ye off – the judge will mak sure she tells where they are.'

Cecilia hoped her mother-in-law was right but a feeling of dread gripped her.

They parted outside St. Giles and made their separate ways home.

Cecilia and Arthur walked, arm in arm, in silence back to their house.

Chapter 2

A week later Cecilia was once more back in the public gallery as the case resumed.

The Court Usher announced -

'Custody Case for the return of the children of Arthur Delaney.'

John MacDonald, Secretary, of the Edinburgh & Leith Children's Aid & Refuge was recalled.

Mr MacDonald – 'Since I was last examined before this Court I have examined a book called, 'Aid and Refuge List of Children Boarded Out.' On page 6 I find the name Annie Delaney appearing as boarding with Miss Gardiner, Fair Mount, Moffat, at 5s a week. Payments are entered as having been made from 30 November 1885 down to May 1886, and they may have been made before that. On the same page is the note – Removed 4th May 1886. The children were removed on the instructions of Miss Stirling to another house. On page 2 Annie Delaney appears as going to Lilly Gray, Greenhill, in May 1886 and board was paid for her up to December 1886. On the same page is the note – removed 20th December 1886.

'There are no entries in the books after that in relation to Annie Delaney. I don't know what became of her after that date.

'James Delaney's name does not appear in the book because he was in one of the Homes, not boarded out.

'On page 4 Robina Delaney's name appears as boarded out with Mrs Williamson, Crawfordjohn. Board appears to have been paid for her there from 30th November 1885 down to May 1886. There is no entry relating to her after that as she went to Nova Scotia.

'It was Miss Stirling who selected these places for the children in the country, and she removed them from one place to another.

'Could I also inform the Court that I have received another letter from Miss Stirling since my last appearance in this court.'

The letter was read out to the Court.

'LETTER EIGHT dated February 5. 1889

Hillfoot Farm, Aylesford, Nova Scotia.

Dear Mr Gray,

I regret that I cannot comply with the request of the Directors, in giving the addresses desired, and I fail to see how the Court can hold them as refusing, or appearing to refuse, information which they do not possess, and have no means of obtaining. They can only say they don't know.

Emma M. Stirling'

Counsel for the Directors put in documents and closed their Proof.

The judge ordered that the Court re-convene on 8th March 1889 and the Court was adjourned.

CHAPTER 3

Cecilia could feel that Arthur was near breaking point as they walked back to the Court of Session on 8th March. She tried to calm him down but she understood his nerves. Today was when he was to appear in the witness box to try and impress the judges to rule that his bairns should be returned to him. So much was at stake.

Arthur was met by his mother and his Uncle Thomas as they arrived outside the Court of Session. Cecilia again climbed up to take her seat in the public gallery while the others disappeared into the Courtroom.

The Court Usher announced 'All rise' as the judge entered and took his seat on the bench. He then declared-

'Petition at the instance of Poor Arthur Delaney, painter, 147 Cowgate, Edinburgh for custody of children.'

Cecilia watched anxiously as Arthur climbed into the witness box and Ross Stewart began his examination.

Mr Stewart – 'Could you please give the Court your name and state your case?'

Arthur Delaney – 'My name is Arthur Delaney and I am the petitioner in this case. After my wife's death I went to reside with my mother and I lived with her for some time. About the same time I gave my children into the custody of the Edinburgh and Leith Children's Aid and Refuge, the agreement being that I was to pay five shillings a week for their board. I paid for them regularly, as far as I could.

'I fell out of work, and when I was not working I discontinued paying.

'I went to visit my children in the homes mostly every Saturday. I continued to visit them more or less regularly for a length of time after their admission. I might say for about two years.

'My mother and sister also visited them.

'After the two years when I went to visit them I did not find them in the home. I was told they had been sent to Moffat.'

Mr Stewart – 'Which home did you go to, Mr Delaney?'

Arthur Delaney – 'It was the home in MacKenzie Place, Stockbridge, that I went to. It was the matron in charge who told me the children had been moved to Moffat for six weeks of the summer.

'At the end of the six weeks I called back again when I was informed that a letter had been received from Miss Stirling that the children would not be home for another fortnight. I called back again at the end of the fortnight. I was told they had received no word from Miss Stirling and they could not say when the children would be home but that they would probably be back in another week.

'They told me to call back in a week and I did so and was told the children were not there. It was the matron who told me.

'I recollect on another occasion, in 1885, being informed that the children were in Burntisland, for the summer.

'That sort of thing continued until I was told that the children had been taken away to America.'

Mr Stewart – 'Who told you the children had been taken away to America?'

Arthur Delaney – 'It was a girl in the High Street, who worked in the same place as my sister, who told me that.

'She told me my children had been sent to America with a lot of others.'

Mr Stewart – 'What did you do then?'

Arthur Delaney – 'I went to the home, MacKenzie Place, the following morning. I was referred to the secretary, Mr MacDonald and I went to him but he would give me no information.'

Mr Stewart – 'What did Mr MacDonald say to you?'

Arthur Delaney – 'He denied at first knowing anything about them. He said I might call again the next day and I did so.

'He told me he had looked up the books and that Robina had been sent away three months before, and that James and Annie were still in this country: but he declined to tell me where.'

Mr Stewart – 'What did you do then?'

Arthur Delaney – 'I went to Father Hannan for advice and was advised to contact a law-agent, Mr Considine. I then went to Mr Considine.

'I left the matter in his hands.

'I received a letter from him dated, 3rd December 1886, in which he said that from what he gathered the children had been brought back.'

Mr Stewart – 'What did you do then?'

Arthur Delaney – 'I went to the Homes next morning and they referred me to Mr MacDonald.

'I also went to Miss Stirling's at Wardie but was refused admission.

'I went to Mr MacDonald's office in the company of my uncle, Thomas Delaney.'

Mr Stewart – 'And what did Mr MacDonald say to you?'

Arthur Delaney – 'At first he denied knowing anything about it, and I called his attention to the fact that he was the secretary, and then he said – "Well, Delaney, my instructions are to give you no information, and to ask more questions is unnecessary" and he ordered me and my uncle out.'

Mr Stewart – 'Did you visit his office again?'

Arthur Delaney – 'Yes, I called on him again shortly after that, and he advised me to wait, and he would get Miss Stirling advised to return the children. He admitted it would be wrong to keep them without my consent. From that time to the end of the year, I called frequently on Mr MacDonald, and when I met him on the street I asked for the children.'

Mr Stewart – 'When did you next see Miss Stirling around this time?'

Arthur Delaney – 'The first time I knew of Miss Stirling being in this country, after I heard the children had been brought back, was when I saw her carriage in the High Street. I cannot say exactly when this was but it would be about January, last year.

'I followed her carriage to one of the branch Homes in the High Street. I went in after her and had an interview with her. There was a detective officer or Court usher present and also a little girl.

'I asked her if she was to give up my children, and she said, "No". I then went to the Police Office and reported that my children were being kept from me.'

Mr Stewart – 'Was this January meeting about a month after Mr Considine informed you the children were back?'

Arthur Delaney – 'At all events I know for certain that it was some time previous to Miss Stirling going away – not very long before she went away.'

Mr Stewart – 'About this time last year?'

Arthur Delaney – 'Yes. After I got Miss Stirling's refusal to give me my children I took steps to get on the Poor Roll.'

Arthur was shown a letter dated 3rd February 1888.

Arthur Delaney – 'Yes, I received that letter. During the whole period from the time Mr Considine ceased to act for me I was too poor to obtain the services of a law-agent.'

Mr Stewart – 'Did you ever authorise anyone to abandon your claim for your children?'

Arthur Delaney – 'I never authorised any one to intimate to the respondents in this case that I had abandoned my claim for my children. I made no such intimation myself.'

Arthur was then cross-examined by Mr Gray, law-agent for the Directors.

Mr Gray – 'With whom did you make the arrangements to pay for board for your children?'

Arthur Delaney – 'It was with the matron of the institution that I made the arrangements to pay 5s a week of board for my children. The matron was Miss

McNee, I think. She was the only person I saw previous to the children going into the home, except the doctor who passed them.'

Mr Gray – 'Did you get receipts for the money you paid her?'

Arthur Delaney – 'I did get receipts for the money I paid her, they were sent to me.'

Mr Gray – 'Did you always get receipts?'

Arthur Delaney – 'I did not get receipts for all the money I paid. After the children had been about eighteen months in the Home, I got three receipts acknowledging payment of £1.17s. These were all the receipts I got.'

Mr Gray – 'How much did you pay in total?'

Arthur Delaney – 'I cannot remember the exact sum I paid. I will produce the receipts I did get.'

At this point Mr Stewart, Arthur Delaney's law-agent intervened.

Mr Stewart – 'I object to this line of questioning, your Honour, the respondents have already admitted it is not relevant to the case in hand.'

The judge upheld the complaint and ordered Mr Gray to desist from that line of questioning
Mr Stewart then rose to question his client, Mr Delaney.

Mr Stewart – 'When did you place your children in the Home?'

Arthur Delaney – 'The children entered the home in December 1882, about six months after the death of my wife. I was working as a painter at the time. I am working at the same trade now. I was working about half-time, making about 15s a week, sometimes less.'

Mr Stewart – 'Have you remained in Edinburgh throughout the time your children were in the Home?'

Arthur Delaney – 'Yes.'

Mr Stewart – 'Who did you see when you went to visit your children in the Home.'

Arthur Delaney – 'Sometimes I saw Miss McNee and on other occasions I saw other matrons or nurses. I cannot tell the names of any of them. As a rule it was a different one every time I went down.'

Mr Stewart – 'Did any other members of your family visit the children?'

Arthur Delaney – 'My mother and my sister visited often. Sometimes I sent them when I could not get myself and sometimes they went of their own accord.'

Mr Stewart – 'Did you always see your children when you went to the Home?'

Arthur Delaney – 'No, sometimes a nurse told me that they were not in MacKenzie Place. They had been sent to the country, to Moffat.'

Mr Stewart – 'Did you visit your children when they were at Moffat?'

Arthur Delaney – 'No, I was told that visiting was not permitted as they were in private homes.'

Mr Stewart – 'Did you visit your children anywhere else, apart from MacKenzie Place?'

Arthur Delaney – 'I have visited the children frequently at Wardie, and also at Joppa; but that was at a later date.'

Mr Stewart – 'Were you ever told they were elsewhere, apart from Moffat?'

Arthur Delaney – 'Yes, I was often told they were in the Home in Burntisland for the summer months.'

Mr Stewart – 'Did you ever visit them there?'

Arthur Delaney – 'I was unable to visit them while they were at Burntisland but my mother went in my place. I was never anywhere else. These are the only places where I got their address.'

Mr Stewart – 'When did you hear that the children had been sent to Canada?'

Arthur Delaney – 'It was two months after I was married that I heard about the children being in Canada. I had been calling at MacKenzie Place but was told the children were away in the country. It will be three years come July that I was married, and it was in September that I heard about the children. It was after that that I went to see Mr MacDonald.'

Mr Stewart – 'When did you first meet Miss Stirling?'

Arthur Delaney – 'My first interview with Miss Stirling was about eighteen months after the children went into the Home. She was going away when they went in so I did not meet her then. It was not I who applied for the children to get in, it was a missionary lady who suggested and arranged it.'

Mr Stewart – 'Did you meet Miss Stirling again?'

Arthur Delaney – 'I had only one interview with Miss Stirling when I went to see the children. I saw James where he was boarded out at Bayton Terrace, in Granton, and he took me to see Annie at, Merleton, Miss Stirling's private residence, at Wardie. Annie was staying there at the time; she was in bad health and later Miss Stirling sent her to the country.'

Mr Stewart – 'Was there anyone else present when you had your interview with Mr McDonald?'

Arthur Delaney – 'There was no one present at my first interview with Mr McDonald. My uncle, Thomas Delaney, was only present at one interview; but on several occasions he accompanied me to the door and waited outside. The occasion he went in with me was the day after I had received Mr Considine's letter, stating that, from what he could gather the children had been brought back to this country.'

Mr Stewart – 'Were you in correspondence with Mr Considine?'

Arthur Delaney – 'I never wrote to him. I called on him in answer to his letter of 28 January, 1887, and explained that Canon Hannan, who had recommended me to him, had said I was to do nothing in the meantime, and he would endeavour to get up a subscription to enable me to proceed with the Petition.'

Mr Stewart – 'And had Canon Hannan been able to help?'

Arthur Delaney – 'I asked him dozens of times, at the chapel, and he always gave me to understand that he was doing what he could. But fourteen months after this I asked if he had succeeded in getting up enough of a subscription but he said he could do nothing further for me.'

Mr Stewart – 'Were you in employment during this period?'

Arthur Delaney – 'I was working a little in the summer of 1887, but in the winter there was very little work available. In the summer I might earn 25s a week.'

Mr Stewart – 'Was Mr Considine intending to proceed with the Petition?'

Arthur Delaney – 'I understood from him that he had everything ready to present when funds became available. I was led to understand by Mr Considine that it would take about £25 to proceed with the Petition. But because Canon Hannan was unable to help further we could not proceed. I had no money and was unaware, at that time, of the Poor Roll.'

Mr Stewart – 'What did Mr Considine suggest you do next.'

Arthur Delaney – 'When he saw that Canon Hannan could do nothing further he recommended that I get on the Poor Roll. This I did and instructed an action be taken against Miss Stirling.'

At this Mr Gray, law-agent for the Directors, intervened.

Mr Gray – 'Was not your reason for proposing to go against her, because Mr Considine told you it was she who was refusing to part with the children?'

Arthur Delaney – 'No, it was because Miss Stirling herself told me that in the High Street.'

Mr Gray – 'And therefore it was to her that you were looking to give up the children?'

Arthur Delaney – 'No, it was not. I was looking to the Directors as well as to her.'

Mr Gray – 'Why then did you instruct the action to be taken against Miss Stirling?'

Arthur Delaney – 'I did not instruct the action to be taken against Miss Stirling only.'

Mr Gray – 'You have already said you instructed it to be taken against Miss Stirling.'

Arthur Delaney – 'I instructed it to be taken against anyone who had to do with the Home, to get my children back again. Mr Considine told me the Directors said the removal of the children was entirely the act of Miss Stirling.'

Mr Gray – 'Why did you abandon the case?'

Arthur Delaney – 'I never abandoned the case. Canon Hannan got a little money with the view of enabling me to proceed with the case, but not sufficient. He told my uncle how much he got, but I don't recollect the sum.'

After this Mr Stewart, for Arthur Delaney, continued his examination.

Mr Stewart – 'How anxious were you to have your children returned to you? Did you continue to press your case?'

Arthur Delaney – 'Between January 1887 and January 1888 I called frequently at Miss Stirling's private residence, at the Homes, and at Mr MacDonald's office about my children. When I went to consult my present agent I left it entirely to him to decide who should be the respondents. Want of money was the sole reason why I did not instruct Mr Considine further.'

Mr Arthur Delaney stood down.
The Court then called John MacPherson to the witness stand.

Mr Stewart – 'Could you state your name and profession?'

Mr MacPherson – 'My name is John MacPherson and I am employed as a detective officer.'

Mr Stewart – 'And what light can you shed on the proceedings of this Court?'

Mr MacPherson – 'I recollect one day in January 1888 being in a room in the High Street with the Petitioner, Arthur Delaney, and Miss Stirling when he demanded his children from Miss Stirling, or to know where they were, and he got no information. She refused to tell him where they were.'

Mr Stewart – 'Would you say that the Petitioner was very anxious to have his children returned to him?'

Mr MacPherson – 'I understood from her remarks that the Petitioner had been bothering her very much to get the children.'

Mr MacPherson stood down.
The Court then called Mrs Ann Delaney to the witness stand.

Mr Stewart – 'Could you please give us your name and your relationship to the Petitioner?'

Ann Delaney – 'My name is Ann Delaney and I am the mother of the Petitioner.'

Mr Stewart – 'When did your son return to live with you?'

Ann Delaney – 'He came to live with me after his first wife's death. I don't remember how long he lived with me; he was away and back again. He was off and on with me certainly over a year.'

Mr Stewart – 'May it have been two years?'

Ann Delaney – 'I think about that.'

Mr Stewart – 'Did you keep in contact with the Petitioner's children?'

Ann Delaney – 'Yes, I used to visit them in the Homes of the Edinburgh and Leith Children's Aid and Refuge. I went to see them frequently. I did not always see them, sometimes they were away in the country. Sometimes I only saw one of them and sometimes two. I remember taking a cab to MacKenzie Place to see Annie and Robina when they were ill with bronchitis as I was not able to walk.'

Mr Stewart – 'Did you visit the children anywhere else except the Edinburgh Homes?'

Ann Delaney – 'I remember seeing James at Burntisland on the Queen's Birthday in 1886.'

Mr Stewart – 'Did your son also visit his children?'

Ann Delaney – 'Yes, he visited them frequently.'

Mr Stewart – 'The respondents argue that your son abandoned his children and never visited them is that true?'

Ann Delaney – 'Certainly not! My son, myself, and my daughter Nellie, visited the children frequently when they were in Edinburgh and even in Burntisland. We could not visit during all the months they were in the country as they were boarded out in private homes and we were not given the address.'

Mrs Ann Delaney then stood down.
The Court then called Thomas Delaney to the witness stand.

Mr Stewart – 'Could you please tell the Court your name and your relationship to the Petitioner?'

Thomas Delaney – 'My name is Thomas Delaney and I am the Petitioner's uncle.'

Mr Stewart – 'Could you describe to the Court your role in this matter?'

Thomas Delaney – 'I recollect on one occasion going with my nephew to call on Mr MacDonald. I had been to Mr MacDonald's with him previously but had never gone in. On this occasion I went in.'

Mr Stewart – 'What did you hear your nephew say at this meeting?'

Thomas Delaney – 'My nephew asked about his children and said he had heard they had been taken away to Nova Scotia. Mr MacDonald asked who had told him that, and he made no answer. My nephew again asked where the children were, and Mr MacDonald said he did not know.'

Mr Stewart – 'And what did the Petitioner say then?'

Thomas Delaney – 'My nephew said he was a strange secretary of a society not to know where the children were.'

Mr Stewart – 'And what was Mr MacDonald's reply?'

Thomas Delaney – 'Mr MacDonald said, "Well, Delaney, my instructions are to give you no information about them."'

Mr Stewart – 'And what did the Petitioner say then?'

Thomas Delaney – 'My nephew said he would compel him to tell by going to law.'

Mr Stewart – 'And what was Mr MacDonald's response?'

Thomas Delaney – 'He said, "Tut, tut, there's no use going to law. How could you go to law about it?"'

Mr Stewart – 'After this visit did the Petitioner continue to demand the return of his children?'

Thomas Delaney – 'Yes, he did. My nephew was repeatedly at Mr MacDonald's office between 1887 and 1888. I was with him on several occasions during that period.'

Mr Stewart – 'Did the Petitioner visit his children while they were in the Homes prior to being taken to Nova Scotia?'

Thomas Delaney – 'Yes, he often told me of his visits.'

Thomas Delaney then stood down and Ross Stewart declared the Petitioner, Arthur Delaney's Proof closed.

Cecilia made her way downstairs and waited until Arthur, Anne and Thomas came through the doors from the Court.

As soon as Arthur saw her he burst out - 'How did a do, Cecilia?'

'You did really well, Arthur, a was so proud of you', she replied.

She turned to her mother-in-law and old Thomas – 'And you were both grand. The judges must have been impressed with you all', she said.

'Sure, a wouldn't like to go through that again', Anne said. 'A was terrified standing up there in the witness box wi all the eyes in the Court on me.'

'Aye, it wis dauntin right enough,' old Thomas said. 'But we told the truth and that's a we could dae.'

'A'm really grateful to ye both for a your support,' Arthur said. 'A ken it was no easy, but surely now they'll believe me.'

CHAPTER 4

Three months were to elapse before, on 7th June, the judge returned to deliver his verdict.

This time Cecilia and Arthur sat together in the Court their hands tightly entwined.

The verdict went in Arthur's favour!

The judge ruled that he was a fit and proper person to have possession of his children, that he was married to a respectable woman and that he had a home to take them to. He ruled that his children had been taken from him illegally. The Directors were ordered to take steps immediately to have his children returned.

Arthur had leapt to his feet as the verdict was announced but Cecilia pulled him back down not wanting him to draw censure from the court officials.

When they arrived back home, family and neighbours crowded into the house to help them celebrate the good news.

A few days later Ross Stewart had delivered to them a copy of the submission to the Court from the Directors' lawyer, Mr. Lorimer, that had been presented to the Court after Arthur and Cecilia had left.

It read –

THE COURT OF SESSION EDINBURGH

7 JUNE 1889

Mr Lorimer agent for the Directors was called to the court. He made the following statement.

Mr Lorimer - 'In consequence of the expression of opinion by the court that the prayer of the petition could not be refused, the respondents undertake to apply forthwith to Miss Stirling for the return of the children to them, and, if necessary to take proceedings in the Canadian courts for that purpose; and they crave that in the meantime any judgement pronounced by the court should be limited to the first finding in the prayer of the petition, namely, that the petitioner is entitled to the custody of his children.'

The Lord President - 'When Arthur Delaney applied to the Court to have his children admitted to the Refuge, they had been received by Miss Stirling and it did not appear that anybody else was responsible for the custody of the children, at that time, except her.

'But it must be quite clear, I think, that when the respondents became Directors of this Institution in the year 1884 they assumed a responsibility for the safe custody of all the children that were in these Homes or in other places belonging to the institution.

And among other obligations and responsibilities which they thus incurred by becoming directors was the obligation to redeliver the children to their parents when they were demanded.

'Now, in point of fact, these children were taken out of the jurisdiction of this Court and out of the United Kingdom in 1886, and that was certainly a most indefensible proceeding. Nothing could justify that without the consent of the parents.

'The respondents, the directors of the institution, seem to have been sensible of that very fact after it took place, and they remonstrated with Miss Stirling, who had carried the children to Nova Scotia, and desired her to bring them back. In that I think they acted quite rightly.

'But, then, I think, they acted very far short of their duty after the children were brought back to this country, because they allowed Miss Stirling, after she had brought the children to the neighbourhood of Edinburgh, to conceal them from their parents, and also from the respondents themselves.

'Indeed, there is an appearance on the part of the respondents of an indisposition to acquire any knowledge of where the children were, and to all applications on the part of the Petitioner for access to his children there could be no satisfactory answer made.

'The consequence was that the children were again carried out of the country. Now, for that I think the respondents must be answerable, because they

were thus violating the obligation which they had undertaken to be responsible for the safe custody of the children while they were in the institution, and to deliver them when the parents required them.

'It is therefore, I think, impossible not to say that the respondents are under an obligation to deliver these children now to the petitioner; and the only question of course which perplexes one in dealing with the case is, that as the children are not here, it may require the lapse of some considerable time, perhaps proceedings in another country, in order to accomplish the object for which this petition was presented.

'I approve entirely of the spirit in which the minute is expressed, which Mr Lorimer has just read, and I am very glad to find from that that the respondents are now fully alive as to what their responsibilities are.

'But I think it would be hardly consistent with the duty of the court to abstain now from pronouncing an order against the respondents for the redelivery of the children. Of course that must be qualified to this extent, that they must have time.

'The order which I would propose, with your Lordships' concurrence, to pronounce, is to ordain the whole parties called as respondents in the petition to deliver to the petitioner his children James, Annie and Robina Delaney, named in the petition, and that on or before the first sederunt-day in October next; and further, appoint the

respondents to report to the court on Thursday 18th July next, what steps have been taken in pursuance of this order.'

Ross Stewart also enclosed a copy of a minute dated 11th June that the Directors had sent to him to show they were complying with the Court's order.

It read –

THE EDINBURGH & LEITH CHILDREN'S AID & REFUGE SOCIETY

MINUTE

MINUTES of a special meeting of the Directors of The Edinburgh & Leith Children's Aid & Refuge Society on 11th June 1889.

That with a view of carrying out in the most stringent form the injunctions of the Court of Session as given in their order of the 7th June, a solicitor be employed at Halifax, Nova Scotia, to wait on Miss Stirling and ask her in a kind, but resolute manner to produce or give needful information toward the production of the Delaney children and send them home, or if she refuses, to take immediate legal steps to enforce the requirements, telegraphing her that in furtherance of this procedure a statement of the whole case should be sent to the solicitor with a copy of the detailed opinion of the judges, and that the directors while wishing every consideration and kindness to Miss Stirling are obliged unavoidably to protect their own position by taking decided measures.

Mr Young strongly deprecated employing a solicitor without first communicating with Miss Stirling, as he felt sure when the matter was fully put before her she would at once give up the children, in his opinion, the Directors object would be more likely to be obtained by such a course than by that proposed by Dr Bell.

Dr Bell objected to writing to Miss Stirling first as in the event of Miss Stirling hiding the children away, the court might look on such action as collusion with Miss Stirling on the part of the Directors. To meet Mr Young, Dr Bell amended his motion by suggesting that a messenger be sent to Nova Scotia with full powers to act. On this motion being tabled, the secretary being referred to and asked whether he could conveniently go to Halifax stated his readiness, if armed with full powers to proceed at once to Nova Scotia and act if need be officially on behalf of the directors, and to take such measures as might be judicious and necessary to bring back the children to this country with a view of carrying out the court's decision. It was resolved accordingly.

Arthur looked at Cecilia, his face full of hope.

'He's gone to bring the bairns home, Cecilia!' he cried.

Cecilia burst into tears – she was so relieved. Then wiping her eyes she became her usual practical self.

'Well, we will have to find a bigger hoose,' she said, 'we won't all fit in here.'

Within a few days they had found a house at 153 High Street, and had bought three truckle beds for the extra room.

HELEN'S STORY

PART SIX

CHAPTER 1

19th July 1889

Helen stood on the platform of the Carlisle Railway Station holding the arm of her son Luke Boylan. They were awaiting the arrival of the train from London carrying the Member of Parliament for Cork, in Ireland, Mr Charles Stewart Parnell.

Luke was the President of the Edinburgh Branch of the National League and for weeks he had been organising the welcome for the Irish leader.

It still seemed unbelievable to Helen, after the long years of struggle, and all the opposition they had faced, that Luke and his members on the Committee of the United Liberal Association, along with the Working Men's Committee, had managed to persuade the Town Council to present Mr Parnell with the Freedom of Edinburgh!

When Luke had finally had it confirmed that the great Parnell would be coming to Edinburgh, to receive the honour, he had burst into Helen's flat on George IV Bridge like an excited child! He had explained that the Committee intended travelling down to meet the train at Carlisle to welcome Mr Parnell and then travel back on his train to Edinburgh with him.

Luke had a request for Helen. Would she travel down with him to Carlisle?

Helen had hesitated.

'You know, Luke, that you should have your wife by your side, not your mother,' she had said, gently.

She had seen the joy drain from his face and a look of bitterness pass over it.

You know, Mother, that is not possible,' he had said. 'Patricia is unwell again.'

Helen knew that Patricia was not unwell. She was drunk again. But Luke would never admit that it was the abuse of spirits that caused his wife's frequent collapses.

'It would be most unsuitable if she was to take one of her fits on such an important occasion,' he had continued.

Helen had known this was true and so, reluctantly, she had agreed to be the lady on her son's arm, for convention's sake.

It was not that Helen did not want to meet Mr Parnell. She had admired his work for many years and she knew how much Home Rule for Ireland meant to her son. But Helen had concerns much closer to home, apart from her worry about Patricia's drinking and the state of the couple's marriage.

Her grandson, Arthur, had discovered that the children he had put into a Children's Home, after his first wife had died, had been taken to Nova Scotia without his knowing. He had been fighting a three year battle through the Courts, both here and in Canada, to have his children returned to him. Helen had been horrified to hear of it and when the woman responsible for abducting the children, Emma Stirling, had claimed she no longer knew where they were, Helen had been distraught.

She well remembered when Arthur used to bring the bairns into her sweetie shop all those years ago, and now they were lost somewhere in the wilderness of Canada with no one to look after them!

She had given a witness statement to Arthur's solicitor as to his character, and his care and concern for his children, when he first took legal advice to have them returned.

How she wished now that she had tried to help him before the bairns went into the Home. But Luke had refused to allow her to offer to look after the children. She was much too old to take on such a commitment, he had argued. Helen had supposed he was right but she still felt guilty, and now this had happened!

Helen had urged Luke to give Arthur financial assistance to bring the Court case. He had given money to Canon Hannan's appeal but Helen didn't know how much. When Arthur said he could not pursue the case because it would take £25 Helen had begged Luke to help.

She remembered his response.

'Mother,' he had said, 'twenty-five pounds is a lot of money, and it wouldn't stop there. You don't understand the law. You haven't seen any poor lawyers have you? They would soon be demanding more and more money to pursue the case. Better not to start', he had argued.

Helen couldn't help thinking that Luke might have been more understanding if he had bairns of his own, but he and Patricia remained childless.

So, Arthur's case could not continue. But her grandson would not give up. He was demented with worry about the lost bairns. He got himself on the Poor Roll and managed to get one of their solicitors to fight the case on a no win no fee basis.

The reason that Helen could not get as enthusiastic as Luke about Mr Parnell's visit was that Arthur had told her that, at last, the Directors of the Home in Edinburgh had agreed to send their Secretary to search for the bairns. The man was in Canada at this very moment. Helen could think of nothing else.

She looked up at Luke. He was craning his neck to see if the train was coming. Helen thought, well, at least Arthur had one blessing that her son lacked, he had a good wife. Arthur's second wife, Cecilia Clifford, was a lovely, devout woman. She came from a highly respected family in the Old Town. She had supported Arthur at every point of his fight to have his bairns returned.

Just then a shout went up from the assembled crowd and Helen saw, down the line, the London train puffing slowly as it approached the platform. It drew up with a screech of brakes amid hissing steam.

As the train came to a halt, Helen saw Councillor Pollard and Mr Train Gray board the train and walk down the row of carriages seeking the one that contained Mr Parnell. They had been deputed by the Edinburgh United Liberal Committee to give the official welcome to the Irish leader. They appeared at the window of one of the carriages that had stopped just opposite where Luke and Helen stood. Beside them, Helen saw a tall, handsome man framed in the window, which was open. His hand was being shaken vigorously by the two men.

The crowd outside surged forward and congregated outside the carriage window. Mr Parnell appeared at the open window and a few people at the front insisted on shaking hands with their great hero. One enthusiastic lady, of middle age, pressed forward, took Mr Parnell by the hand and uttered a fervent, "God Bless you". Her sentiments were taken up and repeated by many other men and women gathered around.

Just then Councillor Pollard spotted Luke and gestured for him to come forward to be introduced. Luke shouldered his way through the crowd, Helen on his arm, and moved up to the window. The Councillor introduced Luke as the President of the National League and Luke, his eyes shining, shook the great man by the hand.

Luke then turned and said – 'Mr Parnell, may I present my mother?'

Helen looked up into the saddest pair of eyes she had ever seen. The man smiled, took her gloved hand and kissed it.

'I am honoured to meet you Ma'am,' he said. 'I hear your son is doing great work for the Cause.'

Luke asked if the gentleman would be prepared to address the crowd and was backed up by the rest of the deputation from the National League.

Helen thought Mr Parnell was disinclined to do this. He suggested that the station authorities might not deem it altogether desirable, and pleaded that after his post lunch nap he had not had time to collect his thoughts. Luke realised that the guards were indeed walking along closing doors, so he hurriedly helped Helen into a nearby carriage lest they be left behind.

Mr Parnell remained standing at the window as the train departed, and above the sound of the whistle Helen heard the crowd left behind on the platform raise a resounding cheer. When she put her head out the window she saw that hats, sticks and handkerchiefs were being waved as the train moved away.

To her alarm Helen also saw half a dozen men clinging to the moving carriage in their desire to see him!

Once the train was underway Luke led Helen through to Mr Parnell's compartment, in the first class carriage, where Councillor Pollard and Mr Gray were already ensconced. Another man was also there, who, Helen later learned, was Mr Parnell's private secretary, Mr Henry Campbell, M.P. for Fermanagh. As they joined them, Helen noticed that only Mr Parnell rose from his seat and gave a short bow when she entered. He remained standing until Helen was seated.

Luke and the other two men began to tell Mr Parnell the arrangements they had made for his brief stay in Edinburgh.

Sitting in the corner, Helen was able to examine the great man as they talked.

He was very smartly dressed in a light check suit and satin hat, but Helen thought he looked very pale and careworn. No doubt his tour was very demanding. However, he seemed touched and pleased with the terms of the addresses that were to be presented to him.

Looking out the carriage window as they approached Edinburgh, Helen could see that Irish flags hung from many windows along the rail route, through Dalry, and people were leaning out of windows waving their handkerchiefs.

Luke had already told Helen about the arrangements he had made for Mr Parnell's arrival in Edinburgh. To avoid overcrowding, Chief Constable Henderson had insisted that a quarter of an hour before the train was due to arrive the police would clear the platform. Admission would be restricted to pass holders, only about fifty of which had been issued.

As the train drew into the Caledonian Station Helen could see that something must have gone amiss with this plan. A huge crowd, far exceeding fifty, crowded the platform, shouting and cheering.

Helen could see a Reception Committee drawn up and she recognised many of them. Bailie Steel was there, and Bailie Walcott, chairman of the United Liberal Committee. As Mr Parnell and his secretary began to gather together their belongings, Luke lent out the window and pointed out two prominent Members of Parliament and several town councillors to Helen.

'Well, well,' he added. 'Looks like the legal profession doesn't want to miss out. There's the solicitors, Thomas McNaught and Ainslie Brown, and Mr McKie, the advocate, and Mr MacKay, the Justice of the Peace.'

Helen herself could recognise the clergy. Canon Hannan and his curate, Fr George Culhane of St Patrick's and Fr Steven Culhane, a priest from Dunfermline, who was very supportive of the Cause.

She could see that many of the Liberal Committee wore green and yellow rosettes on their coats.

Having been held up by the reception at Carlisle, the train had never made up lost time and it was about a quarter to seven when it entered the station.

Luke, Helen, and the others withdrew into the compartment to allow Mr Parnell and his secretary to alight first. Before he left, Mr Parnell bowed over Helen's hand and said he hoped that he would have the pleasure of meeting her again during his visit.

When the door of the carriage was opened and Mr Parnell stepped out, the orderly line of people broke and amid loud cheers and a great deal of jostling and disorder the crowd pressed forward to the edge of the platform.

Mr Waterson was already at the door of the compartment, but before Bailie Walcott and the office bearers of the Liberal Committee had elbowed their way forward, Mr Parnell had stepped down and a loud cheer was again raised.

Helen and Luke alighted from the carriage unnoticed and watched it all unfolding. Enthusiastic admirers pushed forward determined to get within hand-shaking distance of their hero. All ceremony was thrown aside and it took a group of burly constables to clear a passage to allow the party to exit from the side entrance of the station into Rutland Street.

Helen saw two porters trying, in vain, to reach Mr Parnell and relieve him of his luggage. However, they could not get near and he had to carry his own 'Gladstone Bag' to the horse-drawn carriage which waited at the station door.

Helen could not see past the immense crowd, but she realised Mr Parnell had stepped out on to the pavement from the roar that welcomed him from an even larger crowd waiting outside.

Luke ushered Helen into the passageway through the crowd which had been cleared by the police. When they reached the pavement outside they could see Mr Parnell attempting to climb into a carriage, but so many people wanted to shake his hand his progress was slow. Helen could see he was also finding it difficult to shake hands with people as he was hampered by having to hold his travelling bag.

The carriage behind had been reserved for Luke and the other Committee Office Bearers. Luke helped his mother to climb aboard. She could see that the body of stewards from the Arrangements Committee, wearing rosettes of white, orange and green ribbons, had taken up position at the end of Rutland Street.

Seeing Luke, Neil McLean, who was in charge of that Committee, came up and reported that all was in order.

Neil had agreed to marshal the procession of working men and Irish League contingents. They were accompanied by Messrs Miller and Richards's brass band.

When Parnell's carriage at last moved out of the precincts of the station they were faced with the body of stewards and their brass band. They unfurled a banner bearing the inscription – "Welcome to our city, leader of the Irish people".

It was a magnificent banner and Helen, who had a good view of it, could see that the inscription was surrounded by thistles.

As their carriage waited in line, Helen glanced down and saw an itinerant dealer in photographs had laid out his case on the pavement and was calling out his wares. He was attempting to sell photographs of Mr Parnell, Mr Gladstone and other Irish sympathisers. Her mind went instantly to her son, James Delaney, who had also tried to earn a living through photography. Tears welled up in her eyes, for James had died last year in the Union Workhouse in Wigan. He had been working as a photographer in the town, but when he became ill with a heart condition and unable to work, he had been admitted to the workhouse. He had been ill for two months, but it wasn't until he had died and had been buried that his wife, Ann, had received word from the authorities. It broke Helen's heart that her sensitive, gifted son had ended his days in the company of strangers. He was forty-eight years old.

The carriage jolted and brought Helen back to the present for now they were on the move. After allowing Parnell time to read the banner, the group of stewards and the brass band about turned and marched off ahead of his carriage. As they turned Helen was able to read the obverse side of the banner. It read "Self-Government is true unity" above an illustration of clasped hands, while below it continued "We shake hands across the gulf of misrule".

As the stewards and their brass band marched slowly out into Princes Street four mounted policemen rode forward and took up position ahead of them.

When the carriage containing Parnell was spotted a huge cheer went up! The vehicle belonged to Mr Buchanan, the M.P., and the horses sported green favours. Seated beside Parnell were the Member of Parliament, his wife, his elderly mother, and Bailie Walcott.

Waiting on Lothian Road was the Edinburgh Catholic Young Men's Society's flute band. As they marched past, to take up position behind the Irish leader's vehicle, Helen recognised each one of them for this was their very own band from St Patrick's Church.

How her son, John Delaney, would have loved to have been here to see all this, she thought. Most of his own young days had been spent with the Catholic Young Men's Society. But John, too, was dead. He had been dead for five years. He had become a successful actor and had even been given a contract by a Broadway Theatre agent in America. He went on a whistle-stop tour of all the main theatres in the various States, appearing for one night only in his most famous role. But the loneliness and stress of such a lifestyle had ruined John's health and so, when he was touring in a production, he collapsed in Oldham, Lancashire. He was taken to the Union Workhouse there and died shortly after.

He was only thirty-six and he left his wife, Lizzie McAlpine, with a three month old baby, John, and a five year old son, Luke Terence. Luke had been moved when his half-brother had named his first born after him. The two had been close when they were growing up together in St Mary's Street.

Six months later, Lizzie had brought the children to Edinburgh to see their grandmother. Helen was really touched that Lizzie had made such an effort, especially with a young baby. The baby had been baptised in St Patrick's when they were on that visit. Fortunately, Lizzie had a supportive family and they were taking good care of her back down in London and Helen heard from her often.

The jolting of the carriage again brought her out of her reverie. The flute band had marched off and Luke's carriage was allowed to move forward. Marching behind them came the Rose Street flute band and next the carriage containing some town councillors. They were followed by the Leith Nationalists's flute band, then the carriages with the rest of the Reception Committee and bringing up the rear was the Musselburgh Brass band.

The noise was unbelievable and as Helen looked around she saw that the whole area from Shandwick Place to Lothian Road was a teeming mass of people. Constables on foot struggled to hold back the crowds and mounted police rode alongside Parnell's carriage.

Luke looked concerned and scanned the crowds anxiously. He had heard a rumour that a body of two thousand Orangemen, from the west, were converging on Edinburgh. On hearing this, five thousand Leaguers had set off in pursuit. He wanted no trouble to spoil this great day that he had worked so hard to bring about.

The Magistrates had ordered that all carriage traffic on the main thoroughfare should cease after six o'clock to allow the Procession to pass. As they followed

Parnell's carriage along Princes Street, Helen realised it had been a wise decision. The crowd spilled out onto the road, only the rows of mounted police preventing them encroaching on their hero's carriage. Looking out from their own carriage, Helen thought that surely every Irishman and a fair number of the Irishwomen in the city had turned out.

Helen knew that as part of the planning, Luke and the Committee had sent out word to all the Gladstonian and Irish Associations in the surrounding districts, to get their members to come into the town to show support for the great man.

All along Princes Street the windows and balconies of the houses were occupied. Helen suddenly heard jeering from sections of the procession and, glancing up, saw that they were passing the Conservative Club. The balcony was deserted but Helen could see faces at some of the windows.

'Afraid to show their faces,' Luke laughed.

Many ladies were in evidence, on other balconies, dressed in all their finery. It was well known that Mr Parnell was regarded as very handsome and dashing, and so attracted attention from the ladies that perhaps other politicians might not, Helen thought.

The unbroken lines of people extended along both sides of Princes Street but fortunately, in spite of the mass of people, the behaviour was orderly, and to Luke's relief there was no sign of the rumoured Orangemen.

It was a lovely July evening. Helen thought that Mr Parnell could hardly fail to be impressed at the beauty of this broad thoroughfare dominated by its fine castle. She remembered how she had thought the castle like something out of a fairytale when she had first arrived here to marry her beloved Arthur all those years ago.

The smell from the flowerbeds in the gardens was strong on this warm evening and drifted into the carriage as they passed.

They were approaching the fine Royal Scottish Academy building. Its grand stepped entrance provided an ideal viewing point and people stood on every step and some clung for dear life to the stone pillars. A huge statue of the Queen sat above the pediment of the frontage. Glancing up, Helen remembered that it was believed that Queen Victoria was not very fond of Mr Gladstone. She apparently preferred Mr Disraeli, so she would not approve of this large gathering.

The magnificent stone monument to Sir Walter Scott had obviously caught Mr Parnell's eye because, as he passed it, his carriage slowed and his escort could be seen pointing up at the many statues that decorated its facade. Helen remembered how Arthur had explained to her that these statues represented characters from the writer's novels, and also real life people from Scotland's history.

They passed the grand frontage of Register House. The statue, on the prancing horse, that stood in front of the building was the Duke of Wellington, another Irishman. Helen recalled that Arthur had told her that, too. He had known so much about so many things. I suppose it was all that reading, she thought.

Looking ahead, and behind, Helen could see many banners being carried by the hundreds of people who had joined the procession or who lined the route. Princes Street was crowded with people as far back as the eye could see. It was a memorable sight. Helen felt it must have been one of the largest crowds ever brought together on such an occasion.

She saw some trade banners, several Union Jacks, and several friendly society banners. One just ahead of them read - "Scotland and Ireland united" - and behind them another contained an image of Mr Gladstone, while inscribed below was - "Ireland's friend".

They drove on along Waterloo Place and over the Regent's Bridge. Arthur had told her that to make this road they had to lay it right through the centre of the Old Calton burial ground. She had shuddered as he had explained that they had had to dig up all the bodies that were in the way and rebury them in the New Calton burial ground.

Looming up ahead, Helen could see the slopes of Calton Hill. As they passed the Calton Jail it seemed that, if anything, the crowds here were even deeper.

Parnell's carriage swung on to the drive leading up to the summit of the hill and the other carriages followed. Looking behind, Helen saw that as the last carriage turned the huge crowd surged forward and began to follow the carriages up the hill.

The carriages stopped on a grassed area in front of the National Monument and the horses bent and nibbled the grass. Luke suggested that Helen stay in the carriage as she would get a better view of the ceremony than on the ground. Looking at the surging crowds, Helen was happy to agree. She doubted she could have kept her feet in the midst of all that jostling, but Luke jumped down and ran to take up his position on the platform which had been erected at the gate of the New Observatory building.

There were already hundreds of people on the hill. Some had even ascended the Nelson Monument. Helen thought that they must have had a good view of the procession and the scene down in Princes Street, and now they would have an excellent view of the platform. The base of the Nelson Monument was also full of people and others sat along the walls that surrounded the Observatory.

Above her head, Helen could see that the National Monument of Scotland would also provide a wonderful vantage point and it was already crowded with people sitting on its stone steps. The Monument's huge pillars seemed to tower over her. She felt a bit apprehensive. It looked so much like a ruin that she always felt it might fall down one day.

Arthur had tried to reassure her by telling her that it was not actually a ruin, though it did look like something from ancient Greece or Rome.

But, though it had a grand sounding name and an impressive appearance everyone called it "Scotland's Disgrace".

Helen was puzzled at this, until Arthur had explained that it had been intended as a monument to the war dead of the Napoleonic wars. The money for it was to be raised by public subscription throughout Scotland but in the event they had never raised enough to finish it. So the disgrace lay in not finishing a war memorial.

Helen had said that it was indeed disgraceful but, to her surprise, Arthur had disagreed.

He had explained that, when it was erected, each pillar was reputed to have cost £1000. Now, think what that money could have done for the widows and bairns left behind, he had argued. Sure, their lives would be ones of grinding poverty. Grand schemes are all very well but bairns starving – that's the real disgrace.

Her mind had drifted, but thinking about poor bairns had brought it back to wondering how the Secretary was fairing in Canada. Had he found the bairns yet. What if he couldn't find them. What if they never came home! Helen couldn't bear the thought. She was sure it would kill their father.

Just then there was a burst of applause and much shouting and whistling. Looking up Helen saw that Mr Parnell was mounting the stage. Helen knew that the positioning of the stage was important. Luke had explained that he planned to have it erected on the same spot as the one where the great Irishman, Daniel O'Connell, had addressed a huge open-air meeting here, in 1835.

'But how do you know the exact spot?' Helen had asked.

'My father told me all about it,' Luke had replied. 'He brought me up the hill and showed me.'

Of course, Helen had thought, her second husband, Philip Boylan, had never lost his love of his native Ireland or his hope for the betterment of its people. He would have stood here and cheered the great O'Connell, 'The Liberator', and he would never have forgotten that day or the spot were he stood.

'That's a nice thought, Luke,' Helen had said, 'but it was over fifty years ago, I doubt anyone else will remember.'

His reply had caused Helen's eyes to fill with tears.

'It's not for anyone else,' he had said. 'It's for my father.'

So, as Helen watched her son introduce the great Parnell to the cheering crowd she was sure that, somewhere nearby, Philip's loving ghost was looking on with approval.

The noise was deafening, great outbursts of cheering and people waving their hats. By now the rear of the procession had arrived and there were thousands of people on the hill. Helen had never seen anything like it in her life and doubted she would ever see anything like it again.

The platform party contained all the dignitaries. The two Members of Parliament, several town councillors, Liberal Party leaders and a number of priests. There were only two ladies present, Mrs Buchanan, wife of the Member of Parliament, and Mrs Buchanan Senior, his mother.

Luke called James Lochead to the chair and then sat down. James was the Chairman of the Working Men of Edinburgh and had a fine loud voice. Helen could hear every word even though she was some distance from the platform.

He said that the people of Edinburgh had shown that they were in thorough sympathy with the cause to promote, which they had met this evening.

This was met by a burst of loud cheering.

He then invited the party Secretary, Mr Scott, to read the address which had been prepared for Mr Parnell.

Turning slightly towards where Mr Parnell sat, Mr Scott declared –

'To Charles Stewart Parnell, Esq. M.P., Leader of the Irish People.

'Sir,

'We, the Working Men of Edinburgh, take this opportunity of publicly testifying our appreciation of your high character, personal worth and the great ability you have displayed in guiding the great constitutional movement of which you are the head.'

He was interrupted by a great burst of cheering.

'We have watched, with the greatest interest, the way in which you have hitherto conducted this movement. The judgement and firmness you have displayed calls forth our warmest admiration, while the calmness and dignity with which you have borne the calumnies and vituperation of your political opponents is beyond all praise.'

There now took place a prolonged spell of applause.

'We desire, further, to express through you, to the people of Ireland, our heartfelt sympathy with them, in their long-continued struggle, for the right of self-government, which must at no distant date triumph, however bitter, and unrelenting, be the opposition offered to their demand.'

A voice from the crowd called out – 'Thanks to him' - and this caused another outburst of cheering.

'We ask them to rest assured that, the great mass of the people of Scotland, are with them in their struggle, believing that the consummation of their desires, will be the means of more firmly cementing a true and lasting unity of the people of these islands.

'In conclusion, we would express the hope that you would have health, strength, and a long life to guide the destinies of your country.'

Those on the platform called out, 'Hear! Hear!' to this.

'We feel that Ireland, truly free, her energies at liberty from the distraction of political agitation, has great industrial possibilities, and we believe that a proper development of these would be the means of preventing many of her sons being compelled to leave the soil which is so dear to them; to seek, in other lands, the liberty and security they cannot find at home.

'We declare this in the name and by the authority of the Working Men of Edinburgh.'

Helen watched as Mr Scott returned to his seat amidst rapturous applause.

James Lochead now returned to the front of the platform and the crowd grew quiet and attentive.

He spoke out clearly-

'There is one question that came to the front at present, and that was the unity of the Empire. It was mentioned in the address that they were to be a united nation. What else were they but a united nation?' he asked. 'We are united at this meeting which represented all the nations of Great Britain and Ireland. There is not one on this platform who desired separation. Separation was not good for us. We could not be a united nation if we were separated at all; consequently we must be united.

'I regret that this great question of managing our national affairs was to be tainted with party politics.'

Helen saw the men of the platform applaud and call out, 'Hear! Hear!' again.

But she could see that large sections of the crowd were not in agreement with James's statement. There was a low rumble of discontent at his words and a chorus of, 'Sit down, sit down,' issued from some in the crowd.

James was obviously aware of the change of mood and he quickly brought his remarks to a close by saying that he had the greatest possible pleasure, in the name of the Working Men of Edinburgh, in presenting a copy of the address that had been read out by our Secretary, Mr Scott, to Mr Parnell and he hoped he would be long spared to carry out what was contained in it.

The crowd again cheered and whistled their approval.

Luke had told Helen that there were some believed that Ireland would never prosper until it was a free and independent state. For them, Home Rule was not enough, he had explained.

Helen wasn't sure if the mood change in the crowd had come from that element, or if they had just grown impatient and wanted to hear the great man speak.

Another burst of applause caused Helen to look again at the platform and she saw that Mr Parnell had risen from his seat and was about to address the assembled crowd.

He moved forward to the front of the stage.

His voice rang out loud and clear-

'People of historic Edinburgh, in thanking the working men of this great city for the very beautiful address which has just been presented to me, and also for arranging this magnificent demonstration, I shall use but a very few words. It would be impossible for me in the compass of my voice to attempt to reach even a fractional portion of this vast meeting; but it has given me the greatest pleasure and encouragement to come among the people of

Edinburgh and to see that they can understand that justice to Ireland ...'

At this point such an outburst of cheering took place that Mr Parnell had to pause.

He continued-

'......so far from weakening the greatness of the empire must surely consolidate and increase its strength. Ireland has never been rebellious save under the presence of bitter misgovernment and oppression.'

Again Mr Parnell was interrupted by calls of 'Hear! Hear!' from the platform party and loud cheering from the assembled crowd.

He raised his hand to halt the noise and declared-

'It is not the way of peoples to rise against good government – and Ireland would never have risen against England had you done what you did in 1886 – had you followed in the footsteps of your great leader – and offered to Ireland the hand of friendship. I am thankful to think that the old bad times have gone by and that we shall never again see a return to the evil days of the past – that Ireland and England.....'

A voice from the crowd called out – 'And Scotland' – and another prolonged burst of cheering interrupted the proceedings.

Mr Parnell allowed the cheering to die away before continuing-

'I trust we will henceforth be united in the bonds, the strong and enduring bonds, of friendship, mutual interest, and unity. We know that Ireland will prove a source of strength to the Empire instead of a source of weakness, and you will have the knowledge that you have helped Ireland to become prosperous, and that in giving her her legitimate liberty you have benefited yourselves as well as us.

'There is a part of this address which says truly that the material resources of Ireland can be developed. This is one of the things that we wish – that we ardently long to devote our energies to - to finding, for our people, employment at home so that they may no longer flood the labour markets in Scotland and England....'

At this there were loud cheers from some sections of the crowd.

Mr Parnell went on-

'.....so that they may no longer lower the wages of your working men by their competition, but that they may remain at home – that those of them who are here may return to Ireland and help us with the knowledge they have acquired in your workshops and your factories in developing the industrial resources of our own country.'

This was met by prolonged cheering.

He continued-

'Believe me, that for many years to come, we will be fully occupied in the march of progress in promoting the happiness and welfare of our own people, and that Ireland will thankfully, and in good faith, accept the settlement which Mr Gladstone has offered to it – as an end to the strife of centuries - as a real treaty of peace between the two nations, which will bring comfort and happiness to many an Irish house, and which will leave you with the knowledge and the satisfaction that you no longer have to oppress a people who do not really feel any ill-will against you, and that you have been able to do something to settle this great question, and to bring Ireland, Scotland and England into harmony with each other.

'I thank you from the bottom of my heart for this magnificent reception and demonstration. I know that it has not been given to me personally. I know that it is partly because you desire to help your great leader, Mr Gladstone, to settle this question, and because you desire to encourage us to remain in the peaceable and constitutional attitude that we hold today – because you desire to encourage us to refrain from returning to the provocation which the Tory Government ....'

There was a huge outburst of hooting and booing from the crowd at the mention of the hated Tories.

Parnell waited until it had abated before going on-

'....daily inflicts on our people in Ireland – and also because you are convinced from inquiry and reason that this settlement which Mr Gladstone has proposed is a just settlement – that it can be accepted honourably by us, and that you can yield it to us without fear that it will hurt your own interest – but in the confident belief that it will increase and strengthen the unity of the Empire – and enable this great country – this great Empire – to face her foes abroad, if they should ever arise – and I trust that they never will – with the confidence that she is unity and harmony at home – and that there is no oppression towards anybody in any part of these great dominions.

'I am pleased that this demonstration has come from the working men. I shall always be glad to help the working men of Scotland to obtain their just rights and to maintain their privileges – and whenever the united voice of the Scottish representatives demands a reform believe me that there and then you will have no firmer supporters for Scotland, no men who will walk into the division lobby more united and more firmly in behalf of the liberties of Scotland, than will the Irish representatives, whom I have the honour to lead.'

Helen watched as Mr Parnell gave a short bow and returned to his seat.

The crowd erupted into loud cheers and applause and many hats were thrown into the air!

Helen could see that Luke had leapt to his feet and the other members of the platform party followed his lead and stood in a standing ovation, all looking towards the seated Parnell.

Helen saw Neil McLean detached himself from the group and come to the front of the platform.

He held up his hand for silence and eventually the crowd grew quiet.

Neil called out, 'I move that we accord Mr Parnell our heartiest thanks for his presence and for the words he has spoken to us.' He went on to say that he had a request to make from a Mrs Buchanan of Moray Place.

This announcement was met with laughter from the crowd and more cheering.

Helen, like everyone else in the crowd, knew well the lady to whom he referred. She was the mother of the Member of Parliament, Mr T.R. Buchanan, and was well known in Liberal Party circles in the town. Helen had on many occasions attended social gatherings in the lady's magnificent flat in Moray Place, in the New Town.

Neil held up his hand again and the crowd quietened.

'I am sure,' he said, 'they would respond to a request from such a noble lady, who had such a noble son; and he asked them to accord three hearty Scottish cheers for Mr Parnell.'

The crowd roared its approval!

'Hip, hip,' Neil shouted and the crowd responded with a loud hooray.

After the cheer had been repeated three times other voices took up the call – 'Three cheers for Aberdeen and Rosebery' and 'Three cheers for Gladstone'.

The crowd roared their response to each one.

As the last of the cheers died away, Helen saw Mr Parnell leave the platform followed by Mr Buchanan, escorting his mother, and Bailie Walcott escorting Mrs Buchanan.

As they made their way to the waiting carriage they were practically engulfed by the crowd and disappeared for a time from Helen's view.

She stood up in her own carriage, the better to see, and saw Mr Parnell climb into the carriage and turn to give his hand to the ladies and help them into their seats. The two other men joined them, the driver flicked his whip, and they drove off.

Their departure was met with further outbreaks of cheering and Helen saw Mr Parnell stand up in the carriage, raising his hat and bowing to the right and the left as they descended the hill.

Helen watched until they were out of sight then resumed her seat. Her heart was pounding with the excitement of it all. She felt sure she would never forget this day as long as she lived.

She looked across at the platform and saw that Neil was trying to get the crowd's attention.

At last when the cheers of the people further down the hill began to grow fainter he was able to introduce the next speaker.

He was the Member of Parliament, Mr A.L. Brown. Helen had heard him speak many times. He was a gifted orator and a very witty man and she had always enjoyed listening to him.

'Dear friends,' he began, 'this great gathering was not just an Edinburgh affair, but a Scottish one.'

This was met with roars of approval.

'The country of which we are so proud has this night held out the right hand of fellowship to the great Irish leader, and we all trust that the warm grasp which we have tried to give might be some slight compensation for the long years of calumny and wrong through which he had had to pass.

'Our hearts are full,' he went on, 'not so much of the great work which Mr Parnell has done as a statesman but of the great wrongs that he had had to bear.'

This was met by loud applause and cries of, 'Hear, Hear', from the assembled mass of people.

'It is very easy for us to express our admiration for his work as a statesman, but for the unexampled vituperation that had poured out on him, and for the quiet, patient way in which he had borne it all, their feelings were too deep for words.

'But Scotsmen were men not of words, but of deeds,' he declared.

This met with the approval of the crowd and there was an outbreak of cheering.

'Though in some remote corners of Scotland tyranny, and bigotry, and narrow-mindedness would always flourish, yet they might hope that when the day of the General Election came they would be able to show Mr Parnell that Scotland would return even fewer reactionary members to the Imperial Parliament.....'

A voice from the crowd called out, 'Three cheers for Govan,' and the crowd cheered loudly - and another voice added, 'Three cheers for Ireland itself' – again the assembly roared its approval.

Once the noise had quietened Mr Brown continued-

'We have heard a great deal of talk about the retirement of Mr Parnell from the Commission – from the Tory, from the Liberal Unionists Commission – before which he had been dragged.

'Mr Parnell had been in England two days ago and some people were doubting that was a wise step. But we in Scotland, and more especially in Edinburgh, had no doubts, because in Edinburgh we have an infallible guide .....he paused and was met by a gale of laughter from his audience – we have *The Scotsman* newspaper!'

A voice from the crowd called out, 'Burn *The Scotsman*!'

Helen, like everyone else there, had no need for him to name the newspaper. Everyone concerned in the Cause well knew that *The Scotsman* was its sworn enemy.

There was such an outbreak of hissing and booing that it was a while before the Member of Parliament could continue.

At last, he was able to go on-

'We know that *The Scotsman* is our political barometer. It is a barometer turned upside down.'

More hoots of laughter greeted his comment.

He continued, 'For whenever it said it was fair, we knew it was always wet; and whenever it said that it was raining cats and dogs, we were sure that the sun was shining brightly!

'And so on Wednesday morning, when we saw *The Scotsman* newspaper simply foaming at the mouth ......'

More laughter erupted from his audience.

'.... at the wickedness of Mr Parnell for having retired from this fair-minded Tory and Liberal Unionist Commission – he said so with perfect respect for the Commission, but he said so because it was constituted by the Tories and Liberal Unionists – when we saw *The Scotsman* saying it was so wicked and so immoral, of him, we were absolutely sure that Mr Parnell had taken a wise step.'

Loud and prolonged applause met these comments.

He went on, 'You, the working men of Scotland, had never shown how keen your political instincts were as when you gave that glorious reception to Charles Stewart Parnell and I will tell you why – because he is the greatest friend that they had ever had.'

More loud cheers and calls of 'Hear! Hear!' from the crowd.

'Mr Parnell,' he continued, 'was the first statesman of any eminence who had supported Home Rule as a principle, and not as a necessity. There are many of our statesmen who are going to give Home Rule to Ireland because they could not help it – but Mr Parnell supported Home Rule because it was a good thing in itself.

'Mr Parnell,' he declared, 'was also the first of any eminence who had accorded his adhesion to a principle of Federalism.'

His voice rose, 'Home Rule for Ireland first, but Home Rule for Scotland next!' he shouted.

To Helen's amazement, this declaration received the longest, noisiest response of the whole gathering. The cheers, applause and whistles just went on and on.

Luke, so engrossed in obtaining Home Rule for Ireland, had never mentioned to Helen that there were those, in Scotland, who also desired Home Rule.

No wonder this crowd was so large, she thought. It wasn't just the Irish Community who had turned out. There were hundreds, maybe thousands, of Scots here, too. Their hopes pinned on the thought that if Ireland got Home Rule then their desire for Home Rule for Scotland would surely follow!

Perhaps that was why *The Scotsman* newspaper was so opposed to their Cause. Perhaps it was Home Rule for Scotland they feared. Helen could hardly wait to get home and ask Luke to explain it to her.

As the noise subsided the Member of Parliament was continuing with his speech.

'So long as they adhered to the principles which Charles Stuart Parnell had laid down, so long as they returned Irish members to the Imperial Parliament for the management of Imperial affairs, they could give any amount of Home Rule to Ireland, because it would make Home Rule for Scotland an absolute necessity; and they knew that instead of weakening the Empire that would strengthen it, instead of separating; that would consolidate; and they had never shown how well they were to be trusted with the decision of political affairs as when they had given this great demonstration to Mr Charles Stuart Parnell.'

Helen was glad when, at last, Mr Brown returned to his seat on the platform to huge waves of applause.

She watched as Luke rose from his seat and came to the front of the platform.

'I now have the greatest of pleasure in calling Councillor MacPherson, as our next speaker,' he announced.

Councillor MacPherson was a tall, well-made man, with a shock of silvery hair. He was born a Highlander and he had never lost the lilt in his voice in spite of all his years in the city.

'Friends,' he began, 'as a member of the majority on the Town Council I thank you from the bottom of my heart for this magnificent demonstration. The people of Edinburgh, and beyond, have today given an unprecedented welcome to the leader of the Irish people.'

The crowd responded by cheering him loudly.

'You have seen him in the flesh, you have heard him by the ear, and those present who read *The Scotsman* newspaper .....'

More hissing and booing from the audience broke into his address.

'Such readers must have formed a very peculiar opinion of that gentleman. I am glad that you have seen and looked upon the man whom the Irish people revere as their leader. I believe that from this night forward their confidence in him would deepen, and that the day would yet come when Ireland would have an opportunity of putting Mr Parnell in the position of their Prime Minister.'

This produced another bout of applause.

'Here, today, we have heartily shaken hands with our struggling fellow country in Ireland, and we have declared we are only waiting the hour and the opportunity of sending men to Westminster who would grant them all they required.

'We have further strengthened the heart of the Grand Old Man......'

A voice from the crowd called out, 'Three cheers for Mr Gladstone!'

After the cheering had died away the Councillor continued-

'When he looked at the telegrams this evening announcing the great demonstration, we might well imagine that Mr Gladstone would throw up his hat and say, "Three cheers for Edinburgh, three cheers for Midlothian, and three cheers for Scotland".

'As you well know,' he continued, 'the majority of the Town Council had to go through a trial of no mean order. We have been slanderously vilified day after day for months past. I take it that tonight's demonstration was the people's answer to these slanders.'

Voices from the crowd called out, 'It is! It is!'

'We have many grievances in Scotland to rectify; but Ireland occupied the first place. On that question they were united; and when it was out of the way, we will demand those measures which we, in Scotland, have a right to expect.'

This sentiment was greeted with further cheers from the crowd.

'I look upon this great gathering as a strong confirmation of the wisdom of the course which the majority of us in the Town Council had followed.'

He returned to his seat amid thunderous applause.

Luke now rose and introduced the next speaker, Councillor Pollard.

Helen always felt that Councillor Pollard rather liked the sound of his own voice so she was quite relieved when the man began by saying that he did not think much more required to be said.

'Mr Parnell, tonight, delivered to us a very remarkable speech and I would like to emphasis one word in it which I thought was an answer to all the abuse that those of us who proposed the Freedom of Edinburgh, have had to hear during the past few months. We were accused of introducing to the citizens of Edinburgh a man who intended the disintegration of the Empire. We denied that – but Mr Parnell has been here this very night to deny it himself. Mr Parnell had used the words this night - "unity of the Empire". They might rely upon it that Mr Parnell meant unity of Ireland, Scotland, and England.'

Calls of 'Hear! Hear!' came from many areas of the crowd.

'We, the majority in the Town Council, suffered greatly for our views, we have been blamed unjustly, but we have tried to bear it with magnanimity, because we believed that what we were doing was in the interests of the unity of the Empire.

'We believed that we were speaking the voices of the great majority of the people of Edinburgh. We never had any doubt about that, and this meeting was a witness to it. The demonstration of this evening proved that despite their plebiscites, newspaper articles, and their potty persecution notwithstanding......'

A voice from the crowd called out, 'Boycott them!'
Councillor Pollard continued-

'.....the great majority of the people of Edinburgh were in favour of the Freedom of Edinburgh being given to Mr Parnell.'

This was greeted with loud calls of 'Hear! Hear!' from the audience.

Helen groaned inwardly as she realised that the Councillor was in full flow and knew that from past experience that his few words would soon become a flood!

He went on-

'We have welcomed, Mr Parnell, in anticipation of what we are to do next day in our name, and they were not only doing an act of reparation to him who had patiently and so quietly and so magnanimously borne the awful vituperation and calumny of the past two or three years, but we are sending a message of peace to his people.'

A man in the crowd shouted out, 'God Bless ould Ireland!'

Councillor Pollard ploughed on-

'I believe that what we have done this night is an act of the wisest statesmanship because we have helped to knit together the people of Ireland, who were only now beginning to realise that the people – the democracy – of Scotland and of England were desiring to be at one with them.

'We have had our demonstration, and we have proved.....'

A voice from the audience called out, 'To *The Scotsman*!'

'......beyond all dispute,' councillor Pollard continued, 'beyond the very shadow of a dispute, then let them come to us at the November elections.

'Those who said we were not representing the majority of the citizens of Edinburgh – if they would introduce party politics into the Town Council, let them rely on it, they would have more of party politics than they reckoned upon; and if it was to be a party fight, then we would clean the Town Council out of their Tory members......'

Loud cheering from the crowd

'.........and their Unionist member.'

Renewed cheering.
Councillor Pollard's face was growing red in his indignation.

'We have been subjected to a great deal of blame and misrepresentation, and we have had to suffer a good deal but now that we have our victory I hope we will carry it meekly. I hope we will not deal with our opponents as they have dealt with us.

'I trust,' he continued, 'that the Liberals of Edinburgh and their representatives on the Town Council, will never disgrace themselves with the sort of opposition that we have had to bear in bringing forward the proposal to grant the Freedom of Edinburgh to this great man.'

Helen rather hoped he would finish soon because, though it had been a lovely evening, the night was drawing in and it was always breezy up on Calton Hill. She drew her shawl more tightly around her and looking across the Firth saw lights beginning to appear on the ships moored in the river.

'I cannot finish without asking that we express our thanks, in the heartiest way, to Bailie Walcott. I know he has had to suffer in a way that I do not care to describe. Bailie Walcott had had to suffer very great persecution and very great loss, and he had to endure a great deal of pain by reason of the opposition to him. But I believe that Bailie Walcott has our goodwill and the goodwill of the great majority of the citizens of Edinburgh.'

A man in the crowd called out, 'Three cheers for Bailie Walcott – our next Lord Provost!'

As the loud cheers died away, the Councillor, now in the full flood of his oratory returned to the fray.

'Yes, he is worthy to be our next Lord Provost. I believe that those who are at present opposed to him would before long come to see the shame of their attitude and the manner they had borne towards Bailie Walcott.

'As representative of the Calton Ward, I am very glad that the demonstration has taken place in the Calton ward.'

The crowd started to laugh and a voice called out, 'A little bit of electioneering, Councillor?'

The Councillor ignored this and went on regardless-

'It could not have been a more fitting place since everyone knows that the Calton ward has always been thoroughly sound on this matter.'

Helen knew that this was indeed true as it was the Calton ward that Luke had long nurtured on behalf of the Liberals.

He always chaired the meetings in the ward. When Helen had asked him if he would not have liked to stand as a representative of the area on the Town Council he had said he preferred a back room role. Helen felt sure that he did not want to expose his wife, Patricia, to the scrutiny that such a public role would bring.

At last, Councillor Pollard was winding up.

He proposed three cheers for Mr & Mrs Buchanan, and Mrs Buchanan, senior, which were heartily given.

Just when Helen thought the meeting had come to an end Michael Flannigan climbed up onto the platform.

His strong Irish voice rang out proposing a vote of thanks to the Chairman.

'I trust ye will accord to him that which he deserved from this living plebiscite!'

This resulted in further cheering, applause and whistles.

'Let our opponents send their scrutinisers to this evening and we will see whether their "card sharping" or their plebiscite was the real one!'

This was met with gales of knowing laughter.

Helen knew that the opponents of the Freedom being granted to Mr Parnell had organised an unofficial plebiscite by sending out cards for people to return. The returned cards had proved so overwhelmingly opposed to Mr Parnell's honour that it was laughable. Voter fraud was suspected by many and the majority on the town council chose to ignore it. Looking at the vast crowd on the hill Helen felt that such overwhelming opposition could surely not have been true.

Michael Flannigan held up his hand to quieten the laughing crowd.

'I am pleased to see that the prejudices which had existed between the people of Scotland and the people of Ireland has now gone for ever, and that now there would be a union of hearts and nothing else,' he said. 'I have it, on good authority, that of our President, Luke Boylan, and he had it on the good authority of his esteemed father, Philip Boylan, who was there, that fifty-four years ago, a great patriot, and a great leader of the Irish people – Daniel O'Connell –stood on this very spot.

'Today we have had the great leader Charles Stewart Parnell addressing us.'

The noise rose like a crescendo and Helen's eyes filled with tears as she thought of how Philip would have loved to have been here, this night, and heard the roar of this great assembly of people.

Michael had his arms raised above his head, and with his voice breaking, he said -

'Thank ye from the bottom of me heart for the part ye have taken on behalf of me unfortunate country.'

The Chairman came forward and made a brief bow of thanks. Then to loud cheers the platform party descended and made their way slowly through the crowd, to the waiting carriages, shaking hands and being slapped on the back as they went.

Luke, eventually, made it to where Helen waited.

'Mother! Was that not the most amazing thing ye have ever seen,' he said.

Helen looked at her son, his face flushed and his eyes shining. It was a long time since she had seen him so happy.

'It was, indeed,' she said, 'and wouldn't yer father be proud o' you, my fine son?'

Tears started in his eyes, 'This is just the start. Wait until we get Home Rule for beloved Ireland, won't he be proud of me then!'

Helen smiled as he climbed in beside her. Beloved Ireland, she thought, a land that neither she nor her son had ever seen, and yet the blood was strong. She wanted to ask him about the calls for Home Rule for Scotland, too, but decided this was not the time.

'Mother,' Luke was continuing, 'we have been invited along to an "at home" being held at Mrs Buchanan's house at 10 Moray Place tonight at 9.30. You know Mr Parnell is staying with them during his visit to Edinburgh?'

Helen knew this, but her heart sank at the thought of having to go home and change into her finery, and then go out again so late.

'I'm sorry, Luke, but dae ye mind if I don't come?'

She saw the look of disappointment on her son's face, but she went on, 'It's been a long day, and I'm a bit chilled, and to tell the truth a bit tired. But ye must go and then come by tomorrow and tell me all about it.'

Luke was immediately concerned.

'I'm sorry, Mother, it was thoughtless of me, of course ye will be tired.

I'll take ye home,' he said.

By now the other Committee members had arrived and climbed into the carriage. As they drove off they were full of the excitement of the day and the evening Reception that was to come.

Mrs Buchanan had sent invitations to the Executive of the Edinburgh Liberal Association, the Women's Liberal Association and the members of the Town Council who had supported the proposal to confer the freedom of the city on Mr Parnell, and a few private friends.

It sounded like it would be a glittering affair but Helen had no regrets. She was sixty-nine years old now and her days of late nights were past. Besides, she was too worried about Arthur's bairns, lost in Canada, to have any heart for socialising.

Luke asked the carriage to wait, and then escorted his mother upstairs to her flat on George IV Bridge, where Bessie was waiting with a fire in the hearth and some warm soup ready for supper.

CECILIA'S STORY

PART FIVE

CHAPTER 1

The move was in vain.

The Secretary returned without the bairns.

Ross Stewart sent Arthur a copy of a minute he had received from the Directors on the return of their Secretary dated 16th August 1889.

It read -

THE EDINBURGH & LEITH CHILDREN'S AID & REFUGE SOCIETY

MINUTE

MINUTES of a special meeting of the Directors of The Edinburgh & Leith Children's Aid & Refuge Society

Held on August 16, 1889.
Report from The Secretary Mr MacDonald on his visit to Canada in search of the Delaney children.

The Secretary reported that, acting on the instructions he received at the last meeting, he had proceeded to Nova Scotia by the first available ship, viz. the 'Pavonia' to Boston and that on landing he had without any delay travelled to

Aylesford. After six visits, he had succeeded in getting an interview with Miss Stirling, when she had not only declined to give the Delaney children up, or give any information regarding them, but positively declined to discuss the matter with him. He then proceeded to Halifax, the capital of the county, and made application to the Supreme Court there for an order on Miss Stirling to deliver up the children. This the court refused to do on the plea that the directors had no legal right to the children and that the only person entitled to ask for an order was the father. He laid on the table certified copies of all his proceedings. The meeting approved of the Secretary's actions. Mr Gray reported that he had submitted the whole papers connected with the proceedings in Nova Scotia to counsel who strongly recommended that a mandate should be obtained from Delaney in order that the Directors might take proceedings in his name for the recovery of the children. The meeting moved and instructed Mr Gray accordingly and authorised him to assure Delaney's agents that although the proceedings are to be taken in Delaney's name, they are to be at the Directors' expense.

Arthur was distraught. The bairns were lost. How could he ever find them in such a vast country. He would never see them again!

Cecilia urged Arthur to go and see Ross Stewart and ask him what would happen next.

When they met, Ross Stewart gave him some hope. He explained that the Directors intended bringing a case against Miss Stirling in the Supreme Court of Nova Scotia in Arthur's name but at their expense, if Arthur gave his approval.

'Anything to get the bairns back,' Arthur said.

Two months later Ross Stewart came to see Arthur and said he had been informed that a writ of *Habeas Corpus* had been issued in Nova Scotia on 14th October 1889. This meant she would have to explain to the Supreme Court there, why she had not returned the children after being ordered to do so by the Court of Session in Edinburgh. He further added if Miss Stirling did not respond she would be arrested!

This gave Arthur some satisfaction, but Ross Stewart cautioned him that the Law moved extremely slowly, so he would have to be very patient. He promised to send Arthur a copy of the court papers from Nova Scotia as soon as he received them.

EMMA'S STORY

PART SIX

Hillfoot Farm
Aylesford
Nova Scotia

2 March 1891

62 Northumberland Street
Edinburgh

My Dear Miss Auld,

My sincere apologies for the delay in replying to your last letter. Things have been very difficult for me here with regard to the Delaney case.

In August, 1890, the Court in Nova Scotia required me to give the children's addresses, or where I last heard of them, which I did at once.

I was desired to instruct a solicitor to find them, which he failed to do, but did not tell me so until December 23, 1890. I then received a letter from him to this effect, and another from my ordinary solicitor, saying that the court required a man to be sent to look for the children within twenty-four hours.

Two men were suggested - one was my farmer, the other was a detective. To both of these I objected. To the first because having a large stock of cattle in the barn, I could not do without his work; and also because that, being my servant, I could not expect the court to be really satisfied with any effort he might make.

To the second I objected as, being a Roman Catholic, I could not employ him.

I proposed going to Kentville to a well-known solicitor there and ask him to find a man, competent, reliable and without interest either way. This I did there and then, though the date was 23rd December, the hour 7 p.m., the thermometer below zero, the snow lying in drifts seven feet deep on the roads in some places, and I very far from strong in health.

Accompanied by my cousin, I set forth on this expedition to drive in an open wagon to Kentville, about twenty-five miles off. As we might almost have expected in such frost, the bolts of the wagon snapped and we broke down about 16 miles from home!

I think it was a great deliverance and proof of the Lord's care that this happened near a house, and not in the woods and bogs (or uncultivated places) we had just passed, where for miles there was no sign of human habitation. At the house, we got help, the wagon was 'fixed up', and at 12 p.m. we reached Kentville, and sent the man off next morning.

Who can say I did not try to carry out the orders of the court? The man failed to find the children.

I was asked in January, 1891, through my solicitor, I believe by the opposing counsel, if I would advertise for the children. I said 'No'. I had already done all I could to find them. I was then told by one well versed in such things

I had better be prepared to make choice of a prison, so as to avoid the worst.

I do not know what my fate will be but I have good legal brains at my service so I must trust that all will be well. I will write again, dear friend, as soon as I have more news for you.

Yours in haste,

Emma M. Stirling

CECILIA'S STORY

PART SIX

Chapter 1

10th July 1891

Ross Stewart had been right to advise Arthur to be patient. The Supreme Court case in Nova Scotia dragged on for nearly two years!

Arthur could not believe it! He constantly pestered poor Ross Stewart, even though he had explained that the Court of Session in Edinburgh would do nothing until the case against Miss Stirling in Nova Scotia reached a conclusion.

Cecilia and Arthur tried their best to get on with family life with their own children, but the time passing with no news of Arthur's bairns in Nova Scotia weighed heavily on both of them. Arthur was tormented with imaginings of what was happening to them.

At last a bulky envelope was delivered from Ross Stewart. It contained the court papers from Nova Scotia. Arthur and Cecilia read them with growing concern.

SUPREME COURT OF NOVA SCOTIA
HALIFAX

THE QUEEN at the instance of ARTHUR DELANEY, Plaintiff.

Against

EMMA M. STIRLING, Defendant

13 August 1890

Upon hearing read the rule nisi granted by Mr Justice Ritchie, dated the 19th day of June 1890, and the papers therein referred to, the two affidavits of Emma M. Stirling and the affidavit of John Peggie, all filed herein the 5th day of July 1890, and the printed case herein, and after hearing argument of counsel on both sides –

This Court doth order and adjudge that the said rule nisi be, and the same is hereby made absolute, and that the said return of the defendant Emma M. Stirling be, and the same is hereby set aside and quashed, and that a writ of attachment for CONTEMPT OF COURT do issue against the said Emma M. Stirling, commanding the sheriff of the county of Kings, or any other of our sheriffs, to arrest the said Emma M. Stirling, so that he may have her before us in our Supreme Court at Halifax on Tuesday the 9th day of December 1890 to answer to us for certain trespasses and contempts brought against her in our said Court.

And it is further ordered that said writ remain in the office of the Prothonotary for the period of thirty days, and be not delivered to the Sheriff to be executed, if within that period the said Emma M. Stirling shall make a satisfactory return and produce the said children or show that it is impossible for her to do so.

If the children are not produced, any amended return shall give full particulars of how, when, and where she disposed of each of said children, when she last saw or heard of them, and in whose custody and where she believed them to be at the date of the return, and the circumstances to show that she has made every effort and is unable to obtain any of the children in order to produce them in obedience to the writ.

MR JUSTICE RITCHIE

The second document read -

SUPREME COURT OF NOVA SCOTIA
HALIFAX

An amended return to the writ of habeas corpus was submitted by Emma M. Stirling to the Supreme Court of Nova Scotia on 2 September 1890. This contained no new information and so the Court ruled –

An application is now made to this Court for leave to put in force the writ of arrest previously allowed, on the ground that the conditions contained in the order of the 13th August have not been complied with, inasmuch as the children have not been produced, and the new return does not state circumstances to show that Miss Stirling had made every effort and was unable to obtain any of the children in order to produce them in accordance to the writ.

In the case before us this court has already decided that Miss Stirling has illegally parted with the custody of the children. She has not produced them in obedience to the writ, and we are now called upon to decide whether or not the facts and circumstances she has disclosed show that she has made every effort, and is unable to obtain any of the children, in order to produce them in obedience of the writ of habeas corpus.

The last return made to the writ is clearly insufficient on this point. It merely states that she has instructed her solicitor on her behalf to endeavour to obtain the children, and furnished him with all the information in her possession for his assistance.

If we turn to her affidavit we find that the only thing she did in relation to this matter was to write to her solicitors, Messrs Gray & MacDonald, solicitors of this Court, on the 5th September, 1890 two days after the date of the return she submitted to this Court.

If we look at the affidavit of Mr Wallace McDonald to see what his firm did, we find that they wrote a letter to each of the persons mentioned in the return of Miss Stirling, asking where the children were, but obtained no information except that the boy had run away.

They then instructed a Mr Cogswell to proceed to the places of abode of the persons to whom they had written and make all necessary inquiries as to the whereabouts of the children, and use all legitimate means and his best endeavours to find them and bring them to Halifax.

Mr Cogswell states that he went to Middleton and saw Mr Rufus de Wolfe, who told him that James Delaney had run away from him, and that he did not know where he was, and on making enquiries at Middleton he could not find anything as to the whereabouts of James Delaney.

He then saw Mrs Jones at Grand Metis, who told him that she had Annie Delaney, but she did not have her then, and did not know where she was, and on making inquiries there, outside of Mrs Jones, he could get no information.

The next paragraph of his affidavit, referring to Robina Delaney, is similar, substituting 'Mrs Smith of Blacklock' for Mrs Jones of Shemogue' for ' Grand Metis'.

It does not appear that Mr Cogswell had any written authority or credentials from Miss Stirling authorising him to enquire after the children, or requesting the persons with whom they had been placed to give him all the information they possessed in respect of them, and I think it is evident that such information was withheld by the persons best able to afford it without questioning the bona-fides of either Messrs Gray & McDonald or Mr Cogswell their messenger.

It seems to me that sending an utter stranger to enquire for the children was not calculated to obtain information or bring about their restitution but that Miss Stirling should have gone herself, or, if that was impossible sent one of her confidential employees, with proper authority in writing from herself, to make necessary enquiries.

Besides this, the Court has by it's order required Miss Stirling to disclose the facts and circumstances which transpired, so that the Court may judge whether it is impossible or not for Miss Stirling to produce the children.

It would be sufficient in order to comply with the statement in Mr Cogswell's affidavit to go to the house, ask for the child, and when told that she was not there, and his informant did not know where she was, to make enquiries of two or more persons he met in the street. Did he do this? Or were his enquiries bona-fide, and made to persons calculated to give him the information he sought?

If they were, the full particulars and the names and occupations of his informants should have been given to the Court, so that we might judge whether or not his investigations were thorough and calculated to obtain the desired end.

I can come to no other conclusion but that the action taken by Miss Stirling in this matter subsequent to the order of the 13th August falls far short of the requirements of the Appeal Court in England in similar cases, (The Queen v Mr Barnardo), and what should be required by this Court.

In the Barnardo case the Court stated – As a matter of law it is no valid excuse for not producing a child in obedience of a writ habeas-corpus to state inability to obey, if such inability is the result of the previous illegal conduct of the person to whom the writ is addressed. In this case the defendant's inability arises from his having illegally sent the child abroad against the will of the lawful guardian, and that he did this before any legal proceedings commenced is immaterial. Persons who illegally put a child out of their power do so at their peril, and if they are ordered to produce the child no excuse founded on their own ability to comply with the order will be held sufficient answer to the writ.

The English Court was of the opinion that it was not enough to write letters, the person to whom the writ was directed must use every possible effort to get the child, must go abroad, if necessary, and use personal influence for the purpose; and if he cannot get the child back in any other way, he must go after it himself, and assist the parent, if necessary, to recover it by legal process of the country where it is; he must also advertise, and do everything that mortal man could do in this matter.

In the English cases too, it must be remembered, Mr Barnardo did not know where the persons to whom he had given the children were, or their addresses, while in this case the addresses of the persons who had the girls at the time the writ issued, or a very short time before, are well known to Miss Stirling, and their residences are not very far away.

Now contrast the requirement of the English Court with what was done in this case.

Miss Stirling did nothing but write a letter to her solicitors. They wrote a few more letters, and then sent a messenger who was a stranger to the persons who were supposed to have the children, not accredited in any way as coming from Miss Stirling. He makes some enquiries, but with the exception of the persons with whom the children were, and who under the circumstances would be expected to withhold the information, we do not know to whom they were directed.

Having obtained no information, he returns home. Nothing further is done, and Miss Stirling and her solicitors appear satisfied that everything has been done necessary to show that it is impossible for her to produce the children.

If this is a sufficient answer to justify the non-production of a child in obedience to a writ of habeas corpus, such a writ for that purpose is practically worthless, for I can hardly imagine a case in which a judicious shuffling of the child from one party to another would not enable such a return to be made.

There is another point to which I have not averted, but which has somewhat impressed itself on me. Miss Stirling, greatly to her credit, has taken for years an interest in destitute children and spent a great deal of time and money in their maintenance and education, and according to her own statement they are under her charge until they become of age, (which these children certainly were not).

I cannot believe, if this is the case, that it is her usual practice to allow little girls of such a tender age as these children were, and in whose welfare she claims to take a great interest, to be transferred at will from one person to another without her knowing where they are, and that they are being brought up in a respectable manner; and it seems to me very strange that she should take so little interest in the boys she has brought to this country as to allow one who was only twelve years of age to run away from the person with whom he was placed without making any inquiries about him, and endeavouring to trace him in any way, particularly when such a thing happened within a few miles of her residence in this province.

I think it is due to Miss Stirling herself, and the benevolent persons who assist her, as well as the parents and friends of the children brought into this province, that a full explanation should be given to the course pursued in this respect with reference to these children.

For in the face of Miss Stirling's affidavit, I cannot but assume that the particular course followed in this case was for the purpose of removing the children from the jurisdiction of this Court, and enabling Miss Stirling to state in her Return that she does not know where they are.

After Lord Justice Ritchie's summing up the three judges retired to consider their verdicts.

On the Court being reconvened Lord Justice Ritchie made the following statement.

450

Following the decisions of the English Court (in the Barnardo case), I am of the opinion that Miss Stirling has not shown sufficient reason for not producing the children, and that the writ of arrest must be put in force, and she must answer the interrogatories which may be submitted, and this Court can then ascertain whether she has purged herself of the contempt, or is liable to punishment therefore.

Mr Justice Townshend concurred in this judgement, while the Chief Justice was of the opinion she had done everything that was required to get possession of the children.

The verdict of Lord Justice Ritchie and Mr Justice Townshend therefore carried the majority decision and Miss Stirling was ordered to be arrested.

A third document was enclosed which read -

*SUPREME COURT OF NOVA SCOTIA
HALIFAX*

THE QUEEN at the instance of ARTHUR DELANEY, Plaintiff.

Against

EMMA M. STIRLING, Defendant

February 1891

JUDGEMENT of Mr Justice Ritchie in Action in the Supreme Court of Nova Scotia, against

Miss Stirling for delivery of children dated February, 1891.

MR JUSTICE RITCHIE stated -

Miss Emma M. Stirling, in one of her affidavits made in this matter, states with reference to her Home, 'The principle on which it was carried out on was that those children for whom board was paid were kept in Edinburgh, and were to be handed over to their parents whenever requested. Those who were not paid for or regularly visited by their parents, were regarded as deserted, and were considered as thenceforward, until they became of age, as being wholly under my charge and control, and were sent away by me from Edinburgh to homes in the country, and I verily believe that all this was understood by the said Arthur Delaney when he put his children in the Nursery and home and that the said Arthur Delaney only paid board for said children about six weeks and did not visit or make enquires about said children, or any or either of them, except on two occasions'.

Notwithstanding the efforts of Arthur Delaney to get possession of his children they were brought to Nova Scotia by Miss Stirling (as she states in April 1887), and remained on her farm in Aylesford under her control until they were given over by her to respectable persons who undertook to bring them up, and take charge of them until they were able to take care of themselves, James being given over in June 1887, and the others in January 1888.

In October 1889 one of the judges of this Court granted a writ of habeas Corpus, directing Miss Stirling to produce said children before him, to which she made a return to the effect that none of the said children were in her custody, power, or control at the time of the issue of the writ or since.

This reply was quashed and an amended return allowed to be made, which was filed on the 12 May 1890. This amended return was set aside by this Court on the 13th August 1890, when the following order passed -

A writ of habeas corpus was issued at the instance of the said Arthur Delaney out of this Supreme Court of Nova Scotia on the 14th day Of October 1889, addressed to Emma M. Stirling of Hillfoot Farm, Aylesford in the county of Kings, spinster.

The final document was the conclusion of the case. It read -

SUPREME COURT OF NOVA SCOTIA, HALIFAX.

JUDGEMENT of Lord Chief Justice McDonald, Justice Weatherbe and Justice Ritchie, dated 10th July 1891.

On August, 13th, 1890, an order was made directing a writ of arrest to issue against Miss Stirling for contempt of this Court, the contempt being that the non-production of the Delaney children in pursuance of a previous Order of the Court. It was however, directed that the writ should remain in the office of the Court for thirty days and that the same be not delivered to the Sheriff to be executed 'If within that time Miss Stirling should make satisfactory return and produce the said children, or show that it is impossible for her to do so'.

Subsequent to this order on the 2 September 1890, Miss Stirling, made an amended return in addition to the return made by her on 24th October 1889, explanatory of her dealings with the said children and showing how it was impossible for her to comply with the order to produce them, she also filed an affidavit, setting forth the efforts made by her to comply with the order of the Court, and declaring – 'I have not done, so far as I know, anything in contempt of this Honourable Court, and I have used my best endeavours to comply with the order of the Honourable Court, made herein on the 13th day of August last'.

With this amended return and affidavit, were filed the affidavits of William A.B. Ritchie, Robert L. Borden, Wallace MacDonald and Edward E. Cogswell setting out the information received from Miss Stirling by her solicitors, the employment by them of Mr Cogswell, a barrister of this Court, in consequences of these instructions to make search for, and, if possible, find these children, that she might be able to produce them as commanded by this Court, and the efforts made by Mr Cogswell in pursuance of his instructions to find them.

The efforts of Miss Stirling, as detailed in these affidavits and returns, were not, I believe considered satisfactory to a majority of the Court and, under a practice which appears to prevail in England although not familiar here, it was directed that Miss Stirling should be examined before a Master of the Court on a series of questions prepared by the solicitor for the prosecutor, and which she was directed to answer without any opportunity of consulting with or being advised by her own solicitors.

Under this order between ninety and one hundred questions carefully and skilfully framed, covering the whole ground of the inquiry, have been answered by Miss Stirling.

These answers have been returned to this Court by the Master, with his report that Miss Stirling has failed to purge the contempt of Court pronounced against her and that the Court is now to determine whether the report be sustained.

This English practice does not, I believe, require the Master in such cases to give reasons for the conclusions he reports to the Court.

He has not done so in this case, and I am therefore the less reluctant in declaring my own inability to concur with the conclusion he has reported.

It will be kept in mind that the testimony produced by and on behalf of Miss Stirling has not been contradicted. No one has ventured to say that a single statement she has made was untrue.

It is not suggested that Miss Stirling or Mr Cogswell perjured themselves, and yet it is difficult to conceive how on any other hypothesis the conclusion can be arrived at.

It would be an insult to Miss Stirling and those who have aided and assisted her, to discuss such a supposition.

It is shown beyond contradiction or denial that Mr Cogswell made every effort to ascertain the whereabouts of these children. It is not suggested that Mr Cogswell is an incompetent person, that he neglected his duty, or that he was paid NOT to find the children. If she had gone to the expense of employing, eight, ten or a dozen other persons to make this search is there any reason to suppose that the result would have been different?

It was suggested, I think, that she ought to have gone on this exploring expedition herself but I cannot quite see why an elderly lady, apparently not very active or energetic physically, should be a more efficient detective than a young, active man, with sufficient intelligence, to become a member of the legal profession.

I have not the slightest hesitation in holding that Miss Stirling should be purged of the contempt declared against her, and that she has not produced the Delaney children because 'it was impossible for her to do so'.

I come to this conclusion because I believe the statements on which the Court has now to pass to be true, and being true, to be conclusive against any intention on the part of Miss Stirling to deceive or mislead the Court,

It is my opinion that Miss Stirling has purged the contempt declared against her, and that she should be discharged from custody.

Mr Justice Weatherbe concurred with this verdict.

Mr Justice Ritchie stated – In this case the Court has already decided that Miss Emma Stirling is in contempt for disobedience to a writ of habeas-corpus directing her to produce three children named Delaney before one of the Judges of this Court. Three children who she brought illegally to this province, without the permission of their father, and who she claimed to be responsible for until they were of age.

She now states that she does not know where these children are though they are considerably under-age.

This Court has already decided that the different returns made by her to the writ were bad. These returns have not altered.

It is the opinion of the Master who examined her, in detail, that she had not obeyed the injunction of the writ.

It does not appear from her answers to the interrogatories that she has taken any further steps to obtain the children beyond those mentioned in the returns to the writ which this Court has already declared bad.

She has done nothing to purge her contempt.

In my opinion she should be punished for the contempt of which this Court has already found her guilty.

The majority verdict being that Miss Stirling had purged her contempt she was released from custody.

When they had both finished reading Arthur and Cecilia looked at each other in disbelief.

'They let her off with it!' Arthur exploded.

He started to pace up and down holding his head in his hands. He was furious and his face was flushed. Cecilia feared he would have an apoplexy and tried to calm him down.

'Look Arthur, there is a note included from Ross Stewart. He wants you to go and see him tomorrow. He says you can now resume your case against the Directors in the Court of Session,' she said.

'That's good news, isn't it?' she pleaded.

But Arthur was beyond consolation, so bitter was he that Emma Stirling had escaped punishment.

CHAPTER 2

Next morning, after a sleepless night, a worried Cecilia watched from the window as Arthur made his way to his appointment with Ross Stewart. She couldn't settle to anything in the house and was relieved when she heard Arthur's key in the door an hour later.

Arthur told her how sympathetic the lawyer had been. He had said he understood Arthur's anger and frustration at Miss Stirling being absolved from the contempt charge by the Supreme Court in Nova Scotia.

'He tried to raise ma spirits by saying that there was still hope,' Arthur said. 'Now we could return to the Court of Session and demand further action.'

'That's surely good news, Arthur,' Cecilia said.

'Aye, maybe,' Arthur replied.

Cecilia could see he was still very down.

'Will it take very long?' Cecilia asked.

She was thinking of the long drawn out legal processes they had already endured.

'No,' Arthur replied, 'Ross Stewart has already obtained a date for the custody case to resume. It's on the 15th July.'

Cecilia was relieved – just a few days away.

So on 15th July 1891 Arthur and Cecilia sat in the public gallery again, as Ross Stewart presented Arthur's case to the Court of Session in Edinburgh.

To Cecilia's surprise four judges took their place on the bench.

The Clerk of the Court announced–

'Custody case for the return of the children of Arthur Delaney against the Edinburgh and Leith Children's Aid and Refuge Society before the Lord President and Lords Adam, McLaren and Kinnear.'

Cecilia and Arthur looked down as Ross Stewart rose to his feet. He reminded the judges of what the Directors had done to comply with their order of over two years before.

Ross Stewart continued - 'Immediately after that order was pronounced, the Directors sent out their secretary, Mr McDonald, to America, but he failed to obtain the custody of the children.

'It was not expected that he would so, because when they were in this country he travelled with them and Miss Stirling and allowed them to slip through his fingers.'

Reflecting on the outcome of the proceedings against Miss Stirling, Mr Stewart contended that it followed that all the proceedings which the Directors had taken had been futile.

Ross Stewart stated - 'In these circumstances, the Petitioner, Arthur Delaney, had suggested to the Directors that either they employ a detective agency to find the children, or to offer a reward for them, or to advertise for them. None of these suggestions were taken up by the Directors.

'They had also refused to provide the Petitioner, Arthur Delaney, with funds in order that he and his agent might proceed to Nova Scotia to find his children.'

The Lord President intervened – 'And when they found them, what would they do?'

Ross Stewart replied - 'Have them delivered to us in compliance with your Lordship's order.'

The Lord President stated – 'Arthur Delaney cannot get them delivered to himself.'

Ross Stewart responded – 'The present possessors should deliver them to him.'

The Lord President argued – 'The present possessors are not here. Arthur Delaney wants to assume the office of detective. I do not see, even if we were to approve of his doing so, how he could have power to take possession of the children.'

Ross Stewart protested – 'He, as the father, has a title to ask for his children.'

Lord Adam intervened - 'I understand nobody knows where they are. The first step in any future proceedings is to find the children.'

Ross Stewart demanded - 'That is for the Directors to do.'

Mr Lorimer rose to his feet – 'As agent for the Directors I object. The Directors have done all they can to find the children. The suggestion that Arthur Delaney, and his agent, should go out to Canada, at the Director's expense, was not a practical one, because he had not seen the children since 1886 and was unlikely to be able to identify them.'

The Lord President enquired - 'Who is better qualified for identifying them?'

Mr Lorimer responded - 'The secretary of this institution, Mr MacDonald, who saw them in 1889.'

Ross Stewart intervened – 'The secretary, Mr MacDonald, has already been to Canada to trace the children but failed to find them.'

Lord Adam asked - 'Well, Mr Lorimer, perhaps you will state what proposition you have to make in these circumstances.'

Mr Lorimer replied - 'We are in this position - that up to 8th July, we have done all we possibly could do.'

Lord Kinnear intervened - 'That is not stating a counter-proposition.'

Mr Lorimer explained - 'We have not had much time to communicate with our solicitors in Halifax. The Directors are very anxious to obtain these children. If there was anything the court could suggest the Directors could do in consequence of the judgement of 8th July in the Canadian Courts liberating Miss Stirling, from contempt of court, we shall be glad to consider it.'

Lord Adam interjected - 'I gather from this note that the ground upon which the judgement against Miss Stirling was recalled was that, in point of fact, she did not know where the children were and could not produce them. If that is so, the first thing to do is to find the children and then it will be for consideration what are the necessary steps to get them back.'

Lord Kinnear objected - 'It does not seem to me that the Directors should state their readiness to consider any suggestion that may be made by and conform to it as much as possible. Suggestions to court should not be made in that form; but one would like to know what the Directors themselves propose.'

Mr Lorimer protested - 'The Directors wrote to the Petitioner's agent informing him that they were willing to do anything in their power to attain his client's objects. If the court thought that the Directors should take steps by advertising, the directors were quite willing to do so.'

The Lord President stated firmly - 'The position of your clients, Mr Lorimer, is not satisfactory and I think the court is entitled to look to them for further aid in this matter. It may be a very extravagant proposal on the part of the Petitioner that he should go to Canada to hunt up his children among several millions of a population; but we cannot let the matter stand as it is.'

Lord McLaren - 'I should like the Directors carefully to consider whether they can suggest any practical measure to deal with the case as it now stands and whether they will provide the means for taking such a measure.

'It may be that after using their best endeavours to solve the question, they may not be able to propose anything and in that case we should have to consider whether they are to be held in contempt, or whether Mr Delaney is to be left to his remedy of damages.

'In the meantime, they should consider the matter and place it before us in such a way as will enable us to deal with it.'

Mr Lorimer pleaded – 'We have had no opportunity of considering it since the judgement on 8th July, in Canada, the effect of which has reached us by telegraph. If your Lordships suggest that by advertisement, or any other scheme...'

The Lord President interjected – 'You must not fall back upon the court for suggestions. What we are asked to do is to find the Directors guilty of contempt. You must defend that.'

Mr Lorimer argued - 'Up to 8th July, and the Canadian Court's judgement, it could not be suggested that we were in contempt.'

The Lord President stated – 'I am not at all sure about that. The contempt was in a certain degree forgiven, but when you had these children in this country in 1889, I am not prepared to say there was no contempt.'

Lord McLaren insisted - 'Before these proceedings can be allowed to come to an end, the Directors must be in a position to satisfy the court that all practical means of tracing the children have been exhausted.'

The Lord President agreed – 'Some order must be pronounced this session, but what is it to be?'

Mr Lorimer pleaded – 'If your Lordships will allow the case to stand over until Saturday, we shall endeavour to have a meeting of the Directors.'

The Lord President insisted – 'Better make it Friday.'

Mr Lorimer explained – 'There is a large body of Directors and it will take some time to have them convened.'

The Lord President was exasperated – 'The large body of Directors are not going to meet to discuss the thing. They must follow the advice they get from counsel.'

The Court was then adjourned.

When Arthur and Cecilia left the Court she could see that Arthur was looking much more hopeful. At least they had only two days to wait for the outcome.

CHAPTER 3

Two days later, Cecilia and Arthur had just finished their meal when they heard a knock on their door. They had been waiting anxiously for the outcome of the Judges demands on the Directors. When Arthur opened the door Ross Stewart stood there. He came in, sat down and explained that day's proceedings in the Court.

Mr Lorimer, for the Directors, had returned to Court and presented the Minute of the meeting of the Directors at which they had agreed to hire a detective to search for the children in Canada.

The Lords had then retired to consider the Directors' suggestion and had then returned to the Court and announced their decision.

Ross Stewart had obtained a transcript of the decision and handed it to Arthur to read. It stated –

'The Lords having considered the Minute for the Compearing Respondents The Directors Of The Edinburgh & Leith Children's Aid & Refuge Society, No. 67 of process, and heard Counsel for the Petitioner, Arthur Delaney – declare that he is a fit and proper person to have possession of his children illegally removed from him to Nova Scotia.

Thereof, we do Ordain the said Respondents to consult with their solicitor in Halifax, and employ one or more Detectives, and put said Detective or Detectives in communication with a person who can identify the Petitioner's children and send said Detective or Detectives to Nova Scotia to follow up the information as to the last known residence of the children contained in the Affidavits produced in the proceedings in Halifax, and search for, and if possible, find the said children. The Respondents to report to the Court of Session by the first sederunt day in October; and Ordain the Petitioner to furnish said Respondents with Mandates containing his authority for bringing the children to this country, and that the said Mandates may be used if necessary.'

Arthur gave it to Cecilia to read and she could see from his face that the Judges had ruled in his favour. Arthur shook Ross Stewart's hand and thanked him for his good work.

'Ye have nae idea how much this means to me,' Arthur said.

Ross Stewart smiled. 'After all this time and the persistence you have shown I think I do,' he said.

Promising to let them know as soon as there was any news from Nova Scotia, Ross Stewart left.

'Surely a detective will find the bairns,' Cecilia said.

Arthur agreed but later as they both sat staring into the fire they were filled with a nameless dread.

EMMA'S STORY

PART SEVEN

Hillfoot Farm
Aylesford
Nova Scotia

12 July 1891

Miss Auld
62 Northumberland Street,
Edinburgh.

My dear Miss Auld,

I have such good news to report!

On the 10 July past the Supreme Court of Nova Scotia by a two to one majority declared that I be purged of the charge of contempt of Court that had been levelled against me and ordered I be discharged from custody.

The Lord Chief Justice MacDonald declared that I had done all in my power to try to trace the Delaney children and Justice Weatherbe concurred with him.

He gave short shift to the evidence from the Master of the Court who examined me. He said it should be disallowed as it was "a practice which appears to prevail in England although not familiar here". He was obviously not going to be bound by any English law in his Court!

Would you believe that Justice Ritchie continued to argue that I had brought the Delaney children to Nova Scotia illegally without the permission of their father. He stated that since I had claimed I was responsible for the children here, until they were of age, and since they were still considerably under-age I was still in contempt.

Fortunately, the other two judges pointed out that I was not on trial for the illegality of my action or the fact that I had lost the children.

The charge of contempt related to whether or not I had taken every means possible to find the children. They both declared I had.

Mr Justice Ritchie continued to argue that I should be punished for the contempt of which the Court had already found me guilty. Fortunately, he was over-ruled two to one and I am now free.

Thank you for your supportive letter. I will write again soon.

Your grateful friend

Emma Stirling

Hillfoot Farm
Aylesford
Nova Scotia.

10 August 1891

Miss Hope-Johnston,
Marchbankwood,
Scotland.

Dear Miss Hope-Johnston,

I felt I had to reply to your most recent letter immediately.

I realise that the publicity in The Scotsman relating to the Delaney case has caused you some distress and I hasten to reassure you.

I will give my side of the story and hope that will set your mind at rest.

In 1882, a man of notoriously bad character had brought his three children to my care, and deserted them immediately after.

When he applied for their admission, he stated he had been a Roman Catholic, but was tired of the neglect and tyranny of the priests and desired to have them brought up as Protestants.

In the course of four years he only once asked after them and paid only £1 17s. towards their maintenance.

But in 1886, finding that two of the children had been sent by the directors to Nova Scotia in the course of that year, he consulted a priest, who recommended him to a Roman Catholic agent, by whom he was advised to apply for them.

The directors then requested me to bring them home, which I did at once but, knowing what the fate of the children would be, I was naturally unwilling to give them up if it could be avoided; and as the father did not make any further attempt to obtain them, the former application to the directors was allowed to drop.

After waiting five months I sent them out again, and with them the third child, who had not been in the Homes since 1884, but had been supported at my private expense in the country, and in due course they were provided for.

After eighteen months a law suit has been instituted, which has been alike troublesome and expensive. The result has been a breach with the Directors so that for three years I have carried on this work entirely at my own expense.

The decision in my favour given by the Court in Nova Scotia in the above case has been a great relief to me. The Court agreed that since I did not know where the children now were I could hardly be held in contempt of Court for not returning them.

You express surprise that our children are not kept within reach of Hillfoot Farm in their placements. It is perhaps hard to appreciate, from home, that Canada is a vast country, and sparsely populated. Obviously, there are not enough farms in Nova Scotia itself to accommodate all our children.

When we received grants of monies from the Canadian Government to bring out children as migrant workers it was on condition they be sent throughout Canada to wherever there was a need.

We now have children in every province and indeed some have been sent to the States.

The inconvenience and outlay involved in the Court case has been considerable; but, as I was advised to carry it on in the interests of poor children, as well as of the Protestant cause, the risk seemed unavoidable.

I was informed, after the Court's decision, that my whole crime had been taking a Protestant population into Nova Scotia, which would tell at the General Election; that when my boys landed, in September, 1886 they attracted a good deal of attention, and on finding that we had come to found a Protestant colony in the province, the Roman Catholics in Halifax determined to stop it and therefore, wrote home to their friends in Edinburgh, to know if they could find an occasion against me by reason of having Roman Catholic children, with the result that Delaney was brought forward as described above.

After the Judges here freed me, from a charge of contempt of court, a dignitary of the Protestant church here congratulated me warmly. He stated that the whole case was a *piece of Popish persecution and said that my success was the first check that had ever been given to Popish tyranny in Nova Scotia and thousands of Protestants are rejoicing in it.*

Meanwhile, our work goes on. In June we were joined by a party of children from Miss Croall's Home at Stirling. All these are now in good homes and giving satisfaction.

Each year more boys and girls have been placed in suitable homes, and thus enabled to do for themselves, while leaving room for newcomers, and I rejoice to be able still to say that the reports of them which I receive from all directions are most encouraging.

We have also done much to improve the stock of cattle and sheep, since there has been suitable accommodation for them in the new buildings.

By dint of constant care and pains, we hope by-and-by it will be one of the best in the province. We also have a brand new piggery.

Since 1890 we have planted three new orchards of pears, peaches, plums and cherry trees all of which give considerable profit.

So as you can see we continue to prosper!

That The Scotsman newspaper should suggest that child migration is a great and growing evil and that I had no right to deprive a parent of his children without his consent is unbelievable.

I appreciate that the fact that the Court of Session, in Edinburgh, has ruled that I must return Delaney's children, and that they have

declared him a fit and responsible person
to have his children, with a respectable wife,
and a home to take them to, has caused you
some concern. However, I feel sure that now
you know I no longer have his children you
will understand that it is impossible for me to
return them.

Please disregard all you read in the
newspapers and let them not distress you.

Your sincere friend

Emma Stirling.

CECILIA'S STORY

PART SEVEN

CHAPTER 1

Three months later their worst fears were realised. The detective had been unable to find the bairns. Ross Stewart had brought them a copy of the report that the detective had sent to the Court of Session. It read –

REPORT

By

MR H. MELLISH, Detective Officer, Halifax, Nova Scotia,

Of his

SEARCH FOR THE CHILDREN OF THE PETITIONER,

ARTHUR DELANEY.

After receiving your instructions, and perusing carefully Miss Stirling's answers and disclosures in connection with these children, I set about the task of endeavouring to locate the Delaney children.

About the 1st of August, 1891 I went to Little Shemogue, in the county of Westmoreland, in the province of New Brunswick, a farming district

478

about three miles from the nearest station on the N.B. & P.E. Island Railway, and found that Robina Delaney had been living there at the house of Smith Blacklock, under the name of Bessie Whitehead, up to about the month of April in the spring of 1890, when she was taken away by a man who came for her in the company with her brother (James Delaney, I suppose). I could find no clue as to the name of the party who came for her, nor of the place he went, or even the direction he took on going away with the child and from the best opinion I can form, it does not seem likely that the Blacklocks know where the child was taken.

Up to within a few days, not more than a week previous to her being taken away, the child had been staying for some six months at the home of Fred Raworth, a farmer, residing in Westmoreland county, about eight miles from the Blacklocks's, where she had formerly stayed.

She was known in the neighbourhood as a bright child and a good singer.

I then went to Grand Metis, a French settlement on the River St. Lawrence, in the province of Quebec, about three miles from St. Octave, the nearest railway station, and found that a child who gave her name as Whitehead (presumably Annie Delaney) had been living with Joseph Jones, a married man with no family, up to the end of September 1890, when she was taken away by a man, d'une moyenne grandeur et blond, whom the little girl recognised when he came for her.

Mr and Mrs Jones, who were much attached to the child at first refused to give her up, and the child herself was very unwilling to go away, but the man who came for her is said to have represented himself as the child's uncle (not true, of course) and threatened to compel Mr Jones to give her up, and so the latter was forced to give way.

She was then taken hurriedly to the railway station, and put on board the train bound north, but I could obtain no information which could make further search in that direction anything more than mere speculation.

This child used to speak of a sister who was better looking than she. She promised to write to Mrs Jones but does not seem to have done so yet.

I then proceeded to Black Point, in the county of Gloucester, New Brunswick, one of the places named by Miss Stirling as the residence of Mrs Raworth, and found that no person name Raworth resided there, or even in that county.

But I heard of two of Miss Stirling's children there, one a girl named Maggie Cowan, aged fourteen, living with Ebenezer McMillan, and another a boy, named John English, aged sixteen, living with Robert Harvey at that place.

I also visited Black Rock, the other of the places mentioned by Miss Stirling as the residence of Mrs Raworth. It is a small country district near the Caraquet Railway, about thirty miles from Bathurst, in the province of New Brunswick, but found no person named Raworth residing there, and no trace of any children not living with their parents.

A fortnight later I visited Pugwash in this province, and Wallace Bay, about four miles from Pugwash, in search of the children.

John Tuttle, from whom Robina Delaney was sent to Blacklocks's, resides at Wallace Bay but I could get no information of any value at that place.

I found, however, that a child whom I believe to be Annie Delaney had been living a mile from Pugwash with a married sister of John Tuttle about the month of September 1890, but found no trace of her after that date.

Lastly, I visited Middleton in this province in search of James Delaney. I found that he attended a little school about three miles from Middleton Railway Station for some time previous to January 14ᵗʰ, 1890, at which date his attendance, according to the school register, ceases. He is registered as James Delaney, aged twelve years.

At that time he was living at Rufus De Wolfe's, two miles from Middleton Station.

In March, 1890 he ran away from De Wolfe's, but was back there again in September of the same year when he again ran away when Mr De Wolfe was not at home, and since that date his whereabouts are unknown in the community.

Mr De Wolfe made no enquiry or search for him, and never sent any person to look for him, nor did he ever search for him himself after that date, as he himself admitted. Mr De Wolf also stated that he had heard nor seen nothing of the boy since that date, that the boy was not much use on the farm, and was constantly running away.

He is said to have been a bright, smart boy, with red hair and round features.

Mr De Wolfe also stated that the boy was not then in the county of Annapolis (Middleton is in this county).

I have no idea whatever, from any information I have been able to obtain from the most careful enquiry, in what way one should proceed in further prosecution of the search for any of these children.

I have no reason to believe that in any case, except that of the boy, any of the parties interested knew of a search being made for the children, and I also believe that the parties with whom the children were living were not put in possession of any information which would enable their whereabouts to be traced.

I made enquiries in the most cautious manner, staying for days in the different neighbourhoods where it was thought information could be obtained, and working under assumed names, endeavoured in every way known to me to get trace of the present whereabouts of the children, but failed.

I am convinced that the changes in the girl's names and several changes effected in their various residences of late were made with the deliberate intention of avoiding location in case of enquiry and I know of nothing further I can do except to grope around somewhat aimlessly without anything to work upon.

H. MELLISH

Halifax, Nova Scotia
September 9th 1891

Messrs Drysdale, Newcombe & McInnes.
Barristers, Halifax.'

When Arthur had finished reading the report he put his head in his hands and burst into tears.

Cecilia went immediately to comfort him while Ross Stewart stood awkwardly shifting his hat from hand to hand.

At last, Arthur stopped weeping and, blowing his nose and wiping his eyes, he apologised to the lawyer.

'No need for apologies,' Ross Stewart said, 'It is very understandable. But I promise you this is not the end. We will fight on. We will make them pay for this.'

Before leaving he explained that the Judges would meet to consider the detective's report and that he would be informed of their decision on the case. He promised Arthur that as soon as he heard the judgement he would let him know.

Once Cecilia had read the detective's report, she knew Arthur would never rest until he had gone to Nova Scotia to look for the bairns himself.

CHAPTER 2

Two weeks later Ross Stewart again sat in Arthur and Cecilia's kitchen. The judges had met and he had brought the transcript of their deliberations. After Arthur had read it he looked crestfallen and handed it to Cecilia. She read –

THE COURT OF SESSION
EDINBURGH

20 OCTOBER 1891

Petition presented to the court on behalf of the Respondents, The Edinburgh & Leith Children's Aid & Refuge Society.

PETITION

The Directors contend that they have done everything in their power to recover the children of Arthur Delaney. They beg the court to overturn the order of June 7, 1889.

DECISION

Lord Adam stated – This petition is before us upon a report by a detective officer who was sent out by the Directors to search for the children under an order of the court.

I cannot say that the report is satisfactory, but so far as I can gather from its terms the detective officer has done all he could, and he tells us that he does not see any other means of following up his search.

As far, then, as that report goes, I cannot see any practical course which can be adopted to make further search successful.

It has been suggested to us by counsel for Arthur Delaney that in view of the fact that the judgement of the Supreme Court of Nova Scotia was not unanimous we ought to order the Directors to appeal it to the Judicial Committee of the Privy Council.

The judgement of the Court of Nova Scotia has, however, by a majority of two judges to one, declared that Miss Stirling has satisfactorily answered the interrogatories put to her by the Court, and has purged herself of the contempt of which she was formerly found guilty. I do not then see how we could take further any further proceedings as regards the judgement which would be effectual. It is not suggested from the bar that any other effectual course could be taken.

For my own part, I should be very willing to give the fullest assistance to the father in his search for these children. It seems very remarkable that this lady, who may be actuated by benevolent motives, should take the children outwith the jurisdiction of this Court, and should then allow them to disappear in the wilds of Nova Scotia without also being able to say where they are to be found.

I think, however, that the Directors have bona fide done all that they can be expected to do.

In my opinion this petition ought not to be sent out of Court, for it may be that further information will come to the father or the Directors which may make it competent and proper for them to make another motion in the petition.

We ought then, I think, to pronounce no further order in the meantime.

'Well,' said Arthur, once Cecilia had finished reading, 'that appears to be that – there is nothing else we can do.'

'Not quite,' Ross Stewart responded. 'The judges have informed me that they advise you to make a claim for damages for the loss of the children. Are you prepared accept the damages payment?'

Arthur, his nerves strung to breaking point lost his temper.

'What use is the money to me? Money won't bring ma bairns back,' he shouted. 'If I accepted it would be like I had sold them!'

Ross Stewart calmed him down by pointing out that, if Arthur accepted the money, he would be able to go to Nova Scotia and search for the bairns himself, like he had often suggested doing.

Arthur said he would consider it.

Ross Stewart left, saying that Arthur should contact him as soon as possible with his decision.

Cecilia rose and started getting their bairns, Arthur, Bernard, John and baby Cecilia, ready for bed and soon they were tucked up fast asleep.

Arthur stood looking down at them, lost in thought, then he turned to Cecilia.

'Would you manage, Cecilia, if I was to go out to Nova Scotia to look for the bairns?'

Cecilia didn't hesitate. 'Of course you have to go. We have to find the bairns. I'll manage fine,' she said.

Arthur put his arms around her and she rested her head on his shoulder.

Next day, Arthur contacted Ross Stewart and said he would agree to accept the judges' suggestion of damages.

The lawyer explained that they would ask the Court of Session to award one thousand pounds. He said he wouldn't get that amount. The judges would take into account that the Directors had already incurred considerable expenditure. They had sent their Secretary to Nova Scotia, then employed a detective, and finally, they had paid the legal fees to bring the case against Miss Stirling in the Supreme Court of Nova Scotia.

It was four months later that the judges met to consider the damages action. In the event they awarded damages of one hundred pounds.

Ross Stewart brought a copy of the judgement to their flat. It read –

COURT OF SESSION
EDINBURGH

24 February, 1892

Case for compensation for the loss of children called by Arthur Delaney against the Directors, The Edinburgh & Leith Children's Aid & Refuge Society.

The Court orders that compensation of £100, as agreed, should be paid by the Directors of the Edinburgh & Leith Children's Aid & Refuge Society to Arthur Delaney in settlement of his claim.

The lawyer seemed disappointed at the amount, though one hundred pounds seemed a fortune to Cecilia. He explained that they could appeal the amount but it would only delay settlement. He advised Arthur to accept.

Arthur looked at Cecilia and when she nodded, he said, 'Fine, I agree.'

Ross Stewart produced a Settlement of Damages form which read –

COURT OF SESSION
EDINBURGH

8 April, 1892

Final Settlement of case for compensation for the loss of the children of Arthur Delaney.

I, Arthur Delaney, glass-cutter, at present residing at No.4 Niddry Street, Edinburgh, acknowledge to have received from James Colston and others, directors of the Edinburgh and Leith Children's Aid and Refuge, the sum of £100 in full of all claims of damage competent to me under the summons signeted 24th February last, or otherwise against them or the society, past or present, represented by them for or in connection with the loss of my three children, James, Annie and Robina, who were sometimes inmates of the said Refuge and are now believed to be in America, or elsewhere out of Scotland; and my whole claims of every kind for damages in respect of the loss of the said children are hereby discharged, as is also the said summons, and all that has followed thereon.

Arthur signed it.

Just over a month later Ross Stewart returned and handed Arthur a cheque for one hundred pounds.

'What will you do with the money?' he asked Arthur.

'What do you mean? Arthur said, looking puzzled.

Ross Stewart had looked at Cecilia with the baby in her arms and their three sons sitting at her feet.

'Forgive me,' he said, 'but you have a growing family here, that one hundred pounds would make things a lot easier for your wife and these children. It would give you some security.'

Arthur leapt to his feet, his face flushing.

'The money means nothing tae me. A only accepted it so that could go and look for ma bairns,' he shouted.

Cecilia saw a smile appear on Ross Stewart's face.

'That's what I hoped you would say,' he said. 'If you would be willing I could go with you,' he continued. 'I wouldn't charge for my services, just pay for my passage.

It would be a privilege to accompany such an honourable man,' he said.

Cecilia felt relief flood through her at his words. She had known that nothing would stop Arthur going to Nova Scotia to search for his bairns, now that he had the means to do so. She had been apprehensive about how he would fare – a man who had never been out of Edinburgh in his life – making a hazardous sailing across the Atlantic and searching in the wilderness of such a huge country.

She saw the anger drain from Arthur's face and she saw relief there, too.

Arthur held out his hand and the lawyer clasped it in his own.

On the 23rd May 1892, Cecilia and her bairns stood on the platform at the Caledonian Railway Station and waved as Arthur and Ross Stewart set off by train for Liverpool. They were to sail the next day aboard the ship *The Nova Scotian* on the long voyage to Halifax.

CHAPTER 3

They were gone for five weeks.

Then one day the door of the flat opened and Arthur stood there. He was alone.

Cecilia saw that Arthur was exhausted and she made him go straight to bed. She would hear all about the trip after he was rested.

Late that night he awoke and they sat by the fire talking, quietly, into the early hours while the bairns slept.

Arthur told her of the sea voyage. It had taken them ten days to get to Halifax. Both he and Ross Stewart had been terribly sick at first, but later they got their sea-legs. He told of being up on deck and seeing whales and icebergs! He spoke of the strange sensation of being out of sight of any land for so many days, he who had lived his whole life in the narrow closes and the overcrowded tenements of the Old Town. When at last they had reached Halifax it had been a relief to stand on dry land. He described Halifax as a bustling sea-port, but once they were on the train to Aylesford the land grew wilder with few buildings for mile after mile. He began to realise then just how difficult his search was going to be. Looking out the window of the carriage it looked like this was a land where nobody lived. How was he ever going to find his bairns in this wilderness, he had wondered.

He spoke of his gratitude to Ross Stewart.

'A dinnae ken how a would have managed withoot him,' he said.

When they had at last alighted at Aylesford Station, after a journey of a hundred miles, Stewart had hired a horse and cart and they had set off at once for Hillfoot Farm.

Arthur described the countryside. It was right bonnie, he said, with lots of different trees covered in blossom.

Ross Stewart had counselled him to keep his temper when they met Miss Stirling but in the event she wasn't even there!

The Home Supervisor had informed them that she was still in the South of France and they were not expecting her back until summer.

Arthur had been devastated. They had come all this way and she wasn't even there.

Again, Ross Stewart had calmed him down, pointing out that had she been there she would hardly have been welcoming.

From his position as a member of the law profession, he had been able to show official court authorisation for their enquiries, and demand that they be able to search for the children. The supervisor had assured him that none of the Delaney children were there. Indeed they had left Hillfoot Farm a long time ago. But they were very welcome to look for themselves.

Ross Stewart had been a bit concerned that Arthur might not recognize the lassies but Arthur himself had been completely confident.

'A told him a would never forget Annie's wee face, with it's pointed chin, and that Robina's mop of wild black curls could never be disguised.'

They had been allowed to wander freely inside the house and out on the farm.

Arthur became distressed while he was describing it to Cecilia.

'Ye should hae seen it,' he exclaimed. 'Wee bairns that looked scarcely older than our Bernard, all hard at work. There were laddies staggering about carrying piles of logs up the hill to what looked like a saw mill. Inside the hoose, wee lassies were scrubbing floors or busy at wash tubs.

'A couldnae help myself, a said to the supervisor, "Do ye no think these bairns are a bit wee tae be working like that?" and dae ye ken what she said?

'She said, "Miss Stirling believes that the devil finds work for idle hands and they are being trained as farm servants and labourers after all.".

'A just said tae her, "A weel, nae doot Miss Stirling is right familiar wi the devil's ways right enough.".

'It's slavery, that's what it is,' Arthur burst out as he told Cecilia. 'A could see that Ross Stewart was as shocked as me.

'A said tae him afterwards, that nae wee bairn in the worst slum in the Auld Toon would have been expected to work like that. Even if a feckless faither had tried it the neighbours would never had stood for it.

'And the worse thing of a is that a kent that's what ma bairns must have been subjected tae as well.

'We came away then. It was obvious Annie and Robina were not there. They couldn't have hidden them because they didnae know we were coming.'

Arthur explained that they had stayed that night at the Inn in Aylesford and the next morning they had set off for the farm of Rufus de Wolfe which was a few miles away. The farmer was out in his yard when they arrived, and when Ross had introduced himself and Arthur they saw that the man became ill at ease. He was a short powerfully built man with red hair and a bushy beard. He had a strange accent, which Ross later told Arthur sounded French. When Arthur demanded to know what had happened to his son James, the man had just given a shrug.

'He ran away,' he had said. 'He was a bright boy, but not suited for farm work, he was always running away.'

Before Ross Stewart could stop him, Arthur had leapt forward and grabbed the man by the throat.

'A said, "Did you beat him? Is that why he kept running away?".'

Fear had shown in the man's eyes but Ross Stewart had pulled Arthur away.

"For God's sake man," he had said, "do you want to get yourself arrested?"

The man had recovered somewhat but he had taken a step back.

"I only beat him when he deserved it - sitting in the hayloft reading when he was supposed to be working - he deserved it," he had repeated.

Ross Stewart had struggled to keep hold of Arthur as he had strained forward again.

But the man wasn't taking any chances. He had retreated into his farmhouse and slammed the door and they had heard a bolt being pulled.

Ross Stewart had manhandled Arthur back to the cart and he was climbing into the driving seat when the farmer had emerged from his house with a rifle in his hands.

'"Get off my land," he shouted, pointing the gun at us.'

The encounter with the farmer had shaken Arthur badly.

"A gun!" he had said in amazement to Ross Stewart. "A gun, and he looked as if he would have used it. What kind of country is this?"

They had ridden along in silence until at last Arthur had voiced his thoughts. "Ye don't think that he could have beaten James tae death and then hidden his body?" he had asked Ross Stewart. "Maybe ma laddie didn't run away, maybe he killed him! Nobody admits to seeing him in the area after he ran away – the detective asked around – nobody had seen him. Look at this place." He had gestured around the deserted countryside. "There is no place to hide."

Arthur told Cecilia he had felt himself losing control.

"Lets go back," he had urged Ross Stewart, "Give me another go at the man."

"Arthur," the lawyer had said, "He had a gun and this is his country. If he had shot us do you think anybody would care?"

Arthur had had to agree that he was right.

Ross Stewart had tried to reassure him.

"James was a smart boy," he had said, "He would have made for the train. He could have been away from here before anyone had noticed. He could have gone all the way to Halifax."

Arthur had tried to accept this, but anxiety had niggled away at him just the same.

After returning the horse and cart at Aylesford, they themselves had caught the train to Halifax. They had stayed the night in a hotel there and, taking local advice about the best way to travel, they had made their way by train to Little Shemogue, where Robina had last been seen.

They had found the house of Smith Blacklock and had again introduced themselves. The man did not know Robina by her own name, but when Arthur had asked him to describe her it was obvious that it was her, and that the couple had been given a false name. His wife had described how the child had been taken away by a man, in the company of the girl's brother, in the spring of 1890.

Arthur had asked Mrs Blacklock to describe the person the man had claimed was Robina's brother.

"Was he young?" he had asked, "About thirteen years old?"

The woman could not remember clearly what they had looked like, but she had been sure that it was two men, not a man and a boy.

Arthur had asked if Robina had recognised the other man as her brother.

The woman had thought for a bit, and then had said that the girl was not there when they had first arrived, as she had been out on the farm. Mrs Blacklock had, at first, resisted handing the child over without any authority. But the man had said he was her uncle and that the other man was the girl's brother, and she must go with them. It was then that she had sent out to the fields for her, she had explained.

"So Robina never actually identified them as her family?" Ross Stewart had asked.

"No," the woman had replied, "but she obviously knew them. She wasn't happy about going with them, but she had been moved around a lot from farm to farm before she came to us, so I suppose she was used to it."

Seeing Arthur's distress, at hearing this, the couple had obviously felt sorry for Arthur. Before they had left the woman had said, "I hope you find her, she was a really beautiful child with a lovely voice, always singing."

The couple had been sure that Robina was nowhere in their area, but Arthur and Ross Stewart had decided to drive around in their hired horse and cart just to make sure. They had driven around all day, but houses had been few and, though they had stopped and asked at each one, no one resembling Robina was to be found.

Their final journey had been by boat on the St Lawrence River to Grand Metis, in Quebec, where Annie had lived, according to the detective's report.

They found the couple, Mr and Mrs Jones, who she had been staying with. Again they had not known Annie by her own name, but from their description it was obvious it must have been her. For the first time Arthur had felt some comfort. It was obvious the couple had been genuinely fond of Annie and she of them. He had no doubt they had treated her well. On hearing that he was her father, and that he had come all the way from Scotland to look for her, they had been sympathetic and had tried to be helpful.

Mr Jones explained how he had refused, at first, to hand Annie over to the man who had come for her. He and his wife had wanted to keep her.

At this point his wife had begun to weep and Arthur had seen they had been telling the truth. Whoever had sent the man to take Annie away, this couple had known nothing about it.

The husband explained that he had been threatened by the man and that Annie had been forced to go with him.

Ross Stewart had asked Mr Jones if it appeared that Annie had known the man, and he had agreed that she had, but she still hadn't wanted to go with him.

His wife had been still weeping. "She promised to write to me, but she never has," she had sobbed. "She was a good child, she would have written if she could, something must have stopped her."

Her husband had seen that these revelations had been distressing Arthur and he had shushed his wife. "Why was the child taken from us?" he had asked. "Who would do such a thing?"

Arthur knew the answer to that – only Miss Stirling would have had a reason – only she had had the authority to order it.

They had left the couple and Arthur had promised the woman that, when he found his daughter, he would be sure to get her to write. But as they had ridden away, Arthur told Cecilia, he had been feeling sure that he would never see any of his bairns again.

They had journeyed back to Halifax to make the long voyage home.

They had booked their passage and, a few days later, they had been standing at the harbour waiting for boarding to start.

Arthur described to Cecilia how a small cargo ship had been berthed, just below the harbour wall, where they had been waiting.

Down on the deck, out of view, a voice had been singing.

"The wind, the wind, the wind blows high.
The snow comes falling from the sky.
Jamsie Delaney says he'll die
For want of the windy city."

To Ross Stewart's alarm, Arthur had suddenly leapt over the harbour wall and had landed with a thud on the deck below.

A young lad had looked up in amazement as this man had landed at his feet.

A young lad, thin, with a pinched face and black hair.

Not a lad with a round face, freckles and a shock of red hair, Arthur had realised, his heart sinking, all his hopes dashed.

The lad had been coiling ropes and he had frozen, open mouthed, as Arthur had grabbed him by the arm.

'The song,' Arthur had shouted, 'The song you were singing. Is your name James Delaney?' he had demanded, still gripping the lad by his arm.

"No, no," the lad had stuttered, looking frightened, "Jamsie Delaney was a lad that once sailed with me, as a deck boy on this boat. He was always singing that song as we coiled the ropes. It has a good rhythm to it, that song, so I still sing it when I'm coiling ropes," he had explained.

'When? When was Jamsie Delaney on this boat?' Arthur had demanded.

The lad had frowned, trying to recollect.

"I can't remember exactly - a year ago - maybe two," the lad had suggested.

"And did he have two lassies with him?" Arthur had asked.

The lad had shaken his head and Arthur's heart had sunk.

"Where was this boat going then?" he had demanded.

"Boston," the lad had replied. "He was working his passage to Boston."

Arthur had let go of the lad's arm and, reaching into his pocket, he had taken out a silver coin and given it to the lad.

"If ye ever see James Delaney again, tell him his father came looking for him – tell him Arthur Delaney was looking for him – will ye do that?"

The boy had nodded, looking down in amazement at the coin in his hand.

"I surely will," he had promised. "Next time we berth in Boston I'll go looking for him – shouldn't be too hard to find – with that red hair," he had said, smiling.

Arthur had become aware of his name being called and he had looked up and seen the astonished face of Ross Stewart staring down at him. "Have you taken leave of your senses, man?" he had shouted, "Our ship is nearly ready to sail!"

Arthur had seen an iron ladder on the harbour wall and had climbed rapidly to the top.

When he had finished telling all this to Cecilia, Arthur had started to sob.

'He got away! Cecilia, he's no deid! He's out there somewhere and one day I'll find him and the lassies too.'

EMMA'S STORY

PART EIGHT

Hillfoot Farm,
Aylesford
Nova Scotia
20 July 1892.

Miss Auld
62 Northumberland Street,
Edinburgh.

My dear friend,

I write to thank you for a most restful visit to you over the winter. I will never be able to repay your generosity of spirit nor, sadly, your hospitality. How I wish you were a better sailor and could come and visit us here so I could return your hospitality.

After leaving you I spent a very pleasant few weeks in the South of France and so returned fully refreshed.

As I explained to you, when I was with you, I mentioned that I had found it better to buy a saw-mill instead of hiring one, and to continue sawing on my own account.

It proved a most successful venture as after sawing our own lumber we had plenty of work to do for our neighbours. This proved very remunerative and made us a fair sum of money.

I added a grist mill, which could be worked by the same engine by simply adjusting a different belt. As the harvest begins almost directly after the season for sawing lumber is over we were never a day idle with even the smallest children working from dawn to dusk.

Grist is brought in the whole winter and the portion left as payment went a long way towards feeding our cattle.

Sadly, however I have to report that our beautiful mill and convenient building over it, including the joiner's shop, was burnt to the ground, in the middle of the night, in a most mysterious way.

We could not account for it, and there seemed reason to fear unfair play, but we do not know, and so cannot say anything about it, but the loss has been very great, about £600. Not everyone wishes us well here.

I was advised to replace it, in a safer position, as it was so very profitable, and we had established a good lumber trade.

Will you ask among our dear friends and supporters if they will help me to pay for what is an excellent method of training and providing employment for a number of boys?

This summer we must also build a house for the sawyer, close to the mill. Of course, having the wood and machinery of our own enables us to do this at less cost, but I do hope friends who have any money to spare will help those who help themselves as really we and our children do.

The joiner's shop is never idle as we make furniture for the houses, ox-yokes and farm wagons. Even the very little children work. During the winter months, when they cannot be employed outside, they are kept busy making strawberry boxes, which sell very well in the berry season.

Few people, of any age, will be found doing nothing round the doors, as I have great faith in Dr. Watts's statement as to the ingenuity of somebody with a bad name providing employment for idle hands, and I never find it fail when the hands and heads are so left empty.

Play is most desirable. Idleness is destructive.

All boys of eight or nine get something to do with the men, in farm work, or the workshops or bringing in kindling and firewood. The girls have enough to do to cook, bake, clean house, wash, iron and sew for such a party.

Friends who wish to save and train destitute boys and lads of good character, from age ten to fifteen, could not, I believe, have a better opening for them than our farm and workshops. This, I think, is borne out by their success when they leave us.

My dear old friend I seem always to be asking you to do something for us but I know that you have the best interests of our children at heart and will do what you can.

Please write soon and give me all the news from home. I fear my family are poor correspondents as I hear little from them. I rely on you to keep me up to date with how things go in the old country.

Your affectionate friend,

Emma Stirling

Hillfoot Farm,
Aylesford
Nova Scotia

20 August 1892.

Miss Auld
62 Northumberland Street,
Edinburgh,

My dear friend,

It was so good to hear from you.

Thank you for your suggestion for raising money for our new saw-mill and other buildings.

It would be quite splendid if you could have my appeal inserted in the various Christian magazines that are printed in Edinburgh.

I enclose the article, for your approval, and would appreciate all you can do for us.

I will write again with more of our news but meantime I will get this short letter off to the post so that my Appeal can reach you as soon as possible.

Forever in your debt,

Emma Stirling

APPEAL FOR THE CHILDREN'S HOME, HILLFOOT FARM, AYLESFORD, NOVA SCOTIA

I appeal for as many friends as will feel inclined to help me continue my work with destitute children from the old country.

I have established the Home in Nova Scotia in the hope that it will be a real home to numbers of poor children who have no other, and that it will be a safe starting-point for many boys and girls in a new country, where they gave the opportunity offered to them of rising in the world, as well as a home to which they can come, at any time, for counsel or refuge in time of trouble - to say nothing of the place where their success will always be most heartily rejoiced in by all the folks at home!

We have all laboured to make the farm and workshops an efficient training school for lads of good character, from whence they quickly obtain good situations, and therefore hope that many will take advantage of it.

We hope that the same habits of industry, faithfulness, and kindness learned in the house will help to fit many girls for being the good household helpers who are so ardently desired and warmly welcomed on this side of the Atlantic.

I trust that long after my work for children is over, they will be known as heads of godly, righteous and sober families.

I hope that God's people will consider the case of many poor children who are orphans, or worse, by reason of the cruelty of their parents.

No doubt all are not suitable for emigration, but many are. Competent judges say the need is as great as ever in our large cities, yea, even all over the country. I, for one, dare not contradict them.

Much has been done, but much yet remains, and therefore I desire to open the doors of these Homes at Hillfoot Farm, N.S. as wide as possible to every destitute child.

READER WILL YOU NOT HELP ME?

For this I cry to God day and night, for this I have given up my life, and I know that in this work the Lord has blessed me; so I hope by His help to save many, body and soul, to bring sunshine and hope into many poor child's life, and to lead the active steps of many young men and maidens into safe and pleasant paths.

Donations gratefully accepted, on our behalf, by Miss Auld,
62 Northumberland Street, Edinburgh.

2 Main
Street,
Halifax
Nova Scotia

9 April 1895

Miss Auld,
62 Northumberland Street,
Edinburgh.

My dear friend,

Such a tragedy has befallen us. I scarce know how to tell you.

On the 25th March past I received a letter from a well-known and respected doctor, in which he informed me that one of my girls, Grace Fegan, had come to his hands in very serious trouble; that she was in a certain house in the adjoining county of Annapolis about thirty miles from Aylesford; that he thought a most serious investigation should take place, as the girl had received most improper treatment.

That evening I received a telephone call saying the girl was getting worse and begging me to go and see her at once. This I did and found her in a terrible condition. The magistrate was also there who had just taken her dying declaration; the revelation it contained was of the most horrible description.

She had been the victim of a clandestine abortion.

You will remember little Grace. She was in the first party we brought to Nova Scotia in May, 1886 when she was just five years old.

I had placed her with a most respectable farmer four years later but, to my horror, he had subjected her to the most revolting cruelty, the marks of which were still visible on her when I saw her.

When I was listening to her tell of the abuse and degradation she had suffered, the doctor came into the room and said it was not safe to speak for fear of being overheard; he added, it would be necessary to have a legal opinion on the matter, because if the facts were hidden, he and I would be held as accessories after the fact.

I went immediately to Halifax to consult my solicitor, Wallace MacDonald, who said that if the allegations were true, the doctor who performed the abortion and the farmer responsible for Grace being in that condition would have to be arrested.

After going to see Grace and being shocked at her state Mr MacDonald returned to Halifax and together we went for advice to Queen's Counsel, J.J. Ritchie. It was decided that I should lay information against the alleged culprits, Dr Samuel Nelson Miller, and the farmer, Robert Parker.

This I speedily did and the two were thrown into jail in Annapolis on 30th March. They had to send police from Annapolis to Nictaux Falls where Parker lived, and where

Grace had worked as his maid, because the constables in Aylesford were known to be unreliable.

I was advised not to leave Annapolis until the men were safely in jail as they were well known to be desperate characters. When it was safe I left by train, accompanied by my solicitor and returned home.

On the journey, I said to him that, knowing the habits of that part of the country (which are, that if you offend anyone, especially a bad character, your barn is probably doomed to be burnt in less than a week!) I had better look after my buildings.

I must have had a premonition because three nights later we heard talking outside the farm in the darkness. I went out with a lantern but could see nothing.

There were twenty-six of us inside the Big House that night. Myself, six servants, and nineteen children, of these eighteen were below twelve years old. We all went to bed as usual and at 3.45 next morning I was awakened by a large outcry. It was the shrieking of frightened women and children.

I went instantly towards the nursery passage communicating through my dressing room, and was met at the door by all the women and some of the children. I asked what was the matter. One of the women replied that the house was on fire and full of smoke, and the rest of the children were being suffocated and the women could do nothing with them

I went to the children's room, which I found full of dense smoke; and with great difficulty I persuaded some of them to come with me. The others were afraid to move and stayed in bed. We saw no fire then but the smoke was so dense I could not see my hand before me.

I gave the children who had come to me to the women who took them out; I stayed in the room alone to get the rest. The cries and pleading of the poor, terrified little ones, too frightened to get out of their beds were pitiful.

It was hopeless to find them all in the dark quickly enough for safety, as the room was large and the voices in various directions, besides I must keep hold of the baby child I had got. The only hope was to persuade them to come to me. This I did by telling them that if they would ONLY come, God would take care of us all.

This idea of God's actual presence, and power to help them, seemed to comfort them; and they stopped crying and made their way through the smoke to me.

I could not see any of them, only felt their little hands clinging to my nightdress. One of the big girls came back and took the baby child from me, while I sent the others along the passage.

When I got outside I saw to my great relief that Willie Fraser, who is only twelve years old, had rescued thirteen children from the other wing of the house. I gave thanks at the realisation that that meant all were saved.

As I stood there, my feet blistered and bleeding, from the heat from the floorboards in the burning room and the walk barefoot across the rough ground outside I saw the whole of the back of the house collapse.

All the children were taken barefoot through the snow and ice to the nearby Boy's House, were they took the beds which the older boys had left to help fight the fire.

It was all to no avail. As I watched the building began to blaze and by 6.30 a.m. the Big House had been reduced to a pile of ashes.

At first, I hoped against hope that it had been a terrible accident. Surely, no one would be wicked enough to try and burn a house full of children in their beds! Then I noticed that the woodshed was also burning even though it was nowhere near the house.

I knew that not a stick of dry wood was in the house on the night but only wood so green and full of half melted ice as to leave a puddle on the floor. It would not have burned without the addition of paraffin oil, of which there was a strong smell.

A man was later to confirm this as he had seen from a mile off both fires start together. It was no accident.

As the morning light dawned so did the realisation that we were homeless, naked, and without a shred of personal property. No clothes, no furniture, no shelter, no personal possessions or comforts of any kind; no books, no papers, literally NOTHING saved but our lives. Barely twenty minutes elapsed between the first alarm and the roof falling in so I think it a wonder that any of us were saved alive.

The following day we packed up the household and left Aylesford for Halifax where we are now.

I am speeding up the process of placing the children with employers previously arranged for them, and advertising for farmers, to take the others.

Oh, my old friend, what would I not give to have you here to comfort and advise me.

I must get this letter off to the post now. I will write again with news about the upcoming trial. Meanwhile you can reach me at my temporary lodgings above.

Your distraught friend,

Emma Stirling.

2 Main
Street,
Halifax,
Nova
Scotia.

15 July
1895

Miss Auld,
62 Northumberland Street,
Edinburgh.

My dear friend,
Thank you for your most welcome letter. It put me in such good heart to hear from you and realise I was not completely alone. It has helped me bear all the grief that has been visited upon me over the past few weeks.

After I had disposed of most of the children I devoted the rest of my time to nursing little Grace. We had to remove her from her sickbed to another house, in spite of her perilous condition, as a bounty of $2,000 was placed on her head to prevent her testifying against the culprits.

Indeed, two policemen had to be on constant guard at her door in case she was abducted.

It is almost impossible to believe but after the accused had been committed for trial, the county court judge - without informing the prosecutors - had freed Miller on nominal bail. Even before this he had been seen wandering the streets of Annapolis and receiving visitors in the home of his gaoler!

When the case eventually came before the Grand Jury on June 18, the judge opened by telling them, in the strongest possible terms, that they find no bill against the prisoners on the charge brought but that as Miller had gone to another doctor, who had refused to perform the abortion, they might indict him for attempting to have the operation done; which they did.

The jury in the case was most obviously and infamously packed, the judge being aware of it, yet he allowed the trial to proceed, and, of course, the verdict was not guilty.

In order to create a sentiment in favour of his impartiality, the judge fined the sheriff $100, ostensibly for contempt of court but really (he said) because he had packed the jury.

One strong bond among the members of this gang is that they are all Liberals, and most of them very useful to the Liberal interest.

The judge even admitted to me privately afterwards that no one can be convicted in this country unless certain people please.

I have since heard that forced abortions were frequent in Annapolis. I was told by various respectable people, among others an official of the crown, that one woman had been simply murdered from this cause at Middleton in the fall of 1894, and that between the months of January and May, 1895, no less than three graves had been made in Middleton church-yard and filled with three young women from this cause alone.

I never thought that any man could have used a little girl, like Grace, in such a way but I am now aware that gross immorality is rampant in portions of this county.

After the trial I received a letter from J.J. Ritchie, the assistant prosecuting counsel in which he agreed with me that there was no doubt that Parker and Miller were guilty.

He wrote that he could not see how anyone possessing any knowledge of the facts could doubt that I was fully justified in the course which I took in the case of Grace Fegan. Given that before I laid the information against Dr Miller and Parker, I had the declaration of Grace Fegan as to the cause of her condition, taken by J.E. Oakes Esquire, a justice of the peace, and sworn to before him at a time when neither Grace nor the doctor in attendance thought there was any hope of her recovery.

Mr Ritchie reminded me, in his letter, that the law attaches such weight to declarations of this character as to receive them in evidence even in cases of murder, although not sworn to. This is done on the principle that the person making the declaration is at the point of death, and every hope of this world is gone, and every motive to falsehood silenced, and the mind induced by the most powerful considerations to speak the truth.

Perhaps it was naïve of me but up to the time when I heard the verdict I had hoped to be able to return to my farm. However, after the (what I can only call) mock trial at Bridgetown, I felt that unless protection could be obtained from the Dominion Government, as that of Nova Scotia appeared to be utterly powerless or callous in the matter, I felt my position very unsafe, as I had been credibly informed that the gang, or some of them, had sworn in the most horrible manner that they would not have me round that country. That it would be useless for me to think of rebuilding, for, as fast as my houses were built, they would be burned, AS THEY HAD BEFORE!

I despair of this country now and intend to seek refuge among the Quakers of Pennsylvania. I will send you my new address as soon as I am settled.

Ever, your friend,

Emma Stirling.

Drumpellier,
Coatesville,
Chester County
Philadelphia

15 August 1895

Miss Auld,
62 Northumberland Street,
Edinburgh.

My dear friend,

Just, a brief note, in haste, to let you have my new address. I knew you would be anxious to hear from me.

I left Nova Scotia, with never a backward look, on July 19th. I travelled via Montreal and on a terribly hot day in August arrived in Philadelphia.

My only companion was young Willie Fraser. After his heroics in saving so many of our children on that awful night of the fire I could not bear to part with him.

We stayed in a hotel until I had time to look for a house for us and now here we are!

This house has lain empty for almost twenty years and is in a most dilapidated state but it is a most charming house and I am sure we will be able to make it homely in time. It is just habitable enough for Willie and I to live here meanwhile but hopefully it will soon be in a fit state to start welcoming more destitute children from the old country.

I have decided to give the house the name of 'Drumpellier' to remind me of home.

I will write again to give such news as I have. Please do write yourself, now you have my address and give me all the news from Edinburgh

Could you also give my address to Miss Hope-Johnson. I have not heard back from her since her last letter when she expressed concern about the Delaney case. Perhaps she is just very busy.

Your old friend

Emma Stirling.

Colonial House,
Tampa,
Pasco County
Florida.

1 December 1901

Miss Auld,
62 Northumberland Street,
Edinburgh.

My dear old friend,

No doubt you will be surprised to hear from me at the above address!

I had been finding the winters hard in the cold north and my health has been suffering.

On medical advice I have now moved here for the winter. I have bought this house and an orange grove and am most comfortable.

Willie and the remaining children, Bertha Foster and Jessie Martin remain at home in 'Drumpellier' to take care of all our animals.

I have discovered a new 'Cause'. The sponge fishermen, both white and coloured, who work the Gulf of Mexico, have a very hard life. No-one seems to take any interest in their welfare so I decided to build them a church and reading room. It stands in a place called Bailey's Bluff and is much used and appreciated.

I know, I know! I can just hear you saying 'most irregular' but what was I to do. They had nowhere to worship as they are not welcome in the orthodox churches but are still good Protestants. So I did what I could.

Take care of yourself, old friend, we are neither of us getting any younger. I will be at this address for a further six months before returning home to Philadelphia.

Your good friend

Emma Stirling.

CECILIA'S STORY

PART EIGHT

Edinburgh

24th February 1907

Cecilia Delaney sat beside the bed of her husband, Arthur, in their house at 4 Niddry Street.

A strong wind was gusting and rattling the window frame, but inside all was quiet and warm. A good fire burned in the grate and Cecilia rose from time to time to put another lump of coal on the fire. There was no need to stint, because Tammy Bain had come by earlier and emptied a sack of best coal into the coal bunker in the kitchen. He refused to take payment and made Cecilia promise to let him know when the supply was getting low.

Everybody had been very kind, Cecilia thought.

Arthur was propped up on pillows in the high bed with the brass frame.

He was asleep.

Cecilia sat watching him. He was scarcely recognizable as the man she had married twenty-one years ago. He was forty-seven years old but he looked much older. Cecilia was sure that the stress of the long Court battles to regain his lost bairns had aged him.

Even when his attempt to regain his bairns was over there was further tragedy in store for him.

Tears started from Cecilia's eyes as she remembered that awful time in their married life.

Their second bairn, Bernard, had developed cancer of

the blood and had died when he was six years old, at the Sick Children's hospital on 21 September 1893.

When wee Bernard had become sickly, Arthur had been pursuing another case at the Court of Session against Miss Stirling.

He had sued her for damages for the loss of his bairns, hoping, that with any money he was awarded, he would be able to return to Canada, and even America, to look for the bairns.

When the Court of Session had dismissed the case, on the basis that when Arthur accepted the damages from the Directors, he had also given up any claim against Miss Stirling, Arthur's reaction had surprised Cecilia. He had just accepted the verdict with a shrug of his shoulders.

'Wee Bernard is so sick,' he had said. 'A need to give ma energy to looking after the bairns a still have. A've tried so hard for a these years, but now a have tae accept that a will never see James, Annie and Robina again. You and our bairns are ma main concern now,' he had said. 'A must put it all behind me.'

From that day Arthur had never mentioned his lost bairns again. But Cecilia would catch him staring into space sometimes, and she knew that in his heart, and in his thoughts, memories of his bairns continued to haunt him.

When wee Bernard had died they still had three other bairns and they tried to let that be a consolation to them. Young Arthur was now six, their son, John Clifford, was three and their daughter, Cecilia, was just a baby.

Within a year only young Arthur was left to them.

An epidemic of scarlet fever had swept through the Old Town in 1894.

The horse-drawn ambulance became a common sight

in the town. Neighbours watched from their windows, as one bairn after another was removed from their home, wrapped in the scarlet blankets that signified a fever victim. The bairns were taken into isolation at the City Hospital for Infectious Diseases on the outskirts of Edinburgh. No one was allowed to visit them for fear the infection would spread.

When wee Cecilia fell victim and was taken away, Cecilia had thought her heart would break. She had tried to climb into the ambulance with her, wailing, 'She's just a baby, she will be frightened without me.'

Her sister, Mary, had pulled her back.

'Come away, Cissy,' she had said. 'Let them take the bairn and make her better. That's what you want isn't it?'

Every day Arthur had bought the local newspaper. When bairns were taken to the fever hospital they were given a number. In the event of a bairn dying their number was published in the paper. So bad was the epidemic that columns of numbers appeared every day.

Cecilia remembered that awful day when their wee daughter's number had appeared. She had died on 7th May, just four days after she had been taken away. Wee Cecilia had been just nineteen months old.

Arthur just went to pieces, weeping as if his heart would break, but Cecilia barely had time to grieve because their son, John Clifford, took ill.

Cecilia lavished attention and care on her sick son. She recalled how relieved she had been when no rash had appeared on him. It couldn't be scarlet fever and so he was not taken away to the City Hospital. But he started to go into fits, frightening convulsions which shook his wee body. Cecilia remembered how she had plunged him into tepid water, in the tin bath, when the convulsions wracked him, as the doctor had instructed. She had constantly sponged him to try and keep him cool, but his temperature had continued to rise.

Within two days he lay dead in Cecilia's arms. She would never forget how that felt. When the doctor came to issue the death certificate on the 14th May, he stated the cause of death was suppressed scarlet fever and convulsions. John was just four years old.

Arthur had been devastated. He could not take in that they had lost two of their bairns within a week of each other.

Cecilia had tried to find some comfort in her faith. She felt sure the bairns were safe in the arms of the Blessed Virgin and that one day she would see them again.

And there was another reason that forced her to try and control her grief and not let it overwhelm her. She was nursing her two month old son, Patrick. He had been born on the 6 March that year. A strong, healthy bairn with bright red hair.

Arthur stirred and moved his head restlessly on the pillow. Cecilia bent over him and bathed his face. His eyes were puffy, his face swollen and every breath was an effort.

He had become very ill so suddenly that even the doctor was puzzled.

Cecilia remembered that Arthur had suffered a bout of 'flu that had laid him low just before Christmas, but he had recovered enough to go back to work in the New Year. But as January progressed she noticed that Arthur was tiring very easily. He complained of headaches and his vision was blurred.

Cecilia had suggested he get spectacles, and Arthur

had gone and got them, but they didn't seem to help. It was a worry as he was working as a sign-writer at the time.

Then at the beginning of February, he had come home early from work complaining of a sore throat and a bad headache. He was very tired and went off to bed, but in the middle of the night he had wakened feeling nauseous and had later started to vomit. Cecilia had felt there was something seriously wrong and had sent for the doctor.

After examining Arthur he had taken Cecilia aside.

"I think he is suffering from kidney failure," he had said quietly.

Cecilia remembered the dread that had gripped her.

"But what could have caused that?" she had asked.

"Has he been ill recently before this bad spell?" the doctor had enquired.

She had told him about the 'flu.

"Sometimes that can trigger the condition," the doctor had explained. "However, his blood pressure is very high and I suspect there might be an underlying heart condition."

"What can ye do for him, is there some medicine he could take?" she remembered pleading.

"I'm afraid there is nothing we can do if his kidneys fail completely. I'm so sorry," the doctor had said.

Then seeing her distress he had tried to soften the blow.

"It may not come to that, just keep him warm, comfortable and as quiet as possible and let the symptoms run their course," he had said.

Family and friends had rallied round and taken the bairns to stay with them so that the flat in Niddry Street was kept quiet. Usually the house was a noisy, happy place. With six bairns in it how could it be otherwise.

Young Arthur was scarcely a bairn though. He was now twenty years old and working in the printing trade. He was devoted to Cecilia and the special bond she had felt at his birth had endured. With his father ill he was now the sole breadwinner for the family.

Cecilia knew that every shilling he earned was given to her on payday. She had tried to get him to keep a little back for himself, but he had refused, saying he would wait until his father was better and back at work. Cecilia was never sure if he really believed this would happen or if he was just saying it to console her.

Her son Patrick, too, tried to help. He was now thirteen years old, too young for a proper job, but he would run messages for neighbours after school. He went round the barrows and collected the crates they brought the vegetables in from the market. He would chop them into firewood and tie them into bundles to sell round the doors. He also did deliveries for local shopkeepers. He would proudly present the coppers he had earned to his mother. Cecilia was glad of every penny. Money was very tight with Arthur not working.

They now had three daughters. Mary was eleven, Helen, named in memory of Arthur's grandmother, Helen Boylan, who had died in 1890, was nine and Cecilia was six.

When Cecilia had been born Arthur had insisted that she receive her mother's name. Cecilia had been reluctant. She felt it would seem as if the first Cecilia, who had died of scarlet fever, had never existed. But Arthur was a great believer in tradition and had persuaded her that the name Cecilia should be perpetuated in the family.

Knowing how bitterly Arthur had regretted denying his own name to his son, George, by his first wife, she had given in. To avoid confusion the wee one was called Cely in the family.

When the bairns had all gone off to stay with her family it was her youngest bairn, Edward, named after her own brother, Ned Clifford, that Cecilia was most concerned about. He was only three years old and didn't keep good health. But she knew that her sister would take good care of him, and it was necessary if Arthur was to have the quiet he needed to recover.

Arthur slept on. The clock on the mantle piece ticked by the hours as she sat in the quiet room.

Her mind drifted back over the years of her married life.

It seemed to her that the struggle to get back Arthur's children, by his first wife, had dominated the early years of her marriage.

Cecilia had been lost in memories for hours. She came to herself with a start and realised the fire had burned low. She rose quickly and put more lumps of coal on the fire, banking it up for the night.

Returning to the bedside she saw that Arthur was still asleep.

Taking a blanket from the box, she climbed up on the other side of the bed and lay down beside him, covering herself with the blanket.

When the early morning light came through the window Cecilia awoke. She glanced quickly at Arthur lying beside her and realised that he, too, had slept all night. She slipped off the bed and went to the range. She raked up the still glowing embers and added more coal. Once the fire burned up she started to make the breakfast porridge.

She did this every morning, but Arthur had lost his appetite and she was rarely able to get him to take more than a spoonful.

When she went through with the porridge Arthur was still asleep.

She tried to wake him but she couldn't rouse him. His colour was terrible, he looked yellow.

Cecilia was alarmed.

She went across the landing to her neighbour's house and asked her to send one of her sons up to the Bank Street Dispensary to fetch a doctor.

The lad set off at once and Cecilia stood at the turret window, gazing anxiously, up the High Street, until she saw him running down the road accompanied by the doctor.

Cecilia rushed to the door to admit him.

The doctor stooped over Arthur.

Cecilia felt panic grip her throat.

The doctor turned around his face full of concern.

'I'm sorry,' he said, 'but he is fading fast. I don't think he will see this day out.'

A sob broke from Cecilia, and she sank down on the chair beside the bed and took Arthur's swollen hand in hers.

She was vaguely aware of the doctor leaving the room and realised he had gone for her neighbour, Molly.

When he came back into the room with Molly, the doctor said, 'I will call back later tonight.'

Cecilia nodded.

Molly knelt down beside her.

'Dae ye want me tae send for the family, Cecilia,' she said gently.

Cecilia nodded again, beyond words.

Molly left the flat briefly, leaving the door open behind her, and a few minutes later Cecilia saw Molly's many children run off to fetch the family. Molly herself returned and busied herself at the range making a pot of tea. She came to the bedside and, prising Cecilia's fingers from Arthur's hands, she wrapped them around the cup of sweet tea.

'Drink this, Cecilia, ye need it for the shock,' she insisted.

Cecilia, in a daze, did as she was told.

In a short space of time the flat filled up with the family.

Her son, Arthur, had come running from his work, on hearing the news. Cecilia's sister was there and Arthur's brother, James, and his sister, Nellie. Arthur's mother, Ann, had been dead for five years.

Cecilia's sister, Mary, bent over her. 'The other bairns are next door wi Molly, Cissy, do ye want them to come in?' she asked, softly.

Cecilia tried to gather her wits.

'Aye,' she said, 'let them come in for a wee while.'

Young Arthur stood at the side of the bed opposite Cecilia. His brother, Patrick, went and stood beside him. Wee Edward climbed onto his mother's lap and Mary, Helen and Cely clustered around her chair.

Arthur was moving his head restlessly on the pillow, but his eyes remained closed.

Suddenly, he spoke.

'The bairns,' he said, 'where are the bairns?'

Young Arthur took his hand and bent over him. 'We're here, faither, we're a here,' he said, tears running down his face.

But, much as he loved them, Cecilia knew that these were not the bairns he sought. Those bairns were far away across a vast ocean.

He gave a sigh and then lapsed into unconsciousness. Within an hour he was dead.

For Arthur, the long struggle was over.

EMMA'S STORY

PART NINE

Stewart & Stewart
Agents at Law
10 Main Street,
Coatesville,
Philadelphia

10 September 1907

Miss Auld,
62 Northumberland Street,
Edinburgh.

Dear Miss Auld

I regret to inform you that Miss Emma Maitland Stirling passed away at her home, 'Drumpellier', on 2 September 1907.

I am her executor and she requested that on her death I was to inform you, her oldest and dearest friend, of her passing.

I offer my sincere sympathy at your loss.

Yours faithfully,

James Stewart.

THE END

Appendix

Arthur Delaney sued Emma Maitland Stirling at the Court of Session, in Edinburgh, on two further occasions.

Once, in 1892, he sued her for damages for the loss of his children. He lost this case on the basis that the award of damages from the Directors of the Home also absolved Emma Maitland Stirling.

He later sued her for libel, claiming that she had libelled him in an article she wrote for a Christian magazine. We have been unable to find a concluding legal judgement in this case. It may be that, for whatever reason, he simply abandoned the case.

Printed in April 2023
by Rotomail Italia S.p.A., Vignate (MI) - Italy